ARAB NATIONALISM AND
BRITISH IMPERIALISM

ARAB NATIONALISM AND BRITISH IMPERIALISM

A Study in Power Politics

By John Marlowe

FREDERICK A. PRAEGER, *Publishers*
New York

BOOKS THAT MATTER

Published in the United States of America in 1961
by Frederick A. Praeger, Inc., Publishers
64 University Place, New York 3, N.Y.

Copyright © by John Marlowe, 1961
Library of Congress catalog card number 61-8454

Printed in Great Britain by
the Shenval Press, London, Hertford
and Harlow

Prefatory Note

———◆•••◆———

In the past I have sometimes been taken to task by reviewers for having too many footnotes, sometimes for having none at all. This time I have compromised by having a few. Such few direct quotations as I have made are acknowledged in the text itself. Many of the events narrated in the book are too recent to have acquired that documentation which makes footnotes desirable. I have therefore limited footnotes to such explanations and modifications as seemed desirable after reading through the text, and to notes of events which took place after having written the text.

The Bibliography consists only of books actually read or reread while preparing to write and while actually writing this book. It makes no pretence to be a complete Bibliography of all works bearing on the subject. My thanks are due to all those authors whose books are listed, and to innumerable others who have helped me, consciously or unconsciously, in writing this book. I can only hope that the march of events between the time of writing and the time of publication will not make nonsense of too much of it.

DENHAM-BEIRUT-TEHRAN   JOHN MARLOWE
April 1959-January 1960

Contents

————◆————

Chapter		Page
	Introduction	1
I	The Beginnings of Arab Nationalism	6
II	The Ottoman Heritage	17
III	Palestine and The Arab League	31
IV	Interlude	52
V	The Egyptian Revolution	58
VI	Egyptian Lebensraum and Positive Neutrality	78
VII	The Arab World in 1955	92
VIII	Arab Nationalist Propaganda	110
IX	Suez	119
X	The Eisenhower Doctrine	146
XI	Civil War in Lebanon	167
XII	Revolution in Iraq	177
XIII	The Dissolving Mirage	188
XIV	The Twilight of Imperialism	201
XV	The Future	210
	Notes	221
	Bibliography	226
	Index	229

Introduction

During most of the nineteenth century Western European diplomacy was deeply concerned with attempts to preserve the territorial integrity of the Ottoman Empire. During most of the twentieth century it has been at least equally concerned with the problems arising from the collapse of the Ottoman Empire. Foremost among these problems has been that of Western European relationships with the heirs of the Ottoman dominions in Asia and Africa—the Arabs. The history of these relationships has been the history of Western attempts, first to incorporate the Arab territories into their colonial Empires or 'spheres of influence' and, when this had failed, to bind the newly independent Arab nations into the Western network of alliances. For the Arab territories were regarded by the Western Powers as being vitally important, first because of their geographical position on strategic lines of communication, later because of the oil resources of the Persian Gulf, and always because of the brooding proximity of Russia to the north, potentially or actually threatening both communications and oil supplies. These attempts at direct and, later, indirect domination by the West were resisted, and sometimes compromised with, by local nationalist movements which were gradually reinforced by something like a coherent manifestation of Arab nationalism. In a sense then, Arab nationalism is a reaction to Western pressures, developed out of a growing consciousness of a common interest and of a common tradition.

The common interest is the building up of as powerful a political and economic entity as possible in order to resist pressure from and to increase bargaining power against the two Great Power blocs. (In practice, and for historical reasons, the struggle against 'imperialism' has, up to now, been almost exclusively against the Western Powers.) The common tradition is rather more difficult to define. Conventionally, it consists of a common origin, a common language, to a large extent of a common religion and a common memory of a specific civilization. What is an Arab? In the narrowest racial sense an Arab is an indigenous inhabitant of the Arabian Peninsula, with fairly well-defined physical and social characteristics. In this sense the Arabic-speaking peoples outside the Arabian Peninsula are only Arab to a varying but always limited extent. Among the peoples of Jordan, Iraq and Syria there is quite a large amount of Arab blood mingled on the one hand with the original peasant stocks and on the other hand with the blood of various subsequent immigrants from the north —Turks, Kurds and Circassians. Among the inhabitants of Lebanon there is very little admixture of Arab blood; among the inhabitants of Egypt still less. In a more commonly accepted sense, an Arab is one who speaks Arabic as his mother-tongue. But a generation ago hardly any Egyptian regarded himself as an Arab. Today hardly any Lebanese Christian regards himself as an Arab. In truth, being an Arab is not an objective state. It is a subjective idea. An Arab is a person who thinks of himself as an Arab. Many who did not regard themselves as Arabs ten years ago, except occasionally and publicly for propaganda purposes, regard themselves, and are proud to regard themselves, as Arabs today. In ten years' time it is possible that many of these people will no longer regard themselves primarily as Arabs. Alternatively, it is possible that some people who do not regard themselves as Arabs today will regard themselves as Arabs in ten years' time.

Arab civilization in its age of conquest was essentially the imposition of a system of rule, a system of law, a common language and a common discipline, on a number of disintegrating societies, within the framework of which the latent creative ability within these societies had the opportunity to develop. The Arab contribution was primarily a military and administrative, and only secondarily a cultural, one. In that respect it resembled the Roman *pax*. But as it was much less efficient, much less centralized, and much less all-embracing, so it proved less enduring than the Roman *pax* in its military and administrative aspects. But in two of its cultural aspects it proved more enduring. Whereas Roman civilization survived both Roman paganism and the Latin language, Arab civilization was survived both by the Moslem religion and by the Arabic language, the former of which spread and endured far beyond the farthest limits of Arab conquest and the latter of which still remains both the written language and the vernacular in nearly all the areas of Arab conquest. The Arabic language both kept alive and was kept alive by the Moslem religion. For the Quran is not only the Moslem Bible for religious purposes, but also the authoritative linguistic source book. Owing to the central authority of the Quran the language of books, the language of newspapers, as well as the language of prayer varies not at all between Morocco and Iraq, between Syria and the Sudan. Within these vast limits the spoken dialects vary, as indeed they do within the much smaller areas of Europe, such as France, Italy and Germany, within which a common language is spoken. As in these European countries, local dialect differences are much smaller between educated men than they are between peasants, and among educated people in all parts of the Arab world there is evolving, with the spread of cultural and physical communication, something like a standard spoken Arabic. With the spread of education, with the increasing interchange of teachers and experts, and with the increasing popular use of the written word, the radio and the film, it is certain that dialect differences among all levels of Arab society will tend to diminish rather than to increase, just as in Europe and for the same reasons. Although the Arabic language does not, and cannot of itself, impose a sense of unity, it does provide a potent medium through which a sense of unity can be propagated. From this point of view Cairo, with its superior cultural and technical resources for the transmission of the spoken and written word, enjoys a tremendous advantage as a centre for the propagation of Arab unity, far outweighing the disadvantage that, up to very recent times, Egypt has been outside the mainstream of Arabism.

Arab nationalism today, although inevitably rooted in Arab history, is not historically minded. It uses the most enduring heritage of Arab civilization—the Arabic language—as a medium for the dissemination of a common purpose and a common way of thinking, which owes no conscious debt to the Arab past and which only pays that perfunctory homage to the Moslem, which Western statesmen are accustomed to pay to the Christian, religion. Although directed against Western, and to some extent against Russian, 'imperialism', Arab nationalism is essentially a domestic movement within the Arab world endeavouring to convert and to absorb the various centrifugal forces operating within the Arab world. It represents the second stage of the long war of Arab liberation which started with the dissolution of the Ottoman Empire. The first stage was the attainment of sovereign independence. This was attained, in so far as it was attained, within the framework of the various territorial settlements imposed on the Arab peoples by the Western Powers, and was often circumscribed by special treaty arrangements with the Western Powers. The second stage is the completion, consolidation and protection of this precarious and limited independence. In that this second stage limits, for many interests in the Arab world, that liberty and independence which it professes to be consolidating and protecting, it is opposed and resisted by these interests. To some extent, although the parallel is not exact, the argument proceeding in the Arab world today is analogous to the argument between North and South in the American Civil War. And just as the South was supported, more or less overtly, by the ex-Colonial Powers, so, in the Arab world today, Great Britain and France tend to support centrifugal tendencies against the centripetal force of ... nationalism as a means of perpetuating Western influences.

For the time being Arab nationalism is identified with Gamal Abdul Nasr, the head of the Egyptian State, whose policy and whose propaganda have been to develop the centripetal force of Arab unity in opposition to the various forces operating against that unity. Abdul Nasr did not create the centripetal force of Arab unity; but he has given it a coherence and a direction and, by doing so, has probably ensured that 'nasserism' will survive Abdul Nasr. Both the centripetal and the centrifugal forces were implicit in the process of Arab renaissance which the dissolution of the Ottoman Empire made possible. It is the purpose of this book to trace the development, to analyse the components and to assess the importance of these forces in the Arab world.

CHAPTER ONE

The Beginnings of Arab Nationalism

At the beginning of the nineteenth century the Ottoman Empire contained within its dominions most of the territories comprising the former Arab Empires and nearly all those peoples speaking Arabic as their mother-tongue.

The Moslem religion had long since lost its specifically Arab character; the Ottoman Sultan was ex-officio Khalif-al-Islam and, as such, in addition to his temporal authority over Ottoman subjects, claimed and received a shadowy form of allegiance from millions of Moslems in India, in the East Indies and in Africa.

Of the physical memorials of the various Arab Caliphates nothing remained but a few neglected and unrecorded ruins standing in the midst of the deserts to which so much of the Arab lands had been reduced. The Arab cultural heritage had been by-passed in the course of Western Europe's rediscovery of the classics or rendered obsolete as a result of Western Europe's development of the sciences. Nothing specifically Arab remained, either in fact or in human consciousness, but the Arabic language, and this, in an age and area where there were few means of physical, and fewer means of written and verbal, communication, was regarded more as a repository of Islamic lore than as a specifically Arab medium of thought. To such an extent had the Arab tradition receded to its pre-Islamic boundaries that the term 'Arab' was used, both by Arabic-speaking people and others, to describe the nomad and semi-nomad inhabitants of the Arabian Peninsula and the borderlands of the Fertile Crescent.

The beginnings of Arab nationalism can be taken to date from the landing of Bonaparte in Egypt in 1798. This event was the starting-point of a process by which the lands of the Ottoman Empire became more and more exposed to military, cultural, economic and political influences from Western Europe. It was the impact of these influences on a culturally dormant, politically stagnant and economically sterile society which set in train those diverse spiritual, intellectual, social and political ferments which go to make up Arab nationalism as we know it today.

From the ruins of Mamluk power and from the wreckage of Ottoman authority which were left behind in Egypt after, first the French and then the British military occupation, there emerged Mohamed Ali, an Albanian soldier, as the undisputed ruler of Egypt. Ruling Egypt as a vassal of the Sultan, he soon became independent of the Sultan in all but name. By 1834 he was master of Egypt, much of the Sudan, the Hejaz (which included the Holy Cities of Mecca and Medina), Palestine and Syria, and made no secret of his ambition to carve an Arab Empire for himself out of the Ottoman dominions and to become Khalif-al-Islam in place of the Ottoman Sultan. But his ambitions awoke no answering echo from the Arabs themselves. In Syria, which was destined to be the cradle of the new Arab nationalism, Ibrahim Pasha (Mohamed Ali's son and principal General, who was made Governor of Syria), welcomed at first as a deliverer, was soon regarded as a worse tyrant than the Turks themselves. His somewhat laboured patronage of Arabism was regarded with the same lack of enthusiasm as is usually accorded to artificial separatist movements sponsored by foreign conquerors. Nevertheless, the seeds of the new Arabism were sown during the ten-year period of Ibrahim Pasha's Governorship.

The policy, inaugurated by Mohamed Ali in Egypt, of hiring foreign experts and encouraging foreign influences was followed by Ibrahim Pasha in Syria, where the windows opening westwards on to the Mediterranean were opened for the first time since the days of Fakhreddine II, two centuries before. The most

immediately important of these foreign influences were the
Christian missionaries, whom Ibrahim Pasha liberated from many
of the restrictions with which they had previously been encom-
passed. As a result, both Catholic missions, which had been in
Syria since the seventeenth century, and Protestant missions,
which had only recently been established there, were able to continue and extend their work. This work, which was mainly educational, and which greatly increased in scope under the stimulus
of rivalry between the Catholic and Protestant missions, was
necessarily of most benefit to the Christian communities. But at
the same time Ibrahim Pasha, in pursuit of his Arabization policy,
established State schools, attended mostly by Moslems, at which
the language of instruction, as in the mission schools, was Arabic.
Printed books in Arabic, from the Government Press in Cairo,
and from the various missionary Presses in Syria, began to circu-
late and to supply the growing demand for Arabic books created
by the schools.

Meanwhile, the mounting ambitions of Mohamed Ali, encouraged by France, seemed to be threatening the continued existence of the Ottoman Empire. To Great Britain there seemed a
danger lest Russia would occupy Constantinople and that a
French-protected Arab Empire under Mohamed Ali would inherit
most of the Ottoman dominions in Asia. Such a possible development was regarded by Great Britain both as a threat to her own
position as a World Power and as a dangerous disturbance of that
precarious European equilibrium which had been created at the
Congress of Vienna. In 1840, an invasion of Asia Minor by
Ibrahim Pasha (whose army reached the shores of the Bosphorus)
led to a British-inspired intervention against Mohamed Ali by the
European Powers (except for France). The result of this intervention was that Mohamed Ali was compelled to abandon all his
conquests east of Suez as a condition of his remaining Viceroy
of Egypt. His dreams of an Arab Empire were at an end. But the
seed had been sown.

In retrospect the two seminal movements during the nineteenth century which shaped and determined the future develop-

ment of Arab nationalism were (a) the development of a specifically Arab consciousness among the Arabic-speaking inhabitants of Syria, and (b) Orabi's military rebellion in Egypt. There were of course other formative influences, which will be briefly referred to in their turn, but these two movements, the one providing nationalism with a theoretical basis, the other with a practical example, although the one was almost entirely unregarded and the other ignominiously defeated at the time, seem between them to contain the heart of the matter.

Syria is not a nation with defined boundaries enclosing a homogeneous people who regard themselves as Syrians. It is a name given to a region which has never existed as a separate political entity and which has never been precisely defined. It is analogous to, say, East Anglia, or New England. It has generally been taken to include the area lying between the Taurus Mountains and the Sinai desert from north to south, and between the desert and the sea from east to west. In the middle of the nineteenth century this region was inhabited by perhaps two million people. Most of them were Sunni Moslems. Some of them were heretic Moslems—Druzes, Alawites and Metawalis. In the Lebanon Mountain most of the inhabitants were Christians of various sects. Some of the inhabitants were town-dwellers, some were villagers, some were nomads. Some gave their primary loyalty to a religious sect, some to a particular town or village, some to a particular tribe or family. They were all Ottoman subjects and they nearly all spoke Arabic as their mother-tongue. These were the only two things they had in common. In its origins, Arab nationalism in Syria was an attempt, inspired mainly by scholars and intellectuals, to realize, first a cultural and then a political unity based on a common language with the object of securing, first Arab autonomy within and, later, Arab independence without, the Ottoman Empire. Starting as a literary revival arising from the activity of Christian missions in Lebanon, it developed over the years as a coherent political movement which included Arabic-speaking Moslems and Christians in a common Arabism whose members regarded themselves as fellow-members of a

B

noble but oppressed race, 'rightly struggling to be free'. The meaning of 'freedom' varied with varying circumstances. Under the Hamidian despotism, which was administratively tyrannical but racially liberal, 'freedom' was seen as Arab autonomy within a politically reformed Ottoman Empire. Confronted with the pan-Turanian proclivities and the centralizing tendencies of the Young Turks, 'freedom' became synonymous with national independence and, as a necessary corollary, Arab nationalists began to think no longer in terms of reform but of revolt. The sixty formative years of argument, speculation and study, interspersed with some not very dangerous subversive pamphleteering and propaganda, had planted the notion of Arabism pretty firmly among all sections of educated Arabic-speaking people in Syria. Arab Army officers and Arab civilian officials in the Ottoman service, as well as Arab students and professional men, banded themselves into secret societies dedicated to the cause of Arab nationalism and eagerly awaited some external event which might precipitate the fall of the Ottoman Empire and the parturition of Arab independence.

Egypt was a nation in a sense that Syria was not. It had four thousand years of nationhood to look back on. Although ruled by foreigners, it was a nation of itself and not a vaguely defined region within an alien Empire. Whereas in Syria geographical features and religious differences were a cause of division, in Egypt the Nile Valley and the prevailing Sunni Moslem orthodoxy were bonds of union. Thus in Egypt there was no need to create a sense of nationality by appealing to a common Arabism. A sense of nationality—a sense of Egyptianism—was already there, and in Egypt protest against foreign influences took the form of an assertion of Egyptianism rather than an evolution of Arabism.

These foreign influences were of two kinds. There was the Turkish-Circassian-Albanian ruling class, consisting of the Viceroy and his family, most of the larger landlords, all the higher Army officers and the whole of 'society' generally. They bore about the same relation to Egyptians as the Normans must have done to the English in the early days of the Norman Conquest. They spoke Turkish in preference to Arabic and generally regarded themselves as the master race. About the only thing which they had in common with most of the native Egyptians was the Moslem religion. Their attitude towards native Egyptians is epitomized by a remark attributed to Mohamed Ali who was credited with the saying that in the Egyptian Army he never proposed to promote an Egyptian above the rank of sergeant. Ironically, it was the Egyptian Army which was to be the principle vehicle of Egyptianization.

The other foreign influence was imported into Egypt by Mohamed Ali and his successors and consisted of European nationals who, protected by Capitulory privileges[1] and attracted by lucrative concessions and jobs of all kinds, flocked to Egypt in ever-increasing numbers and soon, by means of the banks, trading houses and public utility concessions which they founded and administered, acquired a dominion over Egyptian economic life analogous to that already possessed by the Turks-Albanians-Circassians over Egypt's social and administrative life. The native Egyptian was a second-class citizen in his own country. He was in practice debarred from any position of wealth or influence. He worked not for one but for two sets of foreign masters.

Under Mohamed Ali the European foreigners, in spite of their Capitulatory privileges, which had not attained the luxuriance which they were to acquire as a result of the inauguration of the Mixed Courts[2] in 1875, had been the servants and not the masters of the Egyptian State. By reason of the unwisdom and extravagance of Mohamed Ali's successors, who became so deeply indebted to European creditors that they lost all freedom of action, the Europeans became the masters and, with the advent of the British occupation in 1882, the old ruling class became, in effect, the agents of the British occupiers who, in their turn, were themselves, to a large extent, agents for the European Powers.

Conscious Egyptian protest against this dual domination had developed in the Egyptian Army as being the only organization in which native Egyptians had been able to obtain any effective

influence. In spite of Mohamed Ali's dictum about the eligibility
of Egyptians for military promotion, the campaigns of his successors in the Sudan, together with their considerable ceremonial
requirements at home, had led to a steady increase in the size of
the Egyptian Army and, in view of the low social status accorded
to Army officers, to a progressive increase in the native Egyptian
officer element. After the deposition of the Khedive Ismail and
the advent of the Dual Control, the Egyptian Administration
virtually became a debt-collecting agency, squeezing money
from the Egyptian fellahin for the purpose of satisfying the exigencies of the European bondholders. The Egyptian Army,
purged of its non-Egyptian elements as the result of a number of
threatened and actual mutinies, emerged as the spearhead of
Egyptian nationalism. The Orabi rebellion, was a deliberate and
conscious attempt to replace the rule of the *fainéant* Khedive and
his European masters by the rule of an indigenous Egyptian
Government based on popular support. It was only defeated by
a British military occupation which was to last for the next
seventy years and which was brought to an end as the result of
another, and this time successful, military coup.

The British military occupation of Egypt, precipitated by the
Orabi rebellion, was a decisive factor in the development of Arab
nationalism. For, during and after the 1914-18 war, Cairo was
the base from which Great Britain attempted to extend her dominion over the Arab World. It is not altogether fanciful to see Arab
nationalism in terms of Arab reactions against British manoeuvres
to this end. For nationalism is, in its essence, an assertion of local
unity against foreign power, just as imperialism is an assertion of
foreign power against local disunity.

We must now take a brief look at the ideas underlying Arab
nationalism in its formative stage. These ideas appear to derive
about equally from European liberalism and from Islamic
modernism.

The ideas of nineteenth century European liberalism are best
illustrated from the struggle for Italian independence with which
liberal thought in Europe became particularly identified. There

was in Italy a people speaking the same language, professing the same religion and conscious of a common ancestry. By the standards of the nineteenth century the Italians were a nation in theory. But they could only become a nation in fact by ridding themselves of those disabilities which debarred them from nationhood. These disabilities consisted of Austrian occupation of the northern provinces, of the rule of the Papal States in the centre of the country and that of the Kingdom of Naples in the south. As the popular will for independent nationality was the only justification for and the only means by which these disabilities could be overcome, so it became axiomatic that what could only be achieved by the operation of the popular will must thereafter be sustained by reference to the popular will. An autocratic national State was seen as being almost as much of a contradiction in terms as a democratic Empire. Liberalism was expressed in terms of nationalism, nationalism in terms of democracy. And democracy, in the context of nineteenth century liberalism, meant parliamentary democracy. It was not enough to have a government chosen by the people, a government whose acts were endorsed by the people. The government had to be, in a real sense, the servant of the people in that it was the government's business not itself to be the lawgiver but to implement the laws promulgated by the elected representatives of the people. It was assumed that such a state of affairs was only possible in a national State because it was only in terms of nationality that 'the people' could be regarded as an entity.

Islamic modernism, while undoubtedly influenced by European liberalism, was a conscious attempt to combat European influences on the Moslem world by means of a restatement and re-implementation of the principles of Islam with the object of founding, on the basis of these re-stated and re-implemented principles, a specifically Islamic way of life which would be able to hold its own against all the spiritual, emotional, intellectual, social and economic pressures, allurements and underminings from the West. The pioneer of the movement was Jamal ad-Din Afghani. Among his most influential disciples were Mohamed Abdu, who came within measurable distance of putting the University of al-Azhar, the citadel of Moslem orthodoxy, at the head of the reformist movement, and Abdul Rahman Kawakebi, who was a Syrian from Aleppo and who provided the principal nexus between Arab nationalism and Islamic modernism by presenting one in terms of the other.

Islamic modernism provided a theoretical basis for Arab nationalism in terms of Islam which both supplemented and corrected the European liberal influence which has been described. While the European liberal influence was principally directed against the immediate pressure of Ottoman rule, the Islamic modernist influence was principally directed against the ultimate threat of European domination. The greatest service which Islamic modernism performed, not only for Arab nationalism, but for the Islamic world generally, was to provide a respectable repudiation of the assumption, which had become a commonplace of orthodox Moslem teaching, that submission to temporal Moslem authority was part of the Islamic duty of submission to the will of God. Instead of stressing the duty of the ruled to submit themselves to the ruler, Islamic modernism went back to the early Arab Caliphs to emphasize the duty of the ruler to conform himself to the popular will.

The two conceptions of democracy represented by the liberal and by the Islamic tradition respectively are important in the light of the subsequent development of Arab nationalism. Islamic democracy assumes the existence of, and the ability of the people to find and choose, an ideal ruler with an instinctive knowledge of the popular will. Liberal democracy assumes the necessity for devising machinery to ensure that the ruler does not ignore the popular will. Islamic democracy sees the ruler as the incarnation, liberal democracy as the servant, of the popular will. Both are at one in repudiating the idea of a 'divine right' to govern and both are at one in supporting not only the right but the duty of the people to resist a despotic government.

Racial consciousness had been almost entirely absent from the early literary movement in Lebanon. The Egyptian nationalist movement, although racially conscious, was conscious of a common Egyptianism and not of a common Arabism. But in Damascus, Homs, Hama and Aleppo, as well as in Basra and Baghdad, there was nothing forced or artificial about a consciousness of racial kindred with the Arabs of the desert. In these cities, and in the villages of the Fertile Crescent, the desert is never far away. Meat and fleeces are bought from, tea, sugar, textiles, pots and pans are sold to, desert tribesmen in their markets. Semi-sedentary Beduin with their black tents and their herds of sheep and goats penetrate far into the cultivation. And all through recorded history there has been a persistent process of emigration from the desert to the sown. To the Syrian townsman or villager the Bedu is at the same time an ancestor and someone who is on the way to becoming one of themselves; as such he is regarded with a mixture of respect and condescension, mingled with a certain amount of exasperation. There is no hard and fast line between the desert and the sown, between the Bedu and the cultivator, between the cultivator and the townsman. There is an infinite series of small gradations linking the lawyer in his office with the tribesman in his tent. In the early days of Arab nationalism there may have been, for the urbanized Syrian, trying to realize in himself the concept of Arabism, a certain satisfaction in the contemplation, and even in the exaggeration, of a possible kinship with, and a possible descent from, the Arabs of the desert, just as a clerk in a Glasgow counting-house might derive satisfaction from a possibly mythical descent from Highland crofters. For in racialism it is the myth and not the reality that counts. And so, as Arab nationalism took root among the intelligentsia of the Syrian cities, the concept of racial unity based on a common desert ancestry strengthened and extended the concept of unity based on a common language, a common religion and a common aspiration towards freedom.

Language, religion and race. These were the three basic concepts of Arab unity. Their effects were local in respect of language and race, limited in respect of religion. In default of any realizable sense of Syrian nationality, unity of language had been a means of expressing a unity of aspiration for the various Arabic-speak-

ing sects and tribes included within the geographical region
known as Syria. The Moslem religion, as interpreted in the teach-
ings of the Islamic modernists, was a means of providing a specifically Islamic meaning to the concept of national freedom which
the Arab nationalists had originally learnt from Europe. Consciousness of a common origin was the means by which the sophisticated Arab nationalists of Syria had been able to include within
the orbit of Arab nationalism the warring tribes and principalities
of the Arabian Peninsula, the 'deep south' of a possible future
Arab Union.

In trying to assess the formative influences actuating the early
stages of a movement one must guard against the temptation of
assuming the existence of various influences which are in fact
subsequent rationalizations. Nationalist philosophies are far
more often the decoration of a completed building than the foundations of a building about to be constructed. To a large extent
this is true of Arab nationalism. But in the first Arab Congress
held in Paris in 1913 and attended by delegates from various parts
of the Arab world, but mostly from Syria, we have evidence of a
fairly mature and coherent expression of the ideological bases of
Arab nationalism. The most explicit of these expressions occurs
in an address delivered by Abdul Ghani al-Arisi in which he said,
inter alia:

'In the view of political theorists, groups are entitled to the
rights of nations if they possess unity of language and of race
according to the German school; unity of history and of traditions
according to the Italian school; and unity of political aspirations
according to the French. . . . The right of the Arabs to nationhood . . . finds endorsement in all schools of political theory without exception' (*The Ideas of Arab Nationalism* by Hazem Nuseibeh, p. 52). The extent to which the theoreticians of Arab
nationalism had been influenced by European ideology is
apparent from this extract.

It was only just over a year after the holding of this Congress
that 'the right of the Arabs to nationhood' passed from the
sphere of academic discussion to that of practical politics.

CHAPTER TWO

The Ottoman Heritage

When war was declared between Great Britain and Turkey in October 1914 the Arab lands of the Ottoman Empire occupied a strategic position between the heart of Turkey in Asia Minor and the various outposts of British power in Egypt, Aden and the Persian Gulf. British policy-makers were already thinking in terms, not merely of the course of war against Turkey, but of the shape of things to come after the expected dissolution of the Ottoman Empire. Egypt, the occupation of which had originally been regarded as a temporary and rather tiresome expedient, was already beginning to be regarded as a permanent and vital factor in the British imperial system, and Cairo was beginning to be seen as the administrative centre of a British zone of influence spreading northwards and eastwards over the Arab lands to the Persian Gulf, there linking up with the British zone of influence stretching westward from India to form a continuous British-controlled corridor stretching from Suez to Singapore to provide for the ports, landing-grounds, roads and oil pipelines, as well as for the military garrisons, which were seen as the necessary concomitants of an imperial system of communications. There were even thoughts of reconciling Egypt to membership of the British Empire, and of cementing the allegiance of the millions of Moslems in other parts of the Empire, by transferring the Caliphate from Constantinople to Cairo by virtue of that same right of conquest by which the Caliphate had been transferred to Constantinople some four hundred years before.

But there were other claimants to a share of the Ottoman heritage in Asia. France, who was as mistrustful of British designs in the Arab world as Great Britain had, in the time of Mohamed Ali, been mistrustful of French designs, and who was moreover not yet entirely reconciled to the British occupation of Egypt, was determined that her share of the Ottoman heritage should both be commensurate with her preponderant share of the war effort in the west and be sufficient at least to balance the British share of that heritage. To this end, France had made it clear to her Allies quite early in the war that she laid claim to the whole of Syria in view of her traditional interests in that region.

The third claimants were the Zionists. It is not likely that this claim would have been sponsored, as eventually it was, by Great Britain had it not been for the fact that the French claim to Syria included the area known as Palestine. The British strategic corridor which was envisaged from the Mediterranean to the Persian Gulf required the inclusion of Palestine at the western end, both to provide an adequate 'bridgehead' on the east bank of the Suez Canal, and to enable the development of the port of Haifa, which was seen as an important potential link in the imperial system of communications. An important, and perhaps a decisive, reason for the assumption by Great Britain of what afterwards proved to be the intolerable burden of sponsorship of the Jewish National Home in Palestine was the desire, in return for that sponsorship, to obtain in Palestine that administrative and strategic control which otherwise would have been obtained by France.

The residuary legatees, so to speak, were the Arabs themselves. The Arab claim, which, broadly, was for the recognition and upholding of Arab independence in the rectangle enclosed by the Taurus Mountains to the north, the Indian Ocean to the south, the Persian frontier to the east, and the Mediterranean and Red Seas to the west, was presented to Great Britain by the Amir Husain, Sherif of Mecca, in the course of negotiations with the British High Commissioner in Cairo about the possibility of a

British-assisted Hejazi revolt against the Turks. Husain's only title to speak for the Arab 'nation' was that the fact that, through Feisal, one of his sons, he had been in touch with two Arab nationalist secret societies in Damascus, the leaders of which had authorized Husain to act on their behalf. In particular Husain had not consulted any of his fellow-rulers in the Arabian Peninsula, an omission which was ultimately to be fatal to him.

In view of the subsequent importance assumed by this claim, it is necessary briefly to describe the events leading up to it. It has already been indicated that the Arab nationalist movement, in so far as it existed at all, was based on Syria. After it had graduated from its literary origins to become a political movement, it had necessarily gone underground. Under the Hamidian despotism, when there had been no discrimination against Arabs as such, the aim of the movement had been autonomy in a liberalized Ottoman Empire. Under the Young Turk regime, which was liberal on paper, but which in practice regarded the Turks as a master and the Arabs as a subject race, the Arab nationalists began to see the future in terms of an Arab State separate from and independent of the Ottoman Empire. The movement, although necessarily still underground, gathered momentum. By the time war broke out its principal organization consisted of two secret societies—al Ahd composed of Arab army officers in the Turkish Army, and al Fatat consisting for the most part of Arab students, government officials and professional men. Both societies, whose activities were unknown to each other, to the outside world and, for the time being, to the Turkish authorities, had branches in all the main towns of Syria and in some of the main towns of Iraq, where the movement was slowly beginning to attract adherents. In Constantinople, knowledge of the existence of one or other of the societies seems to have been possessed by some of the Arab deputies in the Ottoman Parliament, including Abdullah, one of the sons of the Sherif of Mecca.

The Sherif of Mecca was one of five autonomous Rulers under Turkish suzerainty in the Arabian Peninsula. The others were the Rulers of Nejd, Shammar, Asir and Yemen. As a descendant

of the Prophet and as Guardian of the Holy Places, he enjoyed
considerable prestige. But he had no primacy, either in theory
or in fact, over his fellow-Rulers in the Peninsula. His status was
different from, and incidentally, somewhat inferior to theirs, in
that he was not an hereditary Ruler but an appointee of the
Turks who, by tradition, had to appoint a descendant of the Prophet as Sherif of Mecca. Husain had spent much of his life in forced
residence in Constantinople and his four sons had been brought
up there. He had been made Sherif by the Young Turks in 1908.
It is not known when he or his sons first became aware of and
first made contact with the nationalist movement in Syria. In
February 1914 his son Abdullah contacted the British authorities
in Cairo to discuss the possibility of an alliance between Great
Britain and the Sherif in the event of a war between Great Britain
and Turkey. Ten months later, after war had broken out, the
British authorities in Cairo opened negotiations with the Sherif
with a view to trying to persuade him to ignore and, if possible,
to oppose the call to Jihad[1] which had just been issued by the
Sultan. Great Britain was understandably anxious about the pos-
sible effect of this call on the Moslem populations of India and
Egypt. The Sherif adroitly avoided becoming embroiled with the
Turks until he was assured of substantial assistance from the
British. In the course of his subsequent negotiations with the
British, and on the sole basis of a statement of Arab territorial
claims drawn up by the secret societies in Damascus, where Feisal,
another of Husain's sons, had been negotiating with them, the
Sherif in July 1915, presented to the British, in the name of the
Arab 'nation', a demand for British recognition of and support
for the independence of all Arabic-speaking territories east of
Suez, in return for an immediate revolt against the Turks in the
Hejaz and the ultimate offer of an alliance between Great Britain
and the Arab 'nation'. At first Husain's claim to act on behalf of
the Arab 'nation' was sceptically received but, after having ob-
tained independent evidence of Husain's connections with the
Arab secret societies, the Sherif was taken at his own valuation.
After considerable correspondence[2] an agreement was arrived at

under which Great Britain undertook to 'recognize and uphold' Arab independence in all the areas mentioned in Husain's state-ment of claim (known as 'the Damascus Protocol') less (a) Mersine and Adana, (b) the Vilayets of Basra and Baghdad where HMG, on the insistence of the India Office, proposed to introduce direct British rule, and (c) an ill-defined area west of a line drawn through Aleppo, Hama, Homs and Damascus to which the French laid claim. The controversies which raged for so many years about the precise meaning of the last reservation have now become irrelevant. The points of enduring interest arising out of the agreement are:

(1) On the basis of this agreement, which placed Great Britain under specific obligations to Arab nationalism in general and to the Sherifian family in particular, the standard of revolt was raised in the Hejaz in June 1916. Although it is probably true to say that, in the course of this revolt, Great Britain obtained no support which she could not have obtained anyway as a result of monetary and military assistance, and although, in any case, the military value of the revolt was very limited, the fact remains that these specific obligations had been incurred.

(2) In fulfilment of these obligations, and as a result of the Allied victory, to which the revolt had in some measure contri-buted, a provisional Arab Government was set up in Damascus, after its capture in October 1918, which, under the general super-vision of the British High Command, administered those areas outside the Arabian Peninsula (where the Allied pledge of inde-pendence had already been honoured) falling unequivocally within the area of Arab independence covered by the British pledge. This provisional Government was later (in 1919), by uni-lateral action on the part of a Syrian Congress, elevated into a 'kingdom' with Feisal, a son of Husain and the leader of the Arab revolt, as King.

(3) In April 1920, at the San Remo Conference, the British Government agreed to a French Mandate over the northern part of the area administered by the Arab provisional Government, including its capital of Damascus. In June 1920 the French occu-

pied this area by force of arms and expelled Feisal. In the same
month the British, who maintained a small military force in the
southern part of the Arab 'kingdom', forcibly prevented Abdullah, Feisal's brother, who was marching northward from the
Hejaz, from attempting to invade the mandated territory which
had been awarded to, and which had just been occupied by, the
French. The British, therefore, having connived at a breach of
their agreement made with the Sherif, had reneged on their obligations both to Arab nationalism in general and to the Sherifian
family in particular. In 1921 the British made their peace with,
and handsomely compensated, the Sherifian family by elevating
Feisal to the throne of Iraq, which was under a British Mandate,
and Abdullah to the throne of Transjordan consisting of the
southern part of the Arab 'kingdom' of which the northern part
had been annexed by France. (As has been related, the Vilayets
of Basra and Baghdad had been specifically reserved to the British
in the pledge made to Husain; the Vilayet of Mosul, originally
claimed by France as part of Syria, was eventually included in the
British Mandated territory of Iraq, a fact which, together with a
similar subtraction of Palestine in favour of Great Britain, made
it almost impossible for the British to resist French claims to the
rest of Syria.) Acceptance of this compensation, which was regarded as acceptance, not only of the French Mandate over Syria,
but also of the British-sponsored Jewish National Home in Palestine, marked the end of such identification as had previously
existed between Arab nationalism and the Sherifian family.
Henceforward, the Sherifian family were regarded as the principal
beneficiaries, while Arab nationalists were regarded as the principal victims, of the post-war settlement of the Arab world. Three
years later, in 1924, Abdul Aziz ibn Saud, the Wahhabi Ruler
of Nejd, invaded and annexed the Hejaz and drove Husain into
exile. From that time onward, and until the process of political
and social evolution produced another set of alignments and
another set of loyalties, the Arab world tended to be divided between the Hashemites[3] and the Saudites, a rivalry which became
analogous in the Arab world to the rivalry between the Guelfs

and the Ghibellines in Renaissance Italy.

As a result of the post-war settlement, a number of Arab States were created, some immediately independent, some eventually to attain independence. But Arab nationalism had for the time being disappeared, to be replaced by more localized aspirations, loyalties and rivalries. In the Arabian Peninsula the previous five autonomous Principalities were merged into two sovereign States —Saudi Arabia and Yemen—as a result of the Amir of Nejd, now to become famous as Abdul Aziz ibn Saud, having conquered and annexed the neighbouring territories of Shammar, Hejaz and Asir. The Fertile Crescent, partitioned between Great Britain and France, was divided into the Kingdom of Iraq, under British Mandate, the British Mandated territories of Palestine and Transjordan, and the French Mandated territories of Syria and Lebanon. As has been related, Feisal became King of Iraq which, in 1932, became an independent State in alliance with Great Britain. Abdullah became Amir, under British Mandatory authority, of Transjordan, which was nothing more than a British-controlled strategic corridor connecting Palestine with Iraq and separating Syria from Saudi Arabia. By the beginning of the Second World War the Republics of Syria and Lebanon, into which the French Mandated area, after some administrative and political vicissitudes, had been divided, were well on their way to that sovereign independence which they attained after the Second World War. Anglo-French ambitions had diverted and delayed, but had not extinguished, the prospects of Arab independence. Except in Palestine.

The effect of the Jewish National Home policy in Palestine, adumbrated in the Balfour Declaration and implemented in the Mandate for Palestine, was not merely to divert and to delay but to inhibit the prospect of Arab independence in that country. For, at all events until the Arab rising in 1936, the British interpretation of the Mandate did appear to exclude the grant of independence to Palestine until such time as the Jews had become a majority of the inhabitants. In the British Mandate for Iraq and in the French Mandate for Syria and Lebanon, the ultimate goal of national independence was acknowledged by the Mandatory Power and the concept of a special treaty relationship with the ex-Mandatory Power (of the kind adumbrated in the British pledge to Husain) after the attainment of independence was, generally speaking, conceded by the inhabitants of these countries. The attainment of that independence and the limitations of that treaty relationship were matters of timing and bargaining, processes which could be and were expedited and modified by actual and threatened insurrection In this way the weight of nationalist resentment was gradually lightened and the extent of nationalist frustration progressively reduced. But in Palestine there was no such issue for this resentment and for this frustration. Thus it was that the insurgent Arabs of Palestine became the focus for the second movement of Arab nationalism on the eve of the Second World War just as the Syrian secret societies had been the focus of Arab nationalism on the eve of the First World War. And, just as the secret societies had been 'adopted' by Husain in an endeavour to create an Arab State, so the Palestinian Arabs were 'adopted' by the Arab League in an endeavour to create an Arab Federation. In this chapter we have summarized what may be described as the Sherifian phase of Arab nationalism. In the next chapter we shall give an account of what may be termed the Palestinian phase. But first we must take a look at the balance of forces in the Arab world as it existed in the years immediately before the Second World War and at the time of the Arab rebellion in Palestine.

After the 1914-18 war it appeared, on the surface, that Great Britain had, with very small concessions to France, secured the whole of her territorial and strategic objectives in the Near East. There was a British Protectorate over Egypt which secured for Great Britain control of the Suez Canal. The Sudan, technically an Anglo-Egyptian Condominium, was, to all intents and purposes, a British colony. The ex-Ottoman Vilayets of Basra, Baghdad and Mosul had been made into the State of Iraq under British Mandate. The corridor between Egypt and Iraq, to which so much strategic importance was attached by the British, was secured by the British Mandate over Palestine and Transjordan. On the south and east coast of the Arabian Peninsula, by the shores of the Indian Ocean and the Persian Gulf, there was a continuous chain of British-protected Sheikhdoms and Sultanates from Aden in the south-west to Kuwait in the north-east. The theoretically sovereign Principalities of the Arabian Peninsula, lying between the British Mandate territories to the north and the British-protected Sheikhdoms to the south, were at least as much subject to British paramountcy as they had previously been to Ottoman suzerainty.

The French Mandate in Syria was an insignificant offset to this British hegemony. The effect of French ambitions had been, not so much to limit the extent of British hegemony, as to bedevil the political conditions under which that hegemony was exercised. As a more or less direct result of trying to provide for both British and French claims Great Britain had (a) broken her pledge to Husain and acquiesced in the breaking up of the Sherifian Kingdom and (b) more inexcusably and, as it turned out, more importantly, had undertaken the sponsorship of the Jewish National Home in Palestine as a means of securing the transfer of Palestine from French to British control. The breach of one pledge to the Arabs and the fulfilment of another (subsquent and conflicting) pledge to the Zionists effectively inhibited the creation of what might conceivably have been a British-protected confederation of Arab States benevolently presided over by a British Viceroy with his capital on the banks of the Nile. As it was, the British rulers in Baghdad and Jerusalem, and the French rulers in Beirut and Damascus, had to try and compound with resentful, divided and defeated nationalists who regarded them as conquerers instead of co-operating with victorious, united and satisfied patriots who regarded them as liberators.

The British interest in the area was primarily strategic. They wished to provide for the unmolested movement through the territory of ships, aeroplanes, troops and merchandise. In so far as troops were to be kept in rather than moved through the area, they were intended as a strategic reserve, available for instant

C

movement in any direction, and not as a chain of static garrisons.
It was therefore desirable that British influence should be maintained, if possible, not by force but by consent. The political problem was therefore to appease, by such concessions as were com-
patible with continued strategic control, the resentments which
had been created by imperial necessities, diplomatic bungling and
inept propaganda. In this matter, as usual, it was the liberal
statesmen who were the realists and the conservative ones who
were the sentimentalists. On the whole, liberal realism prevailed,
both in Baghdad and in Cairo. In 1932 Iraq, under the provisions
of an Anglo-Iraqi Treaty, became an independent sovereign State
having treaty relations with Great Britain which provided for the
maintenance of British forces in and for the movement of British
forces through Iraq. This general pattern which, at the time, satisfied both Iraqi national aspirations and British strategic requirements, was followed in 1936 by an Anglo-Egyptian Treaty on the
same lines. The same pattern was also the basis of negotiations
for treaties between France and the Republics of Syria and
Lebanon (into which, after a series of rather fumbling experi-
ments, the French Mandated area had been divided). While this
pattern was generally acceptable to Great Britain (although less
so to France whose interests in the Levant were sentimental rather
than strategic and who attached importance, as the British did
not, to their 'civilizing mission') it was acceptable to local nationalist sentiment as a matter not of enthusiasm but of realism—as a
recognition of the British (or French) power both to protect or to
coerce. The validity of the treaties was dependent on the continued maintenance of the reality of power. But, as an interim relationship they provided a satisfactory environment in which
British strategic interests were looked after and in which local
nationalism could develop. But in Palestine, the assumed necessity, under the Mandate, for not exposing the Zionist colonists to
the rule of an Arab majority in an independent State (a necessity
which was assumed until 1939, after three years of Arab rebellion) imposed political restrictions on the Arab majority which,
in retrospect, and in relation to what was happening in neigh-

bouring countries, were intolerable and were not in fact tolerated. The Palestine Arabs were in effect being asked to forgo all political development until such time as the Zionists, having obtained a majority, would be able to impose on an Arab minority the sort of political regime which happened to suit them.

In the other Mandated territories of the Fertile Crescent nationalist activity developed, political parties were formed, strikes, riots and insurrections took place within the framework of the frontiers which had been drawn by the victorious Great Powers. These frontiers dictated the scope of nationalist aspiration, just as the regimes set up by the Mandatory Powers (Republics under the French, constitutional Monarchies under the British, Mandates) conditioned the form of nationalist agitation. These frontiers and these regimes were necessarily accepted as conventions within which the struggles for liberation had to be fought. These conventions, which were enforced by the presence of Mandatory forces, while necessarily hindering the growth of Arab unity, also limited the manifestation, and to some extent the development, both of inter-national and of local dissensions. In other words, the Mandatory regimes, while hastening administrative, economic and educational development, hindered the normal process of political development both in foreign and in domestic affairs. This accounts in some measure for the extreme turbulence of Arab domestic and foreign politics after the Mandatory lids had been taken off.

In the Arabian Peninsula no such inhibitions were laid on the various Arab Principalities which became independent sovereign States after the First World War. Except for the British Protectorates on the southern fringe, no State was protected by any external Power from the assaults of its neighbours, no Government from the demands of its citizens. Power politics were allowed to take their course with the result that in a very few years the whole of the Peninsula, except for the British-protected fringe, had become subject to the rule (or in the case of Yeman the influence) of the Wahhabi Ruler of Nejd, Abdul Aziz ibn Saud, who thereby became a powerful factor to be reckoned with, both by the

European Powers and by the Arabs themselves, in the affairs of the Arab world.

Soon after the end of the 1914-18 war, Abdul Aziz ibn Saud, who was on terms of friendly neutrality with the British and who had for some years been sporadically at war with ibn Rashid, the Amir of Shammar, situated immediately to the north of Nejd, finally defeated his rival, entered his capital, Hail, and annexed Shammar to Nejd. This was the first of his series of conquests (unless one counts the recovery of Nejd from ibn Rashid at the beginning of the century, or the annexation of al-Hasa, on the coast of the Persian Gulf, from his Ottoman suzerain, a few years before the war).

Husain, who had proclaimed himself, and had been recognized by the Allies as, King of the Hejaz, had, as a result of his wartime alliance with the British, become easily the most powerful and important of the Princes of Arabia. He was the Ruler of the Holy Cities and as such controlled and received the revenues from the annual pilgrimage. By 1922 one of his sons, Feisal, was King of Iraq and another, Abdullah, Amir of Transjordan. He was reputed to be ambitious to become Khalif-al-Islam. His rule was both inefficient and despotic. His attitude was barbarous towards his subjects and overbearing towards his neighbours. Ibn Saud, who had never forgiven him for having, without consultation with his neighbours, arrogated to himself the leadership of Arab nationalism during the war, and for having thereby secured a throne for himself and for two of his sons, found his pretensions increasingly intolerable. So did the British, to whom Husain was a tiresome old man who had outlived his usefulness to them, and who moreover was regarded by them as having hoodwinked them into making unnecessary promises which they had found it impracticable to keep. When it became apparent that Husain could no longer rely on British protection, ibn Saud (in 1924) invaded the Hejaz and rapidly annexed it. There was some alarm in Islam when it became known that the Holy Cities were subject to the rule of the puritanical and fanatical Wahhabi sect; but ibn Saud knew how to control his fanatics; the pilgrimage continued normally and was rather more efficiently organized than it had been under Husain. More importantly, the conquest of the Hejaz, and the expulsion of Husain and his son Ali, created a delicate situation on the long frontiers which ibn Saud now shared with Iraq and Transjordan. But, by the Treaty of Jidda concluded in 1927 between the British Government and ibn Saud, the latter, in return for British recognition of his conquests in the Arabian Peninsula, agreed to respect the boundaries of the British Mandated territories of Iraq and Transjordan (subject to some reservations about Aqaba and Maan in Transjordan) as well as agreeing to keep friendly relations with the British-protected Sheikhdoms of the Persian Gulf. On the whole, these promises of good neighbourhood were kept.

The Sherifian episode had come and gone, having shaped Arab affairs during the First World War and having left its mark on the Arab world in the ruling dynasties of Iraq and Transjordan. Now a new and considerable figure had emerged from the Arabian Desert who was destined, by reason of his character rather than by reason of his material power, to have an important, sometimes preponderant, and usually beneficent influence on Arab affairs during the remaining 25 years of his life. He possessed to a considerable degree a quality in which most Arab statesmen are lacking—a lack which is responsible for many of the misfortunes which have beset the Arab cause—in that he had a keen appreciation of the truth that politics are the art of the possible, that ends must be related to means, that the best must be made of what is beyond one's power to change. Another facet of his influence should not be underestimated. The predominant and increasing influence of this bearded, Bedu figure, with his flowing robes, his classical Arabic speech and his traditional Arab ways, all in sharp contrast to the cosmopolitan appearance and manners of nearly all the other Arab sovereigns and statesmen, was, both for the Arabs themselves and for the Western statesmen who dealt with them, a perpetual reminder of the common origin from which Arab nationalism derived both its inspiration and its justification.

This, then, was the situation towards the ends of 1936 when the eyes of the Arab world were beginning to be concentrated on Palestine. An independent and united Arabia, small in population, negligible in material power or cultural influence and backward even by comparison with the other Arab countries in twentieth century amenities, but ruled over by a King in friendly relationship with the British Government whose moral stature and political influence in the Arab world were out of all proportion to the material resources at his command. An independent Iraq in treaty relationship with Great Britain and ruled by a dynasty at bitter enmity with the House of ibn Saud. The small, mainly Beduin State of Transjordan, an artificial creation of British policy, autonomously administered under British Mandatory supervision by a Sherifian Prince, also at bitter enmity with the House of ibn Saud. The Republics of Syria and Lebanon, still under French Mandate but, apparently, about to achieve a similar status vis-à-vis France to that already achieved by Iraq vis-à-vis Great Britain. An independent Egypt, in a similar treaty relationship as Iraq to Great Britain, which did not as yet regard itself, nor was regarded, as part of the Arab world, being intensely conscious of its 'Egyptianism' but as yet unconscious of any connection between Egyptianism and Arabism. And in the middle, the tiny land of Palestine—about the size of Wales—with about a million Arab inhabitants in insurrection against the British Mandate on account of the Jewish colonization which was being imposed on them under the conditions of that Mandate. The Palestine Arab revolt was in the nature of a challenge to the common Arabism of their Arabic-speaking and mainly Moslem neighbours. This common Arabism was glibly acknowledged in theory but had never aroused much practical enthusiasm and had never, except in the British-inspired and mainly British-led Sherifian revolt, been realized in practice.

CHAPTER THREE

Palestine and The Arab League

In 1936, as in 1916, Great Britain's interest in what was coming to be known as the Middle East was primarily strategic. What she essentially required was the power to maintain military bases, ports and airfields, and to move military forces and commercial supplies freely through the area by land, sea or air. It was important as a base and as a corridor. In addition it was beginning to be important as a source of petroleum.

After 1918 an attempt had been made to hold the area by military force and direct rule. But an insurrection in Iraq and serious rioting in Egypt led to a change in tactics. Instead of military force and direct rule an attempt, inaugurated at the Colonial Office Conference in Cairo in 1921, was made to preserve the strategic essentials by substituting consent for force and indirect supervision for direct rule. So long as the alternative possibility of coercion existed, as it did, for use in case of necessity, the prospect of collaborating with the occupying Power was a sufficiently attractive one to secure the consent of a sufficiently large body of influential collaborators. It was a collaboration which was, in appearance and to some extent in fact, so reluctant as to seem almost indistinguishable from resistance. For it was necessary for the collaborators, by hard bargaining, to justify the results of collaboration to political opponents and personal rivals and to try and demonstrate that these results had been obtained not by collaboration but by resistance. Conventionally, resistance to the occupier was a compulsory gesture and the Anglo-Iraqi Treaty of 1930 and the Anglo-Egyptian Treaty of 1936 were greeted in these countries not as signs of reconciliation but as tokens of successful resistance, not as final settlements of differences but as instalments of liberation. Indeed, the reluctant collaborationists could be regarded as realist nationalists in that, with the opportunities then at their disposal, their limited collaboration produced infinitely better results, in terms of nationalist achievement, than intransigent resistance would have done. Nevertheless, like Laval a few years later, they would have been, and proved ultimately to be, extremely vulnerable in the event of a withdrawal or a decline of British power which would have exposed them, and ultimately did expose them, to accusations of treason. For this reason a vested interest in the British connection grew up among the Sherifian family and the big Sunni magnates who ruled Iraq, and among the big landlords, professional politicians and rich lawyers who ruled Egypt. For the same reason the British found themselves more and more committed to, or at all events identified with, the existing rulers of these two countries. This meant that when the social changes set in train by Western European connections, fostered by nationalism and accelerated by the Second World War began to take effect, feudalism and imperialism—the old ruling class and the British connection—were inseparably linked in the minds of the new middle class nationalists. But in 1936 this was far into the future.

In 1936 the main resistance to the British connection in Iraq and Egypt and to the French connection in Syria and Lebanon, and the main opposition to the 'treaty' politicians in these countries, came from two sources. First, there were the Islamic traditionalists who objected to the impact of Western manners and Western economics on Islamic life, who regarded the actual disadvantages of contact with the West as outweighing any potential and actual advantages, and who wished as far as possible to decontaminate the Arab world from the infection of the West and to seek a way of development on purely Islamic lines. This traditionalism really represented a de-intellectualized Islamic modernism. It was of course essentially Islamic; it was modernist in that it realized that a rigid application of the Sharia Law[1] to the problems of modern life was impracticable; it was de-intellectualized in that it was uninterested in or incapable of devising the sort of society which it wished to see develop as a result of successful resistance to the West. Secondly, there were the agnostic, intellectual, Europeanized but anti-Western nationalists, bitterly aware of their own frustrated abilities and limited opportunities, bitterly resentful of foreign domination and bitterly distrustful of 'imperialist' intentions. Just as their forbears had, on the eve of the First World War, looked towards the liberalism of Western Europe as a possible instrument for their liberation from the Ottoman Empire, so the young nationalists of the thirties, on the eve of the Second World War, looked towards the fascist regimes of Central Europe as possible instruments for their liberation from that Western European liberalism which had deceived and (as they saw it) enslaved them.

There was no possibility of Arab collaboration with the British over the Mandatory policy in Palestine. Thus, those Arab Governments which, formally like Egypt and Iraq, or informally like Saudi Arabia, had established a *modus vivendi* with Great Britain, either had to ignore the position of the Palestine Arabs or try, if possible by persuasion, if necessary by threats, to induce the British Government to a change of policy in Palestine. After the Arab rebellion had broken out in April 1936 it became impossible for the independent Arab Governments to ignore Palestine, and it became urgently necessary for them to try and influence events in Palestine since the popular insurrectionary forces in Palestine—the pan-Islamic traditionalists and the agnostic pan-Arab intellectuals, united in a common xenophobia—were precisely those forces which represented the principal domestic opposition to these Governments and to their pro-Western policies. The events in Palestine, therefore, in that they exasperated and emboldened these forces, posed a possible threat to these Governments and to these policies. The existence of this threat was recognized both by the Arab Governments and the British

Government. As early as 1922 the British Government had recognized that the provisions of the Palestine Mandate were incompatible with that policy of collaboration by consent which, after the troubles in Egypt and Iraq in 1919 and 1920, had been tacitly substituted for a policy of force as a means of securing British imperial interests in the Middle East. But it was not until the Arab rebellion in 1936 that the British Government began to realize that the whole laboriously constructed edifice of consent was being threatened by their Palestine policy. This realization marks the beginning of a new phase in Anglo-Arab relations. It is this phase which we shall now examine.

Within a few weeks of the outbreak of the Arab strike and rebellion in April 1936 the Palestine Arab cause was already attracting attention in Arab lands beyond the boundaries of Palestine, and particularly in Syria, Transjordan and Iraq. This was a new phenomenon. Earlier outbreaks in Palestine, in 1929 and in 1933, had aroused no such interest. In Syria, the home of Arab nationalism, and, moreover, a country which had still not attained its independence from the French, the interest was particularly intense and it was from Syria that the majority of Arab volunteers from outside Palestine were later to be recruited. The French, who were not displeased to see some Arab nationalist odium transferred from their heads to those of the British, and whose local officials in Syria had a traditional distrust of the British, did nothing to prevent and may even have encouraged this Syrian interest.

The first official Arab move came in August 1936 when Taufiq as Suwaidi, the Prime Minister of Iraq, with the connivance, and possibly at the invitation of, the British Government made an unsuccessful attempt to persuade the Palestine Arab Higher Committee to call off the strike which had been declared at the beginning of the disturbances. Two months later, the strike was called off as the result of an appeal to the Higher Committee by Amir Abdullah of Transjordan and by Abdul Aziz ibn Saud, who declared their conviction that Great Britain would do justice to the Palestine Arabs. The wording of this appeal, which had clearly been made after prior consultation with the British Government, made it apparent that the British Government had become committed to find a solution to the Palestine troubles which would be acceptable to moderate Arab opinion as represented by the independent Arab Governments. From that time on, consultation between the British Government and the Arab Governments over the future of Palestine was continuous, and accompanied by a continuous pressure on the Arab Governments, from the Arab side, in the form of resolutions, demonstrations, 'Palestine Days', etc. The rejection by the British Government of the Report of the Peel Commission, which recommended the partition of Palestine into Arab and Jewish areas, was the result of intimations received from the independent Arab States that such a solution would be unacceptable to them—or rather to public opinion in their countries. The solution imposed by the British Government in 1939, according to the provisions of what has become known as the 1939 White Paper, was promulgated after consultation with the Governments of Egypt, Iraq, Transjordan, Saudi Arabia and Yeman, representatives from which had attended the Conference in London preceding the issue of the White Paper, although these Governments felt unable publicly to commend this solution to the Palestine Arabs. Under the provisions of the 1939 White Paper Jewish immigration into Palestine was to be limited to a further 75,000, to be admitted during the succeeding five years, after which there was to be no further Jewish immigration without Arab consent. Land sales to Jews were to be forbidden over most of Palestine and restricted over most of the rest. After an interim period of ten years, during which self-governing institutions were to be gradually built up under the British Mandate, Palestine was to become an independent bi-national State within the British Commonwealth with an Arab majority and with special guarantees for safeguarding the interests of the Jewish minority. This Statement of Policy, like the Anglo-Iraqi and Anglo-Egyptian Treaties, contained sufficient concessions to the Arab nationalist viewpoint to serve as a logical extension to the policy underlying these Treaties, which was to secure the Middle East as a strategic base and as a corridor of communication for the military and commercial purposes of Great Britain and her allies by finding a *modus vivendi* with the increasing exigencies of Arab nationalism. The growing certainty of a Second World War increased both the urgency and the difficulty of maintaining and widening that *modus vivendi*. It increased the urgency for obvious reasons. It increased the difficulty because this *modus vivendi* was based on the reality of British power. The only justification for each act of collaboration lay in the certainty that, as an alternative to collaboration, Great Britain could impose submission. Any diminution of this certainty reduced the justification for and increased the domestic resistance to collaboration. The military and diplomatic successes achieved by Germany and Italy since 1935 had reduced this certainty and had begun to undermine the collaborationist position.

The consultations with and between the Arab States arising out of the Palestine rebellion had the effect of restoring the Arab world as a psychological entity both in the minds of outsiders and in the minds of Arabs themselves. The effect on the Arabs was seen in the assistance to the Palestine Arab cause given by Arab volunteers from Syria, Iraq and elsewhere and in the two pan-Arab Conferences held in Bludan in 1937 and in Cairo in 1938, both of which put heavy pressure on the Arab Governments who, in their turn, put heavy pressure on the British Government. Arab nationalists in all countries were beginning to look once more beyond the strait boundaries which had been imposed on them by the Peace Treaties.

This new Arabism was not a homogeneous movement; implicit in it were all the dynastic rivalries, xenophobic resentments and prudent calculations which had marked and marred the previous twenty years. The picture is a complicated one. It is perhaps best presented on the one hand in terms of the dynastic Arabism of the past, and on the other hand in terms of the popular Arabism of the future.

Amir Abdullah of Transjordan, the senior surviving, the most able and the most ambitious of the Hashemites (the family name

of what has up to now been described as the Sherifian family),
had never regarded Amman as more than a staging post on the
way to Damascus. His loyalty to the British connection was
largely grounded in the conviction that the fulfilment of the
British pledge to Husain had been delayed but not aborted by the
exigencies of the peace settlement after the First World War. He
looked forward to the day when Iraq, Syria, Lebanon, Palestine
and Transjordan would be united in a Greater Syria under
Hashemite rule. He regarded the approach of independence in
Syria and Lebanon, the rebellion in Palestine and even the
imminence of a second world war mainly in their relation to the
possible fulfilment of this dream. To that end he became increasingly active in the internal affairs both of Palestine and of Syria,
hoping to gain sufficient support in these countries to obtain
recognition for himself as the heir of the French Mandate in Syria
and of the British Mandate in Palestine.

Inflexibly opposed to this Hashemite dream of a Greater Syria
was Abdul Aziz ibn Saud. Such an accession of power to his
Hashemite rivals would have reduced him once more to the status
of a desert chieftain. With a view to blocking Abdullah's ambitions, he established particularly close links with the leaders of
the National Bloc in Syria, who formed the majority Party in that
country and who could reasonably be expected to control its
Government as soon as the French Mandate had come to an end.
More importantly he seems to have persuaded the British Government that British support for Hashemite ambitions was incompatible with a policy of friendship with the Arabs as a whole.

In this task of persuasion he was assisted by the appearance of
Egypt on the stage of Arab affairs. Until the signature of the
Anglo-Egyptian Treaty in the summer of 1936 Egypt had been
occupied entirely, as regards external affairs, by her relations
with Great Britain. On her emergence as an independent nation
Egypt, as a Moslem and as an Arabic-speaking country, inevitably began to take an interest in Arab affairs and, just as
inevitably, in view of her population, her comparative wealth
and her technical and cultural maturity in comparison with the

other Arab nations, aspired to leadership in the Arab world. Abdullah's ambitions for a Greater Syria, which would have challenged and probably defeated any prospect of such leadership, were therefore as unpopular in Egypt as they were in Saudi Arabia.

This division between Saudites and Hashemites, with the new Arab Power of Egypt throwing its weight on to the side of the former, was to shape Arab affairs for the next ten years. But beneath their surface differences the rulers of these countries were united in their determination to arrest the spread of popular movements in the Arab world.

The immediate effect of the Palestine Arab rebellion on these popular movements was to give a new lease of life both to the pan-Islamic and to the intellectual agnostic species of xenophobia which formed a permanent opposition to the social status quo in the Arab countries and to the pro-Western policies of the Arab Governments. Of these two tendencies the pan-Islamic was infinitely the more powerful and it received immense reinforcement from the personality and achievements of Haj Amin al Husaini, Mufti of Jerusalem, President of the Supreme Moslem Council of Palestine and leader of the Palestine Arab rebellion. Moslem fanaticism, expressed as a reaction against Western techniques and Western ways of life exemplified by the Zionists, was the mainspring of the Palestine rebellion and might well have become a much more important factor than it did in Arab nationalism. As it was, it proved a dead end, like the secular Syrian nationalism represented by the Syrian Popular Party, founded in 1935 by Anton Saade, a Lebanese Christian. The PPS (Partie Populaire Syrien) was in the true line of succession from the Syrian nationalists of the nineteenth century and, just as the nineteenth century nationalists were influenced by the liberalism of Western Europe, so the PPS were influenced by the Fascist ideas then current in Central Europe. Like Abdullah, the PPS advocated a Greater Syria, but as a Republic and not under a Hashemite king. It is only interesting historically as a stage in the development of that intellectual, Syrian Arab nationalism which has always been such an important factor in the shaping of Arab nationalist thought and, to some extent, in the forming of Arab nationalist policy.

In spite of the immediate encouragement which the Palestine rebellion gave to Arab radicalism its intermediate effect was not to strengthen radical but to consolidate conservative tendencies in the Arab world. For the conservatives, the princes and the pashas, who were identified with the British connection both in the popular mind and in fact, had been able to use the Palestine rebellion to persuade the British Government to a major change of policy over Palestine and had thus been able once more to justify the policy of collaboration, in terms of realism, as giving results which resistance would not have achieved. For there could be no doubt that the considerable concessions to the Palestine Arab case contained in the 1939 White Paper were the result, not of the fighting qualities of the 'fedayin' but of the negotiating finesse of the pashas, galvanized, as they undoubtedly had been, by public opinion.

During the Second World War, the British Government had every reason to be satisfied with that policy of appeasing Arab nationalist sentiment which had culminated, just before the outbreak of war, in the issue of the 1939 Palestine White Paper. Apart from the abortive Rashid Ali coup in 1941 Great Britain was, throughout the whole period of the war, able to use the Arab Middle East as a base and as a channel of communication with the co-operation of the Arab Governments and without opposition from the local populations. In return the Arabs were, by a narrow margin, protected from the ravages of war. In utilitarian terms, the bargain seemed a fair one. But, hidden beneath the censorship, the restricted political activity and the other restraints imposed by martial law, and in spite of the outward success of a policy of collaboration, a tremendous force of resentment was growing up during the war years in Egypt, in Iraq, in Syria, and, to some extent in Lebanon and Palestine and Transjordan, both against the foreign occupiers and the domestic rulers. There were various reasons for this. First, the exigencies of war had en-

abled, and to some extent compelled, the foreign occupier to re-
assert measures of detailed control over nominally independent
countries, which underlined the illusoriness of that independence
and seemed altogether to vitiate such justification as there
apparently had been for a policy of collaboration with the
occupier. Secondly, these same exigencies had enabled and to
some extent compelled the occupying Power, with the connivance
of the domestic Government, to suppress not only violent but also
peaceful manifestations of opposition and discontent, and consequently to ignore or to minimize such legitimate reasons as there
might have been for this opposition and discontent. Thirdly, the
process of inflation, arising from shortage of supplies combined
with heavy military spending, while it had made large fortunes
for a few had, in general, made the poor poorer and the rich
richer and had, in particular, borne heavily on the salaried middle
class, who found their means straitened just at the time when, in
accordance with the normal process of social development, their
aspirations were increasing. By the end of the war, therefore,
there was a mounting pressure on the Arab Governments, and on
the occupying Powers, in some ways reminiscent of that which
had developed in Egypt and in Iraq after the First World War.
But with a difference. Then the demand had been for national
independence as an end in itself. Now the demand was for independence as an essential preliminary to domestic reform. The
identification between foreign occupation and the existing social
order was complete.

The weight of this opposition pressure varied from country to
country. In the dominions of ibn Saud it existed not at all and in
the Amirate of Transjordan, soon to be elevated into a Kingdom
as a reward for Abdullah's war services, hardly at all. In Palestine
everything else was overshadowed for the Arabs by the menace of
Zionism. In Lebanon the traditional ties of the Christian population with the West on the one hand and the economic advantages
possessed by a progressive Christian over a backward Moslem
population gave this nascent discontent a special confessional
character. In the protectorates of the Persian Gulf the first stir-

rings of middle-class discontent, imported from Iraq, were beginning to make themselves felt. But in Egypt, in Syria and in Iraq, something like a revolutionary situation was beginning to develop.

Long before the end of the war it had become apparent that the Arabic-speaking countries were destined to occupy a key position in the power politics of the post-war period. Until the battles of Alamein and Stalingrad in the autumn of 1942 had made the ultimate issue of the war certain, Arab statesmen had understandably tried to conduct themselves in such a way as both to avoid the immediate displeasure of the actual occupiers and the possible vengeance of potential occupiers. The simultaneous retreat of the German armies across the plains of Russia and the deserts of North Africa enabled them to resume what might be termed a policy of positive collaboration in the light of what could now be discerned as the shape of things to come. It was already clear, both to the British Government and to the Arab leaders, that two cardinal factors—the re-emergence of Russia as a World Power and the increasing importance of the Middle East oil deposits to the future industrial needs of Western Europe—fortified the validity and necessitated the continuance of Great Britain's traditional policy of ensuring for her use the countries of the Middle East, both as bases and as lines of communication. What was required, from the British point of view, was an up-to-date version of the 'Arab State or Confederation of States' adumbrated in the pledge to Husain. The Arab leaders, who saw quite clearly the dangers, as well as the advantages of the increased importance of the Arab world both as a strategic area and as a potential source of raw material essential to the West, concentrated their policy on an attempt to build up the diplomatic strength of the Arab States so as to ensure that they were in a position to exploit this increased importance instead of being exploited because of this increased importance. The history of Arab nationalism since 1942 is the history of a series of attempts to exploit, instead of being exploited as the result of, the fortuitous importance which the accidents of history, geography and geology have conferred on

D

the Arab peoples. It is part of the peculiar fascination of Arab
nationalism that this importance was conferred on the Arab
peoples at a time when they were on the one hand sufficiently
developed politically to resent and to resist exploitation and on
the other hand insufficiently developed socially or technically to
make that resistance wholly effective.

The first condition of effective resistance was unity—the trans-
lation of a common tradition and common aspirations into a
common policy which would present something like a united
front to the outside world. The 1939 White Paper, representing a
major change in British policy towards Palestine and constituting
a reversal of the policy laid down in the Palestine Mandate, was
an earnest of what could be achieved as the result of a united
Arab front on a particular issue, supported by public opinion and
uninhibited by dynastic, personal or political rivalries.

This lesson had not been lost on the Arab leaders. As soon as
the Battle of Alamein, in the autumn of 1942, had relieved them
of more immediate political preoccupations, there began a busy
to-ing and fro-ing by Arab politicians between Cairo, Baghdad,
Amman and Riadh which was eventually to issue in the formation of the Arab League. There were two general points of agreement. First, the independence of Palestine by means of an ac-
celeration of the policy laid down in the White Paper. Secondly,
the immediate independence of Syria and Lebanon, in implementation of the promise made by the Free French in 1941. Beyond
this all was rivalry and dissension. Abdullah in Amman saw
Arab unity entirely in terms of a Hashemite Kingdom of Greater
Syria, Nuri as Said in Baghdad saw it in terms of an Iraqi hegemony over a Greater Syria from which Egyptian and Saudi influence would be excluded. Abdul Aziz ibn Saud in Riadh objected to any access of influence either to Iraq or to Transjordan.
In Cairo, Nahas Pasha, the Egyptian Prime Minister, objected to
the aggrandisement of any Arab Power, except Egypt, east of the
Suez Canal. In Damascus, Shukry Kuwatli, the President of the
Syrian Republic and leader of the Syrian National Bloc, was a
faithful and, it might almost be said, slavish adherent of Abdul

Aziz ibn Saud. In Beirut the Christians were fearful of any scheme for Arab unity which might expose them to the domination of a Moslem majority. It was clear therefore that any fruitful scheme of co-operation would have to be conceived in terms of the unimpaired sovereignty of each of the Arab States within their existing boundaries. There was no reason why this limitation, in itself, should have prevented a fairly comprehensive unity *vis-à-vis* the outside world. The immediate reason for failure to achieve this external unity was the question of the future of Palestine. Assuming the emergence of Palestine as a mainly Arab State in accordance with the provisions of the White Paper, would it become an independent State in its own right under the inevitable dominance of the Husaini family, or would it unite with Transjordan and possibly become the nucleus of a Greater Syria? Failure to agree over this was to paralyse united Arab action, not over Palestine only, but over almost everything else. For failure to agree over Palestine was a symptom of that double rivalry, between the Nile and the Euphrates on the one hand and between the desert and the sown on the other which has always imposed its inexorable pattern on the inhabitants of the Middle East and which is the principal reason for the endemic dissension and disunity in the Fertile Crescent.

Unity, whether in Arabia or anywhere else, can be achieved either as the result of the imposition of unity by a single dominant State or as the result of a tacit or formal agreement by all the sovereign States concerned to abandon any attempt at hegemony over the others by way of either invasion or subversion. Such unity as has been attained in Western Europe since the Second World War in face of a common danger has been achieved as a result of this abandonment. The Arab failure to achieve unity in pursuit of a common aspiration has been due on the one hand to the failure of any one State to achieve hegemony and on the other hand to an unwillingness, first on the part of the Hashemites and then on the part of Egypt, to abandon the attempt to do so.

Ever since the early days of the Palestine rebellion the principal protagonist of Arab unity had been Nuri as Said. This was due partly to personal predilection and partly in order to counter actual Saudi and potential Egyptian pressure against Iraq. For although Nuri, like Abdullah, saw Arab unity primarily in terms of a Greater Syria, he was thinking not so much of an Hashemite Kingdom as of an Iraq which, by virtue of becoming the sponsor would also become the master of a Greater Syria and thus, among other things, be able to safeguard the passage of Iraqi oil by pipeline across Syria to the Mediterranean. By 1944 the revenues from oil production in northern Iraq were becoming increasingly important; the only practicable way of exporting this oil was by pipeline across Syria and Lebanon to the Mediterranean and Iraq had a legitimate interest in trying to ensure that these countries remained friendly to her. The subsequent and at first rather reluctant Egyptian and Saudi interest in Arab unity was largely due to a common desire to counter Iraqi ambitions for a Greater Syria which would, in the case of Egypt, have hindered potential Egyptian expansion in that direction and, in the case of Saudi Arabia, have advanced Hashemite at the expense of Saudi influence.

Thus to a very large extent, Arab unity, as it developed from 1942 onwards, was a façade which concealed the reality of a struggle for power within the Arab world for the control of Syria. But it was necessary first of all to free the maiden from captivity before fighting for her hand. The wartime collaboration between Great Britain and the Arab States was based on the understanding that Great Britain would, by securing the evacuation of the French from Syria, and by the implementation and, possibly, the expediting of the White Paper proposals, redeem the Arab interpretation of the promises made to the Arabs in the First World War. The fact that neither Egypt, nor Iraq nor Saudi Arabia had any prospect whatever of securing the liberation of Syria themselves, either by armed invasion or by popular insurrection, necessitated a continuance of reluctant and precarious co-operation with Great Britain until this liberation had been achieved. The British Government, aware on the one hand of the importance and on the other of the precariousness of this co-operation was, to all appearance, on the advice of the Minister of State in Cairo, prepared to purchase its continuance at the expense of Zionist and of French interests. In the event it was as the result of British military action that the French unconditionally evacuated Syria and Lebanon in the summer of 1945. Thus was British acquiescence in the expulsion of Feisal from Damascus handsomely requited almost exactly twenty-five years later. The other half of the British undertaking—the implementation and expedition of the White Paper policy in Palestine—remained unfulfilled. Just as, in the years immediately before the war, Arab pressure from within and from outside Palestine had caused the British Government to abandon the task of trying to impose Jewish colonization on to reluctant Arabs, so, in the years immediately after the war, Zionist pressure from within and from outside Palestine (and particularly Zionist pressure exercised on Great Britain via the US Government) caused Great Britain to abandon the opposite task of trying to impose minority status on to reluctant Jews. This double refusal led inexorably to an abandonment of the Mandate and to a tacit invitation to the Arabs to try and do for themselves what the British Government no longer found it practicable to do for them. The reluctant acceptance of this invitation exposed the Arab States to humiliation and defeat, confronted politically conscious Arabs with a moment of truth which was to usher in a decade of revolution, and put an end to any serious prospect of Anglo-Arab collaboration in the affairs of the Middle East.

The Pact of the Arab League, signed in Cairo in March 1945, was the result of some two years' negotiation between the Governments of the independent Arab States. The original members of the Pact were Egypt, Iraq, Transjordan, Syria, Lebanon, Saudi Arabia and Yeman. During the course of the negotiations leading up to the Pact the initiative in Arab unity had gradually passed out of the hands of Nuri as Said and into those of Mustafa Nahas, the Egyptian Prime Minister. By the time the Pact was signed it had become little more than a hollow instrument of Egyptian prestige, voided of all real content. Instead of being an instrument for the recording and implementing of the highest common factors of Arab unity it became a mirror for depicting Arab dissensions.

During the first few weeks of the League's existence an opportunity occurred for demonstrating its effectiveness as an instrument for common action. In May 1945 a crisis arose in relations between France on the one hand and Syria and Lebanon on the other. France was demanding Treaties with these two countries, on the lines of the Anglo-Iraqi and Anglo-Egyptian Treaties, as a condition of the grant of effective independence which Syria and Lebanon had been promised at the time of the entry of the Allies into Syria and Lebanon in 1941. The treaty terms proposed by France were unacceptable and France was reinforcing her garrisons in Syria and Lebanon as a probable preliminary to coercion. There were serious disturbances in Damascus. A meeting of the Council of the Arab League was announced to discuss the situation, but the fact that it was not held for over a fortnight indicated a desire to avoid precipitate, or indeed any, action at all. By the time the Council did meet the British had already occupied Damascus and secured the evacuation of French toops. There was therefore little left for the Council to do except to thank the British for their intervention. Thereafter, the pressure applied to France for complete and accelerated evacuation from the two States was applied by the British Government and not by the Arab League. The reason given by the British Government for their intervention in Syria was that the French had created a situation in which the Syrian people 'must either surrender to force or call in the help of their Arab neighbours which would have been freely given. In that case the Middle East would have risen and would have dislocated the work of the Middle East base'. (*The Times* of 12 June, 1945, reporting a statement by the British Minister Resident in the Middle East.) As a result of this British intervention and as a result of the British themselves having subsequently withdrawn from the Levant States, thus demonstrating that their intervention had been dictated by no crude imperialist considerations, relations between the British

Government and the Arab League reached a point at which they could be compared to those of a master and his dog. If the Arab League had in any way reflected the aspirations of the Arab peoples, or had in any way been used as an effective instrument of policy by the Arab leaders, this would have been a signal triumph for British policy. As it was, it was rapidly becoming what it has since remained—a branch of the Propaganda Section of the Egyptian Foreign Office.

Official Egyptian interest in Arab affairs had grown steadily since the 1936 Treaty. Nahas Pasha, the principal architect of the Arab League, had seen Arab unity mainly in terms of his personal prestige with the British *vis-à-vis* that of Nuri as Said and of Egypt's prestige with her neighbours *vis-à-vis* that of Iraq. When Nahas was dismissed from office in October 1944, two days after the signature of the Alexandria Protocol which led to the Pact of the Arab League five months later, his interest in, and his motives for being interested in, Arab unity were adopted by King Faruq (who at about this time grew a beard in order to emphasize his Arabism). But behind these considerations of prestige there were more cogent reasons for Egypt's interest in Arabism. Egypt had a rapidly growing peasant population which could not be absorbed into employment either on the land or in industry; she had a rapidly increasing out-turn of secondary school and university graduates who could not be absorbed either into government service, or into the professions, or into commerce and industry. Egypt desperately needed land for her peasants, economic opportunities for her educated middle class, capital for the industries which she hoped to create. It was natural and inevitable that, as Egypt emerged from British tutelage into national independence, successive Egyptian Governments should cast their eyes beyond Egypt's frontiers at the broad and underpopulated territories all around them. It was likewise natural and inevitable that the common language and religion of the inhabitants of these lands, combined with their endemic domestic feuds, should provide the opportunity and temptation to exploit both for the benefit of Egypt's domestic needs.

Iraq's needs for expansion were much less imperative. With a small population and with ample land available for development, Iraq's main need was capital for such development, and there seemed a fair prospect that this would be forthcoming from future oil revenues, provided that access across Syria for that oil to the Mediterranean could be safeguarded. Iraq's purposes in the Arab League were therefore much more genuinely defensive than those of Egypt, and the presence in a liberated Syria of a National Bloc Government, hostile to Iraq and in close relations with Saudi Arabia and, later, with Egypt, was a matter of legitimate concern to the Iraqi Government.

For Abdul Aziz ibn Saud, Egypt's leadership in the Arab League and Egypt's increasing interest in Arab affairs generally was a welcome offset to Hashemite influence. But at the same time the machinery of the Arab League threatened to replace his well-established role as a mediator and elder statesman in the Arab world. Therefore, while quite prepared to see the Arab League as a convenient forum for discussion and consultation between Arab rulers and Governments, he was no more prepared than was any other Arab ruler to assist it to develop any independent authority of its own.

Lebanon was almost equally divided numerically and politically between the Christians, who had almost a vested interest in a divided Syria since their continued favourable status in Lebanon depended on a perpetuation of this division, and the Moslems, who had an almost equal vested interest in a united Syria since this alone would deliver them from what many of them regarded as Christian domination in Lebanon.

King Abdullah of Transjordan, still dreaming of a recreated Hashemite Kingdom under British protection and embracing the whole of geographical Syria, found himself almost unanimously opposed by the members of a League which, while ostensibly devoted to the cause of Arab unity was, in practice, and by the wish of the majority of its member States, becoming a means of preserving the status quo at all events until such time as Egypt should be in a position to alter it.

In this complicated situation Palestine occupied a key position. On the assumption of Palestine becoming an independent Arab State (with a Jewish minority) as envisaged in the 1939 White Paper, it could either remain a separate State, or join with Trans-jordan, or become part of a Greater Syria. In view of the jealousies which inhibited the possibility of a Hashemite Greater Syria, it was obvious that the possibility of a union between an Arab Palestine and Transjordan would be opposed, and for the same reasons, by all those Arab States which objected to the larger Hashemite plan for a Greater Syria. This division between the Hashemites and the rest was reflected among the Arabs of Palestine who displayed, in miniature and in public, a picture of all the dissensions in the rest of the Arab world which were, on the whole, concealed beneath the façade of the Arab League. The Husaini[2] faction, which had been the backbone of the rebellion and which, in spite of its wartime Axis affiliations (Haj Amin, after having helped to engineer the Rashid Ali coup, had spent most of the rest of the war in Germany and was still not permitted to return to Palestine) was still the strongest single group in Palestine, was committed to the idea of an independent Palestine without any more intimate connection with Transjordan than would be provided by common membership of the Arab League. In fact, any sort of amicable relationship, either political or personal, between the Husainis and Abdullah, had long been made impossible by the murderous feud which the Husainis had been carrying on in Palestine since 1937 against their political opponents, most of whom were supporters or clients of Abdullah. This meant that all those Arab States which, for one reason or another, were opposed to a Greater Syria—Egypt, Saudi Arabia, Lebanon and Syria—became committed to the support of, and in practice compelled to connive at, the mindless excesses and follies of the Husaini faction in pursuance of their domestic feuds in Arab Palestine. In this way the Arab States, steadfast only in their refusal to face the implications of the policy to which they were committed, found themselves imperceptibly but inexorably drifting towards a war for which their armies were physically and their people psychologically unprepared.

The British Government, harassed by Zionist terrorism and by American pro-Zionist pressure, were gradually retreating towards that point which they reached in the autumn of 1947, when they announced their intention of abandoning the Mandate after six months and, in effect, of leaving the Arabs and Jews to fight it out.

In the liberation of Syria and Lebanon from the French, the British had done the work of the Arab League for them, leaving the member States, by their raucous resolutions, to provide background music for the clash of arms which extruded the French from the Levant States. This had followed the precedent, set in the First World War by the British, when they had handed over Damascus to Feisal's Arabs after having themselves captured it from the Turks. There seemed to be a general disposition among the Arab Governments to assume that the same thing would happen over Palestine, leaving the Arabs to dispute possession of the carcase among themselves after the animal had been slain. When it became apparent that this was not going to happen the Arab Governments and peoples were faced with an exacting test of their political maturity, military preparedness and capacity for united action. Their complete failure to pass, or even seriously to attempt, this test, marks the end of what we have called the Palestinian and the beginning of what may be termed the Nasserite phase of Arab nationalism.

In 1947, and for the next thirteen years, the Arab Governments refused to face the clear-cut choice between fighting and negotiation which was presented over Palestine. Either fighting or negotiation demanded a measure of unity which they proved unable to achieve in face either of a common danger or of a common opportunity. But, even allowing for this state of disunity, something could have been made of the situation. The facts of geography, and the possession by Abdullah of the best-trained and best-equipped of the Arab armies, made it inevitable that Transjordan should be the major partner and probable major beneficiary of a firm decision to fight. This prospect was intolerable to most of the member States of the League. But the alternative prospect of negotiation by these States—with the United Nations and with the British Government—with a view to some compromise which would provide for some form of partition was debarred by their association with the Husaini faction in Palestine. What, in effect, was done was to leave Abdullah's Arab Legion to do most of the fighting in the hope that the other Arab armies, hanging like vultures on to the outskirts of the battle, would be able to appropriate the fruits of victory after it had been won. As a result of this refusal either to fight or to negotiate collectively, the Arab States were first compelled ineffectively to fight, and then humiliatingly compelled to negotiate, separately.

CHAPTER FOUR

Interlude

---◆◆◆◆◆---

The various armistices by which active hostilities in the Palestine war were terminated during the first half of 1949 led to a temporary eclipse of Arab nationalism in the same way as the expulsion of Feisal from Damascus had done twenty-nine years previously. On the Arab League it had the same effect as the Abyssinian war had had on the League of Nations. It destroyed its effectiveness and prestige without terminating its existence. Thenceforward it was to be regarded neither by its members nor by the outside world as a viable instrument of action or of policymaking. The ageing Abdul Aziz ibn Saud, who had prudently kept aloof from,[1] without altogether being able to avoid implication in, the consequences of the Palestine fighting, withdrew for the short remainder of his life from the mainstream of Arab affairs and concentrated on the profitable development of his relationships with the American oil companies. Lebanon, whose material and emotional involvement in the Palestine war had been likewise minimal, began to concentrate on the attainment of that delicate and precarious balance between east and west, between Moslem and Christian, which was the essential condition of its continued existence as an independent State. Abdullah of Transjordan (now known as the Hashemite Kingdom of the Jordan), the only Arab victor in the Palestine war, found himself ruling, in face of almost unanimous Arab nationalist hostility from without, and vigorous Arab nationalist opposition from within, an abbreviated caricature of that Greater Syria which

had originally been regarded as the apotheosis of Arab nationalism. The Governments of Iraq, Egypt and Syria, which were
much more deeply committed over Palestine than either Saudi
Arabia or Lebanon and which, unlike Jordan, had no satisfactory
results from the Palestine campaign with which to appease public opinion, found themselves faced with a dangerous domestic
situation, arising from the effect on an already discontented
middle class of the evidences of governmental weakness, corruption and misjudgment which the Palestine affair had revealed.
In order to understand subsequent events in these countries it is
necessary to have some idea of the revolutionary forces which
were threatening the continued existence of the by now almost
completely discredited parliamentary regimes.

In Egypt easily the most powerful of these forces was the
Moslem Brotherhood. Founded in the late twenties by a school-
teacher named Hasan al Banna, it had had little importance
until, as a result of the Wafd's collaboration with the British,
first over the negotiation of the 1936 Treaty, and later when
Nahas was put into power by the British in 1941, it had gradually
succeeded the Wafd as the principal militant nationalist organization in Egypt. The ideal of the Brotherhood was a theocratic State
based on what it regarded as the primitive principles of Islam.
This involved a complete extrusion of all Western and non-
Islamic influence and a return to a way of life based on the Sharia
Law and the five 'pillars' of Islamic conduct.[2] Up to 1946, its practical policies, as distinct from its theoretical beliefs, had been
opportunist. Variously, as occasion offered, the Brotherhood
accepted support and received subsidies from both the Wafd and
the Palace. But at the same time, under the able leadership of
Hasan al Banna, its organization was being built up, until in 1946
it claimed to have a membership of about two-and-a-half million, closely organized into semi-secret cells covering the whole
country. By the end of 1948 the Brotherhood was as dominant
as, and even more xenophobic and addicted to terrorism than, the
Wafd had been twenty-five years earlier. It eschewed any attempt
at parliamentary opposition, having no more use for parliamen-

tary democracy than it had for social reform; what it wanted was a revolution to be achieved by violence as a preliminary to the setting up of theocratic State. Early in 1949, after the armistice with Israel, the Prime Minister, Noqrashy Pasha, was murdered by a member of the Brotherhood. In consequence, the Brotherhood was forcefully, and temporarily suppressed by Noqrashy's successor, Ibrahim Abdul Hadi. During the course of this suppression the Brotherhood leader, Hasan al Banna, was mysteriously murdered.[3] His successor, Hasan al Hodeibi, was a much less skilful leader and a much less uncompromising revolutionary than Banna and, under the new leadership, the Brotherhood was never to regain its former influence. (If indeed Ibrahim Abdul Hadi, as was popularly believed, had connived at the murder of al Banna, he deserved more thanks from the military regime than he was subsequently to receive.)

Ahmed Husain, the leader of the Egyptian Socialist Party, had followed much the same course of development as other Arab revolutionaries in that he had been pro-fascist in the late thirties and had become pro-communist in the late forties. This was partly opportunism, the worship of an apparently rising star, but also partly, and perhaps mainly, the result of a consistent search for a viable totalitarianism to replace the democratic institutions which they disliked for emotional as much as they despised for practical reasons. In the 1930s Ahmed Husain had founded the Misr al Fatat—the Greenshirts—in Egypt as a para-military organization run on consciously fascist lines. After the war he changed the name of the Party to the 'Egyptian Socialist and Democratic Party'; in domestic affairs he advocated the evolution of a socialist State by peaceful means and in foreign affairs an alliance with Soviet Russia as a means of offsetting British influence in the Middle East. In spite of the Party's outward moderation and professed devotion to constitutional procedure (unlike the Moslem Brotherhood they contested parliamentary seats) their real strength was, not in parliament, where they never had more than one representative, but in the trade unions and on the streets.

In Egypt, the Communist Party, split into half-a-dozen or more disputing factions, was of little importance, overtly or covertly. In Syria, on the other hand, there was a strong Communist Party, led by Khaled Bikdash, the most able communist organizer in the Middle East. There was also in Syria an 'Islamic Socialist Front' which had started as the Syrian branch of the Moslem Brotherhood, but developed less on exclusively Islamic and more on socialist lines and, moreover, unlike the Moslem Brotherhood, contested parliamentary seats and claimed to be a constitutional party. By 1948 it had more affinity with Ahmed Husain's Socialist Party than with the Brotherhood and, like the Egyptian Socialist Party, advocated alliance with the Soviet Union in order to neutralize 'Anglo-American pressure'.

In Iraq there was a strong and well-organized Communist Party. But the principal overt 'revolutionary' opposition was the Istiqlal Party. Like Misr al Fatat in Egypt, this Party had originally been pro-fascist and had been one of the principal forces behind the Rashid Ali coup in 1941. After the war, again like Misr al Fatat, it had become pro-Russian and advocated alliance with the Soviet Union as a means of offsetting 'Western domination'. It was, overtly, a constitutional Party and had a handful of Deputies in the Iraqi Parliament.

It will be observed that there was a common pattern in the 'revolutionary' parties which were developing in the 'democratic' Arab countries. The pattern was nationalist, totalitarian and anti-Western; their various ideological attitudes, ranging from extreme Islamic puritanism to extreme communism, were dictated by this nationalist, totalitarian, anti-Western obsession rather than by any disinterested faith either in Islam or in communism, both of which were regarded primarily as aids to the expulsion of Western influence and to the establishment of a totalitarian State. This made co-operation easy between the various revolutionary parties. Except for the Moslem Brotherhood and the communists, these 'revolutionary' parties were overtly constitutional but their real power lay, not in parliament, but in the streets, and the real basis of their organization was not parliamentary but popular.

The role of the various communist parties was to activate, and to promote common action between, the other 'revolutionary' parties—the 'united front' policy adopted by Western European communism during the thirties against fascism and adapted by Middle East communists during the thirties against parliamentary democracy and Western imperialism.

In this situation, with defeated and discredited parliamentary democracies on the one hand and active, clamant revolutionary parties on the other, the attitude of the various national armies was obviously likely to be decisive. In all three countries the army was reformist rather than revolutionary, although in all three countries some officers had naturally become adherents of one or other of the revolutionary groups. In all three countries the army officers represented a cross-section of the middle class,[4] they had no traditional loyalty to the ruling House or to the local 'establishment' generally; on the other hand that sense of hierarchy and order on which any army is based made them dislike and distrust those tactics of mob incitement characteristic of the 'popular' parties, since they were afraid of the effects of such mob incitement on the rank and file of the army which was as much a cross-section of the workers and peasantry as the officers were of the middle class. So, when the army took over in these countries, as they eventually did, they took over, not to create a revolution but to avert one; they took over when they considered that the weakness or oppressiveness of the Government on the one hand, and the militancy and organization of the revolutionary groups on the other, had reached a point at which it was necessary to overthrow the Government and to inaugurate those social and administrative reforms which had become a necessary condition of preserving the existing social order. For, it is repeated, the army 'revolutions' in the Middle East, whether in Syria, in Egypt or in Iraq, were not revolutions in the sense that they aimed at overthrowing the existing order; on the contrary, they aimed at reinforcing it by, so to speak, cutting away the dead wood, as they saw it, in the shape of kings, pashas, political parties and parliaments, by effectively appeasing whatever they regarded as legitimate popular aspirations and by ruthlessly suppressing revolutionary popular discontent. In Syria, the army took over in 1949, soon after the end of the Palestine war. After an initial period of confusion and turbulence, during which two army leaders, Husni Zaim and Sami Hinnawi, successively seized and were thrown out of power, Colonel Adib Shishakli succeeded in establishing a stable and reformist military regime which lasted for five years and ended, relatively peacefully, in 1954, in what proved to be a transient return to civilian constitutional government. In Egypt, the army took over in 1952, with momentous consequences both for the Middle East and for the world in general. In Iraq, as the result of a succession of Governments, either presided over or dominated by Nuri as Said, which devoted themselves to the ruthless and temporarily successful suppression of the various revolutionary parties, the intervention of the army was delayed until 1958. The effect of this delayed intervention was not to avert but to precipitate a revolution, with the results of which the army then had to try and deal.

The principal consequence of the Egyptian army coup was the revival, under Egyptian leadership, of that Arab nationalism which, to repeat a phrase used by Abdul Nasr himself,[5] had, like a character in search of a hero, vainly been seeking realization since the beginning of the century. It is this consequence which we shall now proceed to examine.

E

CHAPTER FIVE

The Egyptian Revolution

After the Second World War a number of circumstances combined to promote the Middle East from its previous position on the periphery to its present position of being somewhere near the centre of international power politics. The emergence of the Soviet Union as a major World Power and the existence of an endemic state of tension between the Soviet Bloc and the Western World made it inevitable on the one hand that the Western Powers should endeavour to associate the Arab States with that world-wide system of alliances which was designed both to block Russian expansion and to provide, in case of necessity, military bases for use against Russia, and on the other hand that Russia should endeavour to deny to the Western Allies the use of the Arab countries for these purposes. The strategic importance which the accident of geography had conferred on the Arab States in connection with what came to be known as the cold war was enhanced by the accident of geology which provided that the littoral States of the Persian Gulf should contain the world's largest known reserves of petroleum, the production from which was becoming increasingly vital both to the expanding industrial economy of Western Europe and to its potential military requirements in the event of war. In the case of petroleum, as in the case of military bases and alliances, the Western Powers were positively interested either in retaining such control over or in fostering such co-operation with the Arab States as would enable them to continue using relevant resources in the way of communications, bases and raw materials, while the Soviet Bloc were negatively interested in that they required, not to use these resources themselves, but to deny (or in the case of petroleum to be able to deny) their use to the Western Powers. The Soviet Bloc had the advantage in that their ends would to a large extent be served by the encouragement of existing manifestations of nationalism while the Western Powers had the far more difficult task of trying to reconcile the aspirations of Arab nationalism with their own strategic and economic requirements. This reconciliation became the grand object of British and, later, of Anglo-American policy in the Middle East. The Arab League was seen as an instrument, by means of which it might be possible, in exchange for military and economic aid, to perpetuate, to extend and to co-ordinate the treaty relationship which already existed between Great Britain and Iraq and Great Britain and Egypt. But it was precisely against this treaty relationship that post-war Arab nationalism became directed. The immediate cause of France's extrusion from the Levant States, forcibly insisted on by the British in 1945, was France's attempted insistence on concluding treaties with these States based on the Anglo-Iraqi and Anglo-Egyptian models. In the autumn of 1947 the Egyptian Government appealed to the UN Security Council against the 1936 Treaty.[1] In 1948 an Iraqi Government, having signed with the British Government a new treaty which, while modifying, renewed the clauses in the 1930 treaty which gave the use of military bases in Iraq to British forces, was forced to resign office as a result of the clamours of the Baghdad mob against the treaty, which was never ratified. The only Arab country where the government was in conformity with and where public opinion did not (until after the Palestine war) object to those relationships which Great Britain regarded as being basic to her Middle East policy and necessary for the interests of the 'free world', was Transjordan, whose ruler was regarded by most of the other Arab Governments, and by most Arab public opinion, as a creature of the British, and whose treasury was almost entirely dependent on a British subsidy.

In fact, British policy in the Middle East, based as it was on a network of treaty relationships with independent Arab States, at harmony with each other and with Great Britain, would have made these States satellites of Great Britain. This policy had already collapsed under the weight of adverse opinion in the Arab world before the Palestine war gave it its *coup de grâce*.

The emergence of an effective public opinion in Egypt, in Iraq and in the Levant States, but not as yet in the Arabian Peninsula or in the Sudan, was a decisive factor in determining the future policies of these States. Before the war public opinion had been largely a matter of personalities. Opposition to the government and pressure on the government were exercised by individuals who had either to be effectively placated or effectively suppressed. In so far as mobs or newspapers incited to violence, they did so as paid agents of individuals. When the paymaster turned or became silent, they all turned or became silent. It is not easy, either in the Middle East or elsewhere, to discern the exact point at which public opinion becomes an anonymous, unpredictable force in its own right, and when 'subversive elements' can no longer be effectively controlled either by the bribery or imprisonment of individuals. But there is no doubt that, during the war years, this change had, almost unregarded, taken place in most of the countries of the Middle East and had confronted the governments of these countries with the alternatives of reform, repression and revolution. For the time being this public opinion could be diverted from domestic matters by a sufficient degree of anti-imperialist zeal on the part of governments.

From 1945 to 1948 the main threat to Western interests seemed to be the Soviet pressure on Turkey and Iran which had, as its intended effect, the reduction of these countries to Soviet satellite States. These threats were resisted by these two States with the assistance of American arms, American advice and American money, and it was behind the umbrella provided by this resistance that the Arab States were enabled to pursue their disputes with Great Britain and with each other without serious damage either to the Western alliance or to themselves. Nevertheless, the 'power vacuum' which existed in the Arab world in 1949 was full of potential dangers, not only to the Arab peoples themselves but to the peace of the world generally. British and French forces had evacuated the Levant States. British forces had evacuated Palestine, leaving behind them the new State of Israel, in an endemic state of war with her Arab neighbours, and a million Arab refugees, distributed among the neighbouring Arab countries. The only substantial British base was in the Canal Zone. In Iraq and Jordan there were small RAF forces who could only be regarded as detachments from the main Middle East force on the Canal Zone, and whose continued presence would become meaningless if the Canal Zone were evacuated. Only along the southern rim of the Arabian Peninsula, from Aden to Kuwait, in the British-protected Sheikhdoms bordering on the Indian Ocean and the Persian Gulf, did there exist those treaty relationships with local governments and those British and British-trained forces which British policy had envisaged as the desirable pattern for the whole Arab world.

The responsibilities which Great Britain had all but relinquished had not been assumed by the United States, whose interests in the Arab world were still mainly confined to Saudi Arabia, the output of whose oilfields now exceeded those of the British-controlled oilfields of Iraq and approached those of the British-owned and British-controlled oilfields of Iran, and where the Americans had, with the agreement of the Saudi Government, established a military airbase. Neither had they been assumed by the Arab States themselves, whose military defencelessness and whose mutual dissensions had just been advertised to the world by the Palestine campaign.

A 'power vacuum' may be defined as an area where one or more politically immature, socially backward or militarily defenceless States, occupying an area which is either strategically important or rich in some vital raw material, or both, provide a standing temptation for military intervention and occupation by some outside power. Apart from abolishing a power vacuum by filling it, there are, broadly, two ways in which it can be maintained without endangering peace by provoking international rivalries. The first, of which the Monroe Doctrine is the classic example, is for a neighbouring Great Power to place an effective shield of protection round the area. The second, of which traditional British policy towards the Low Countries is the classic example, is for all neighbouring Great Powers to guarantee the neutrality of the area and to refrain from unilateral intervention in it. In the Middle East, the first of these methods was impossible because Great Britain had not the means and the United States had not the will to provide the protective shield; the second was impossible because the state of cold war inhibited such an exercise in self-denial by any of the Powers concerned.

Inability to provide for the policing of this power vacuum led to a British determination to fill it as far as possible by an attempted insistence on the implementation of existing treaties with Egypt, Iraq and Jordan, by the maintenance of British garrisons in Cyprus, Libya, Aden and the Persian Gulf, and by renewed attempts to secure American participation in the defence of Western interests in the Middle East. This British decision, which was in effect a conscious decision to swim against instead of with the tide, to resist instead of attempting to co-operate with the forces of nationalism in the Middle East, to perpetuate the divisions rather than to encourage the unity of the Arab States, to sustain reactionary rather than to come to terms with progressive forces in the Arab world, was no doubt in part the instinctive reaction of a declining imperial Power in retreat before the forces of nationalism. But there was more to it than that. In the days before the cold war had achieved a relative equilibrium, and in the days before the United States was less wholly committed to the defence of the West outside the Western hemisphere, any further erosion of the British military position in the Middle East, in deference to the demands of a distracted and divided Arab nationalism, would have been a virtual invitation to Soviet intervention, if not in the form of physical invasion, at least in the form of ideological and political penetration. Such intervention would not only have adversely affected the balance of forces in the cold war, but would also have endangered the flow of Middle

East oil which was becoming an increasingly important factor in the British and in the Western European industrial economies.

These fears were greatly accentuated, first by the outbreak of the Korean War in 1950, which seemed to be a precise example of the sort of communist action to be expected in an unpoliced power vacuum, and secondly by the nationalization of the Anglo-Iranian Oil Company in 1951, which seemed to emphasize, not only the probable result of a military withdrawal in the face of xenophobic nationalism, but also the impossibility of effective defence against such action once military withdrawal had taken place. More than ever it seemed necessary to maintain and even to reinforce the Canal Zone base, both as an assurance to friends and as a warning to enemies.

The Canal Zone base was in appearance the largest visible symbol and in fact the essential condition of British military control of the Middle East. Quite apart from any strategic value which it may have possessed in terms of the cold war, it provided the British with the possibility of military intervention in the internal affairs of the Middle East by enabling them to fly troops and supplies at a few hours' notice to any spot in the Middle East and by enabling them to build up reinforcements at will in the Middle East area. The fact that the British had not used the base for intervention either at Abadan or in any of the numerous domestic crises with which the countries of the Middle East had been afflicted since the end of the war did not affect the nationalist feeling that the mere existence of this base was a limitation on their independence. This feeling was of course far stronger in Egypt than in the rest of the Arab world. The base was on Egyptian soil. Its existence meant that Great Britain and not Egypt was in effective control of the Suez Canal. Egyptian troops could not move into Sinai and up to the Israel frontier without in effect receiving British permission to do so. Egyptians were subjected to search by British sentries on Egyptian soil; Egyptians were liable to be confined in British prisons on Egyptian soil. For a country with aspirations to leadership in the Arab world the position was intolerable and, from 1945 onwards, with varying

degrees of insistence, successive Egyptian Governments had demanded either a cancellation or a drastic revision of the 1936
Treaty.

Arab nationalists, in Egypt and elsewhere, were almost certainly convinced that British insistence on retention of the Canal
Zone base was motivated, not by considerations of cold war
strategy, but by a determination to retain the Arab States as
British satellites. It was, in fact, impossible to distinguish between
the two motivations. Cold war strategy, as seen by Great Britain
at the time, required, not only the provision of airbases in the
Middle East from which bombing attacks could be made on Russia
in the event of war, but also the possibility of local intervention
in the Middle East in the event of a threat to oil supplies or, probably, in the event of a threatened communist coup. It was undoubtedly true that the presence of British forces in the Canal
Zone, and the knowledge that they might be so used, did have
some effect on domestic Arab politics. The concept of alliance,
which Great Britain was continually trying to press on Egypt and
on other Arab countries as a justification for the treaty relationships which the British were trying to perpetuate and extend,
necessarily involved a certain degree of subordination by the
weaker partner to the stronger partner, and necessarily involved
the possibility lest the stronger partner might use the powers
conferred on him by the alliance to intervene in the domestic
affairs of the weaker partner. In these circumstances there has to
be a sharp awareness on the part of the weaker partner of the
peril from which the alliance is intended to protect him, a con-
fident belief that the alliance does provide efficacious protection
against that peril and a feeling of trust that the stronger partner
will not abuse the powers conferred on him by the alliance. These
conditions more or less existed between the United States and the
nations of Western Europe; they existed not at all between Great
Britain and the Arab States of the Middle East. Nine-tenths of
Arab nationalists believed that the communist menace was a
British excuse to perpetuate British control of the Middle East.
The other one-tenth were communists themselves. For seventy

years the Egyptians had been hearing a variety of British reasons explaining why the continued British military occupation of Egypt was necessary; first it was Egypt's finances, then it was the protection of foreigners and minorities, then it was Mussolini, then it was Hitler, then it was the Japanese, and now it was the Russians. They were getting tired of it.

Inextricably associated with the Suez Canal base was the status of the Anglo-Egyptian Sudan. The Sudan had originally been Egyptian territory.[2] It had seceded at the time of the Mahdist revolt, which coincided with the British occupation of Egypt in 1882, and it had been reconquered by Anglo-Egyptian forces and in the name of Egypt in 1898. On its reconquest it had not been reincorporated as part of Egypt, ostensibly in order to avoid the necessity for having to apply to the Sudan the Capitulations and other international privileges applicable to Egypt.[3] When, by the end of the Second World War, all these privileges had been swept away,[4] there was a general feeling in Egypt that there was no further impediment to a reunion between Egypt and the Sudan. But the 1936 treaty, as well as providing for a British base in the Canal Zone for a period of twenty years, also provided for a continuation of the existing dual regime in the Sudan (which virtually amounted to British rule over the Sudan) until such time as the Sudanese were able to decide on their own future. As in the case of the Canal Zone, where the British were regarded as using high-minded expressions like 'the free world' and 'the democracies' to perpetuate and extend British domination over the Arab world, so in the Sudan the Egyptians were convinced that the British were using expressions like 'the right of the Sudanese to decide their own future' as a cloak for Egyptian extrusion from and for continued British occupation of the Sudan.

The truth—and a realization of this is essential to an understanding of the third (or Egyptian) stage of Arab nationalism—is that, perhaps unconsciously or half consciously as yet, Egyptian nationalism, borne forward by population pressure, was interested, not merely in removing British hegemony from the Middle East, but in replacing British by Egyptian hegemony.

Egypt had emerged from what we have earlier termed the cocoon of the Ottoman Empire a full century before the rest of the Arab world (excluding for the moment North Africa, which was later to be drawn into the orbit of the Arab world mainly as a result of the Egyptian renaissance). After a brief period, first of French and then of British occupation, it had experienced, under the nominal suzerainty of the Ottoman Sultan, about thirty years of imperial expansion by Mohamed Ali. Egyptian imperialism under Mohamed Ali had followed the two classic routes of Egyptian expansion—southwards up the Nile Valley and down the Red Sea to the Sudan and the Horn of Africa, and westwards across Sinai to the Arabian Peninsula and the Fertile Crescent. At the apogee of his power Mohamed Ali was in effective occupation of most of the Sudan, part of the Horn of Africa, all of Syria and part of the Arabian Peninsula. Ambitious to become the ruler both of an African and of an Arab Empire, Mohamed Ali overstrained his comparatively slender resources by attempting both. If he had pursued the line of least resistance by concentrating on Africa and the Nile Valley, and avoided entanglement in European power politics by the pursuit of an Arab Empire, it is arguable that the course of Middle Eastern history would have been different. As it was, his Arab ambitions threatened the dissolution of the Ottoman Empire, which might have led to a Russian occupation of Constantinople and a consequent disturbance of the delicately poised balance of power in Europe. This provoked European intervention and compelled Egyptian withdrawal from Asia and ended Mohamed Ali's ambitions of an Arab Empire. Thereafter Mohamed Ali and his successors concentrated their imperial ambitions on the Nile Valley and the Horn of Africa. But the financial extravagance of his successors invited European loans; failure to service these loans led first to European interference, then to European financial control and finally, in 1882, when European control had provoked a popular rising, to British military occupation, which was to last for seventy-two years. During that time a variety of causes, including principally the development of perennial irrigation, and the improvement of medical and sanitary services, led to a progressive increase in population which, pressing upon a country where the cultivable area was limited and the extent of industrialization negligible, was to provide the driving force and justification for future manifestations of Egyptian imperialism.

Egypt's long struggle with Great Britain for independence is marked by four principal milestones. The first is the unilateral British Declaration of Independence in 1922, when Great Britain conferred on Egypt a limited independence subject to British responsibility for defence, foreign policy, protection of foreigners and minorities, and the Sudan. The second was the 1936 Treaty, by which Egypt became an independent sovereign State, but subject, within defined limits, to continued British military occupation and continued British control over the Sudan. The third milestone is the Sudan Agreement of 1953 whereby Great Britain, in effect, relinquished the special British position in the Sudan, leaving the Sudanese to choose between independence and union with Egypt. The fourth and last milestone is the Anglo-Egyptian Agreement of 1954 which provided for the evacuation of British forces from the Canal Zone base. The last two milestones were attained by the revolutionary regime which seized power in Egypt in July 1952, and were an indispensable preliminary to and preparation for the wave of Egyptian expansionism, and its identification with Arab nationalism, which followed.

From 1919 until 1945 the external defence of the Arab States was the responsibility of Great Britain and France. Serious internal disorders were also, in practice, dealt with by the European occupiers. The various armies of the Arab States, in so far as they had a function at all, acted either as an internal police force, or as auxiliaries to, and under the command of, European forces. This subordinate status was almost entirely unaffected by the various instalments of independence which were achieved for, so long as the various 'independence' treaties provided for the presence of foreign military commands, for so long were the indigenous armies subordinated, for military purposes, to the control of these military commands. During the Second World War no

Arab army, except the Transjordan Arab Legion, played any active fighting role, and all of them emerged from the conflict scathless, outmoded, humiliated and unregarded. It was not surprising that ambitious officers in these armies, deprived of the possibility of any worthwhile military experience, responsibility or achievement, should turn their attention to political activity, and hardly surprising that, shorn of their normal military responsibility for external defence, they should think in terms of using such arms and organization as they possessed for internal intervention.

The object of such interventions was always seen as reformist rather than revolutionary and was, generally speaking, delayed until such time as imposed reform of the *status quo* was the only alternative to revolution. In Syria the absence of any 'popular' alternative to, and the extreme weakness of, the National Bloc, precipitated an army coup immediately after the Palestine war. In Iraq a series of strong and resolute reactionary governments delayed an army coup for ten years. In Egypt the coup was delayed for four years. The principal reason for this was that the failure in Palestine and the discontents of the immediate post-war period generally had been associated entirely with the succession of Palace coalitions which had ruled Egypt since 1944. The Wafd was still able to pose as the 'People's Party', capable both of achieving internal reforms and of ridding the country of the 'foreign oppressor'. It was not until the Wafd, which was returned to power at the general elections in 1950, had been tried in the balance and found wanting that the reformist potentialities of parliamentary democracy in Egypt were seen to be exhausted.

Up to 1945 the rivalry between the Palace and the Wafd had, on the whole, been advantageous to the British occupiers in that either party had usually been prepared to compound with the British in order to secure power for itself. But from 1945 onwards, such was the mounting strength of public opinion against the British connection that each side was compelled to try and outbid the other in nationalist zeal. At the end of 1944 the Wafdist

Government, which had been put into power by the British in 1941 and which remained there on British insistence for three and a half years until the end of active hostilities in the Middle East area, was dismissed by King Faruq. Thereafter, until 1950, there was a series of Palace coalitions which tried to divert increasing popular discontent, first by an increasingly chauvinistic attitude in their relations with Great Britain and, later, by an excess of extreme and ineffective bellicosity over Palestine. In both these matters domestic rivalries prevented the accomplishment of anything useful by making compromise impossible. It had to be all or nothing. The two points at issue with Great Britain were the presence of British forces in the Canal Zone and the future of the Sudan. There is no doubt that, before the British evacuation of Palestine, and before the Korean War had stiffened the British attitude towards the Canal Zone base, the evacuation of this base could have been secured by negotiation had not the Egyptian negotiators insisted on linking evacuation of the Canal Zone with the future of the Sudan, and on insisting that the Sudan was an integral part of Egypt which should be restored to Egypt without reference to the wishes of the Sudanese themselves. In the midst of all this sterile and acrimonious negotiation, the rulers of Egypt were, apparently unconsciously, drifting towards a war over Palestine, in which their Arab League policy demanded that they should take a major share and for which they had made no attempt to prepare themselves. Their foreign policy resolved itself into a series of raucous gestures designed, not to accomplish anything, but to provide opponents and critics with irrefutable evidence of their impeccable patriotism.

This opposition and this criticism were increasing. There was the parliamentary opposition of the Wafd, which had once been the only serious opposition with which a 'Palace' coalition had had to contend. But far more formidable than this was the extra-parliamentary opposition. In retrospect it can be seen that the Palestine campaign precipitated the end of pashadom, whether represented by the Palace or by the Wafd. Its existence was threatened on the one hand by a disaffected army whose officers, as in the days of Orabi, reflected the more or less sophisticated and reasonable discontent of the urban middle class, and on the other hand by the Moslem Brotherhood, which represented the inchoate fury of the masses with royal extravagance, governmental incompetence and British occupation.

The Palestine war and the subsequent necessity for dealing with the Moslem Brotherhood temporarily relegated Anglo-Egyptian relations to the background. So menacing had the internal situation in Egypt become that Palace and politicians might have preferred to leave them there. But the very menace of the internal situation demanded a quarrel with and, if possible, a success against, Great Britain as a diversion. It was not long before the Wafd Government, elected to power in 1950, decided that negotiations were unlikely either to achieve results or appease popular excitement. The People's Government, as they termed themselves, were just sufficiently in touch with the people to realize that something spectacular and successful was required to rehabilitate the credit of constitutional government in Egypt. In October 1951 the Anglo-Egyptian Treaty was denounced, on the Government's motion, by an unanimous and enthusiastic vote in the Egyptian Parliament and to the accompaniment of delirious comment in the Press. An offer to replace the treaty by a NATO-type alliance which would provide for the continued use of the Canal Zone base manned, not by the British only, but by the forces of an alliance which would include Egypt, was contemptuously rejected. There followed several weeks of sporadic violence and sabotage in the Canal Zone accompanied by a mass withdrawal of Egyptian labour. The Egyptian army took no part in the violence and appeared to be a neutral 'third' between the Egyptian Government and the British. Their moment was near at hand. On 26 January, 1952, there was a serious riot in Cairo provoked by the news of a British attack on Egyptian auxiliary policemen in the Canal Zone. Matters rapidly got beyond the capacity of the police to control. The army refused to move without orders from the King. These orders were, at the despairing request of the Government, rather belatedly given. The army moved into Cairo, order was rapidly restored, and the Wafdist Government dismissed from power.

Momentarily it appeared that the Palace had won a victory for royal autocracy against both mob rule and constitutional government. But in reality the army were the masters of the situation, and they were prepared neither to use nor be used by a King whom most of them had come to detest and to despise. The military coup of July 1952 was brought about by a group of young army officers who, while sharing the popular discontent with British imperialism on the one hand, and with domestic corruption, inefficiency and injustice on the other, had no clear programme of action prepared after they had seized power. It appears that the Free Officers Movement which engineered the coup quite genuinely believed that their function was, by overturning the existing regime, to liberate all those beneficent and constructive forces which were assumed to be awaiting the opportunity to express themselves in action. But these forces, when liberated, had nothing constructive to offer. When people or nations are suffering, or believe themselves to be suffering, from oppression, there is an almost universal tendency to believe that the removal of the causes of the oppression will lead automatically to a solution of all the real ills with which they are afflicted. Thus, national liberation creates the necessity for some form of dictatorship as the only alternative to chaos. Sometimes, if this liberation has come about by constitutional means, there is a period of chaos, followed either by a civilian or a military dictatorship; alternatively, if liberation has come about as the result of a military coup, the coup is immediately followed by the setting up of a military dictatorship. In Egypt, the popular view was that liberation had only been half achieved by the military coup. Domestic tyranny had been abolished; British imperialism remained. Since British imperialism had been sustained by its alliance with domestic tyranny, the abolition of the latter opened the way to the abolition of the former. What was required was a determined blast of trumpets which would cause the collapse of the already undermined walls of the imperialist Jericho. And when they had fallen, all the poverty, the dissension, the social, technical and economic backwardness, all the mundane difficulties with which Egypt was afflicted, and which had for so long been attributed to the machinations of imperialists and to the corruption of pashas, would automatically disappear, and everybody would live happily ever after. It was very much the same mood as that in which many British working-class people approached the prospect of a Labour Government in 1945, and very much the same mood in which an otherwise sophisticated individual might face the prospect of being cured of a serious disease or relieved of an overwhelming burden. In these circumstances, even a government with a clearly thought-out political and economic programme is tempted to rely primarily on a mixture of repression and promises, on a combination of discipline today and jam tomorrow. When a government has no such programme in view the temptation is almost irresistible. It is to the credit of the revolutionary regime that the temptation was, to a large extent, resisted.

Certain immediate reforms were necessary. Faruq was deposed and sent into exile. Parliament was indefinitely prorogued. The titles of Pasha and Bey were abolished. More importantly, all landed estates in excess of 200 feddans were expropriated and distributed to peasants. Party political activity was banned. All this took most of the second half of 1952. The military regime had established itself. It enjoyed both popularity and authority, which is more than could have been said of any of its immediate predecessors. Unlike its predecessors it was able to tackle the question of relations with Great Britain without much fear of the violence of mobs or the machinations of political rivals. It did so realistically. It separated the two great questions of the Sudan and the Canal Zone and agreed to negotiate these two issues separately and one at a time. It avoided the previous, and hopeless, recipe, used both by the Palace coalitions and by the Wafd, of dilatory negotiation accompanied by ineffective violence. Within a very few weeks an agreement had been reached over the Sudan. Under the previous regime such an agreement had always been prevented by continued Egyptian insistence that the Sudan was a part of Egypt and must be treated as such. The military regime, having conceded the principle of self-determination, came to an agreement with both the principal Sudanese political groups —the Ashigga group of parties favouring union with Egypt, and the Umma favouring independence both from Great Britain and from Egypt—which provided for immediate elections, for a three-year transitional period during which all powers remaining in the hands of the British were to be handed over to the Sudanese, and, at the end of the three-year period, for a referendum to decide whether the Sudan should be independent or united with Egypt. Having thus secured in advance the agreement of the two principal parties to this accelerated programme of self-determination, and having therefore trumped the British ace, an agreement on these lines with the British Government was almost inevitable and was arrived at during January 1953. Almost immediately following this agreement, negotiations were started with the British Government over the Canal Zone base. These negotiations took rather longer and were complicated by two factors.

On the Egyptian side domestic divergencies had begun to appear within the military Junta. General Neguib, the titular leader of the revolution, and Head of State after a Republic had been proclaimed in July 1953, was in favour of a gradual return to constitutional life, with the military regime, having got rid of the King, having 'abolished corruption' and having accomplished a few urgent and overdue reforms, fading from the scene like the Cheshire cat, leaving nothing but a benevolent grin behind. This had been the original concept of the Free Officers who brought about the coup. But Gamal Abdul Nasr, at this time a comparatively unknown figure, and most of the other members of the Junta, had soon come to realize that a return to constitutional life would involve in all essential respects a return to the *status quo ante* 23 July, 1952. The bloodless and outwardly silent struggle for power between Neguib and Abdul Nasr, between reform which would have meant reaction and revolution which would have meant reform, lasted until April 1954, when Abdul Nasr became Prime Minister and Chairman of the Revolutionary

F

Command Council and the real power in the country. Neguib, who remained for some months longer as President, without power or influence until he was removed and eliminated altogether from public life, had, with the assistance of modern methods of publicity, become a popular 'father figure' in Egypt and had done much to commend the new regime to the people. By way of contrast, Gamal Abdul Nasr appeared unsympathetic, a saturnine, unsmiling figure who had not yet, in the public mind, established his ascendancy over the other members of the Revolutionary Council—Salah Salem, Gamal Salem, Abdul Latif Boghdadi, Hassan Ibrahim, and Zakaria Mohieddin—who were themselves only just beginning to become known to the public.

This ascendancy was soon to be established, both in fact and in the imaginations, not only of the Egyptian people but of the whole Arab world. Whether consciously or otherwise, the media of mass communication were used, first in Egypt and later throughout the Arab world, to build up a quite specific, clear-cut and well defined image of 'Big Brother'.

On the Egyptian side these domestic adjustments had delayed the process of negotiation with Great Britain over the Canal Zone. On the British side, within the Conservative Party which was now in power, an emotional resistance to the idea of evacuation from the Middle East was beginning to build up. This emotional resistance was best expressed by Churchill himself when, in one of his wartime speeches, he said, 'I have not become Prime Minister in order to preside over the liquidation of the British Empire.' After the war it did appear to many Tories that the British Empire was being liquidated. To these Tories, as was to appear later, the Suez Canal had an almost sacramental significance as the 'imperial life line'. Egypt, although never technically part of the British Empire, was regarded by many Tories as such, and as a particularly insubordinate and undeserving part at that. The Middle East was still regarded as a British sphere of influence and the maintenance of that influence was considered more than ever necessary in order both to keep out communism and to 'keep the oil flowing'. The Arab was still regarded as a

British client, ungrateful, perhaps, and misguided, but one who could, under proper direction, be drawn towards the light. And the Egyptian was most emphatically not an Arab. The Canal Zone base, quite apart from its undoubted strategic importance, was regarded by the right wing Tories rather as a medieval baron might have regarded a chastity belt, since it guarded the integrity of the 'imperial life line' and prevented the Arabs from getting up to any serious mischief. These feelings, which appear to have been shared to a certain extent by the British Prime Minister himself, led to a certain lack of enthusiasm in the pursuit of the Canal Zone negotiations.

But, in spite of this lack of enthusiasm on the British side, agreement between the British and Egyptian Governments on the future of the Base was arrived at in July 1954. This Agreement provided for the evacuation of the Base by British troops within eighteen months, for the maintenance of the Base in time of peace by civilian technicians and for the 're-activation' of the Base, i.e. for the return of British troops to the Base, in the event of war or the threat of war in the Middle East. (The exact circumstances in which British troops should return to the Base were the subject of long and wearisome negotiation; eventually it was agreed that the Base would be reoccupied in the event of an armed attack by any outside Power on Egypt, or on any other Arab country, or on Turkey.)

In Egypt the Agreement was hailed as 'our final liberation from imperialism'. In Great Britain it was justified on the ground that atomic developments had made the Base less important than before. The right wing Tories showed a prescient scepticism about Abdul Nasr's future intentions and, quite correctly as it proved, regarded the complicated arrangements for the replacement of soldiers by civilian contractors as a face-saving gesture to cover the fact of the practical abandonment of the Base.

It seems doubtful whether, at this time, Abdul Nasr had any precise future intentions. In terms of popular mythology, the British and the Pashas had been the two root causes of the various disabilities which afflicted Egypt. Both the British and the Pashas had now, to all appearance, been removed, and the military regime found itself face to face with the realities of the domestic situation.

These realities were fairly grim. The least unmanageable part of them, for a military government, was the growing opposition from the militant wing of the Moslem Brotherhood which, to- gether with the communists, turned against the regime, having originally greeted it with approval, after the elimination of Neguib. (It is at first sight paradoxical that a revolutionary party should have approved of moderate and disapproved of radical reform; but neither the Moslem Brotherhood nor the communists wanted a strong, reformist government; they wanted a reversion to a weak and reactionary one which would have re- created the revolutionary situation which existed at the begin- ning of 1949.) Abdul Nasr's first task, therefore, after the con- clusion of the Anglo-Egyptian Agreement, was to tame the Moslem Brotherhood. Seizing, or creating, the opportunity of an attempt to assassinate Abdul Nasr by a member of the Brother- hood, some four thousand members were arrested, several tried and sentenced to long terms of imprisonment and six condemned to death and subsequently hanged. This purge destroyed, for the time being, the last semblance of active domestic opposition to the military regime. At the same time Neguib, who was alleged to have been the conscious or unconscious Brotherhood nominee as Head of State after Abdul Nasr's overthrow, was placed under house arrest and faded into an obscurity from which he has never emerged.

The drastic treatment meted out to the Moslem Brotherhood was ill-received in other Arab countries, notably in Syria and Saudi Arabia. The Syrian Government gave asylum to those members of the Brotherhood who managed to escape from Egypt and King Saud (his father, the illustrious Abdul Aziz ibn Saud, had died the previous year) expressed his displeasure at an Egyptian proposal to hold an Islamic Conference in Cairo as being an attempted challenge to his position as Guardian of the Holy Places. All this was an unpropitious prelude to that pan-Arab

Egyptian foreign policy which seems already to have been maturing in Abdul Nasr's mind and which may be said to have had its beginnings in the autumn of 1954.

CHAPTER SIX

Egyptian Lebensraum and Positive Neutrality

It is necessary to try and make some estimate of the motives underlying that sponsorship of Arab nationalism which became the principal characteristic of the military regime in Egypt and with which the name of Gamal Abdul Nasr will always be associated. At first, the military coup in Egypt, like the previous military coup in Syria and the subsequent military coup in Iraq, seemed to presage a turning away from the Arab nationalism represented by the Arab League and a concentration on the internal affairs of Egypt and the future relationship between Egypt and the Sudan. It was not until after the signature of the Anglo-Egyptian Agreement in 1954 that Abdul Nasr showed himself interested in trying to regain for Egypt that predominant position in the affairs of the Arab League which she had enjoyed up to the time of the Palestine war.

Egypt's domestic circumstances were such as almost to impose on its rulers the necessity for looking for 'lebensraum' outside the borders of Egypt. Egypt's cultivable area consists of the land which, by natural or by artificial means, is irrigated by Nile water. This cultivable area is one of the most densely populated parts of the world and the rate of population increase one of the highest in the world. In order to accommodate and to feed this rapidly increasing population it is necessary (a) progressively to increase the area of cultivable land by means of expensive irrigation works and (b) to supplement Egypt's agricultural resources by a progressive increase in the rate of industrialization. Both these processes demand capital, which Egypt was unable to generate from her own productive capacity. In order to relieve this continual and mounting pressure it was desirable to have the possibility of settling Egyptian peasants on the half-empty land with which Egypt was surrounded—in the Sudan, in Syria and in Iraq. Arising from this general population pressure there was a particular problem presented by the chronic under-employment of the Egyptian middle class who could not find sufficient economic opportunities in Egypt's overcrowded cities and villages. This chronic under-employment was a large part of the reason for the political turbulence displayed by the student class in Egypt and also part of the reason for the enormous Egyptian bureaucratic machine since, by an insidious process of patronage from the top and intimidation from the middle, Egyptian Government service, in its lower echelons, was converted into a gigantic system of outdoor relief for the under-employed 'white collar' class.

These domestic circumstances provided, on two counts, a classic incentive for attempted expansion beyond Egypt's borders. First, such expansion, by providing land for Egypt's surplus peasants, employment for Egypt's surplus graduates and clerks, and (from a share in the increasing revenues being derived from oil royalties) some of the capital required for increasing Egypt's agricultural and industrial resources, would help to solve Egypt's pressing domestic problems. Secondly, such expansion could play the political role of diverting public attention from these problems.

If the incentive for what might, without abuse of language, be called an imperialist policy was great, the opportunities, at first sight, seemed even greater. On the assumption that rulers and governments, in their expansionist policies, are swayed purely by economic considerations, expansion towards the Sudan seemed to offer the most fruitful possibilities. The Sudan was a large, under-populated, underdeveloped country with a backward population. There was ample land for Egyptian agricultural settlement, there were obvious advantages for Egypt in a unified and Egyptian-dominated control of Nile water, and there was a good potential market for Egyptian industrial and agricultural production. Moreover, once British influence had been eliminated, there was no serious fear of international complication arising as a result of Egyptian penetration.

Politically, the regime had, up to a point, been remarkably successful in its Sudanese policy. The Sudan Agreement with the British in February 1953 had neatly turned the tables on the British by making it appear that it was the Egyptians who had succeeded in, while the British were trying to retard, the attainment of Sudanese self determination. The elections which followed in the summer of 1953 resulted in a victory for the Ashigga group of parties who favoured ultimate union with Egypt. But the elimination of Neguib, who was himself half Sudanese and who was popular in the Sudan, and some extremely tactless propaganda by Salah Salem, who was the member of the Junta[1] responsible for Sudan affairs, caused the original pro-Egyptian enthusiasm steadily to diminish.

The allocation of water between Egypt and the Sudan was governed by the Nile Waters Agreement of 1929 which had, in fact, been very largely a British-imposed arbitration between the two countries. In 1929 there had been no serious difficulty about such allocation as the amount of water available was much greater than the means available for its use. Twenty-five years later, however, actual and projected irrigation plans in both countries made a new agreement desirable. What was required was an agreement which would increase the relatively very small share of the Nile waters allocated to the Sudan under the 1929 Agreement without encroaching on the amount of water which Egypt would need for storing behind the High Dam at Aswan, if and when it should be built. (The High Dam, rather like the Channel Tunnel in England, had been a subject of intermittent study in Egypt for the previous twenty years. It was a project which would enable the amount of water stored behind the existing dam at Aswan to be increased sufficiently to provide for a 30 per cent increase in

Egypt's cultivable area and so make a really fundamental contribution to Egypt's endemic population problem.) In this matter of Nile water, the Sudanese held the whip hand in that, in default either of effective Egyptian control or of an amicable agreement with Egypt, the Sudanese were in a position to appropriate such water as they required without reference to Egypt at all. It was therefore a vital interest for Egypt that she should either assume control of or establish close and amicable relations with the Sudan. Successive Egyptian Governments had, as a matter of course, always assumed the necessity for control and had taken the view that, since Egypt and the Sudan were one country, which had only been separated as the result of imperialist intervention, the only opposition to such control which might be apprehended from the Sudan would be opposition fomented and financed by the British occupiers, which opposition would automatically wither away once the British had departed from the Sudan. By the middle of 1954, however, it was becoming apparent that the Egyptians had greatly overestimated the attachment of the 'unionist' parties to Egypt, and had greatly erred in assuming that the Umma or independence party was a separatist creation of the British. In reality, both groups of parties, while quite prepared to use Egyptian good offices in expediting the departure of the British, were at one in their determination not to exchange a British for an Egyptian master.

One of the decisive factors in shaping the course of policy, both domestic and foreign, pursued by the military regime in Egypt was Abdul Nasr's personal lack of interest in the Sudan. For example, in his book, *The Philosophy of the Revolution*, the Sudan is hardly mentioned. He may have resented the lack of enthusiasm displayed in the Sudan for himself as compared with Neguib. He may have calculated that a successful pan-Arab policy, which firmly established Egyptian leadership in the Arab world, would automatically involve the subordination of the Sudan. For whatever reason, Abdul Nasr never appears to have placed relationships with the Sudan in the forefront of his foreign policy, and was never prepared either wholeheartedly to pursue the unionist line in face of growing Sudanese resistance, or un-reservedly to substitute for it a policy of co-operation and alliance between neighbours. Instead, he was to pursue a half-hearted policy of propaganda (which was much less efficient and effective than his pan-Arab propaganda), of bribery (which was lavish enough to provoke resentment from those who did not receive it, but not lavish enough to stimulate any active response from those who did), and of attempted subversion. The end-result of this policy was a military coup in the Sudan at the end of 1958 which had, as one of its avowed objects, the protection of the Sudan from attempted Egyptian domination.

This failure to adopt a clear-cut policy, either of attempted domination or of conciliation, towards the Sudan was all the more remarkable in that, during the second half of 1954, the military regime not only started making serious studies of the High Dam scheme but also started putting the near prospect of such a scheme being undertaken in the forefront of its domestic propaganda. And the feasibility of such a scheme was dependent, *inter alia*, on a prior agreement with the Sudan over the allocation of water.

But the ghosts of all the Egyptian conquerors of the past, from the Pharaohs to the Fatimites, from the Mamluks to Mohamed Ali, were imperiously beckoning Abdul Nasr towards the perilous prospects and glittering prizes which lay eastwards from Suez. Arab nationalists all over the Fertile Crescent, frustrated by corrupt, or tyrannized over by oppressive, rule were waiting in the shadows, like 'characters in search of a hero'. It was demonstrable that the failures and humiliations which had afflicted the Arabs since the end of the Second World War—the humiliating failure of the Palestine war, the almost total failure to exploit for their own advantage *vis-à-vis* the Western Powers either their strategic position or their oil wealth—had been due to lack of unity and to lack of popular leadership. Instead of exploiting their geographical and economic advantages, instead of exploiting the circumstances of the cold war, they were, because of this lack of unity and of popular leadership, being exploited because of these geographical and economic advantages and in spite of the potential bargaining position conferred on them by the cold war. Attempts to secure that unity by means of the Arab League had failed miserably, and it was easy to attribute this failure to the corruptions of reactionary pashas and to the dissensions of feudal kings. A newly regenerated and a newly liberated Egypt, under the leadership of one who was already beginning to regard himself as a man of destiny, seemed almost pre-ordained to bring about the unity and to provide the popular leadership which had been lacking.

It is doubtful whether Abdul Nasr, in 1954, envisaged the full amplitude which his pan-Arab ambitions were eventually to attain. It is doubtful whether he ever consciously formulated to himself the concept of replacing British by Egyptian hegemony in the Arab world. He almost certainly did not foresee that his ambitions would lead to an intensification of that age-old rivalry between the Nile and the Euphrates, and that the most potent opposition to his ambitions would come, not from a 'feudal' Baghdad in alliance with London but from a 'democratic' Baghdad in alliance with Moscow.

There was one serious difficulty, which Abdul Nasr may have underrated, in the pursuit of a successful pan-Arab policy by Egypt. The existence of the State of Israel. Apart from the physical existence of Israel on the flank of communications between Egypt and the Fertile Crescent, it had, in the years of humiliation between 1949 and 1954, become part of the Arab mythos that any aspirant to Arab leadership must constitute himself the spearhead of the Arab movement for 'revanche' against Israel. Before the Palestine war the Palestine issue had never been a source of much emotional excitement to Egyptians and a strong, although not universal, Egyptian reaction to the Palestine war had been resentment against the King and Government for having dragged Egypt into a quarrel in which she had no particular interest. Up to the end of 1954 the attitude of the military regime towards Israel had been, by pan-Arab standards, one of almost treasonable moderation. In retrospect it can be seen that one of Abdul Nasr's most serious miscalculations was a failure to appreciate that ability to restore Arab honour by a successful war of 'revanche' against Israel was an essential qualification for Arab leadership. For, to the Arabs, Palestine had become Alsace-Lorraine, Danzig, the Six Counties, Gibraltar and Cyprus rolled into one.

The first tentative move which Abdul Nasr made in pan-Arab affairs was in August 1954 when Salah Salem went to Baghdad to discuss foreign policy with Nuri as Said. In the following month Nuri paid a return visit to Cairo. It was already apparent that there existed a fundamental disagreement between Baghdad and Cairo about defence relationships between Arab States and the non-Arab world. The Egyptian attitude which Abdul Nasr had inherited (without acknowledgment) from the old regime, was that the cold war was no affair of the Arabs, that the communist menace was a British invention designed to perpetuate British control of the Middle East, and that the Arabs were quite capable of defending themselves from the only attack likely to be made on them, which was from Israel. The Iraqi Government, on the other hand, whose country was much nearer to Russia, which had seen at closer quarters than Egypt the Russian attempts to subvert Turkey and Iran, and which traditionally (e.g. in the pre-war Saadabad Pact) had closer ties with Turkey than did the rest of the Arab world, was not inclined to subordinate her defence needs to a conception of Arab solidarity which, if it came to the point, could do nothing to satisfy those needs. There was also the Iraqi suspicion, analogous to the suspicion that the Egyptians had of the attempted British insistence on defence treaties, that Egyptian ideas about mutual Arab defence were a cloak to cover predatory Egyptian designs in the Fertile Crescent.

The exchanges with Nuri arose from the knowledge on the part of Egypt that the Iraqi Government was contemplating an alliance with Turkey. Abdul Nasr, who was already beginning to see himself as a Middle Eastern Nehru, after some apparently fruitless but outwardly good-tempered negotiations with Nuri in Cairo in September, summoned, in October, a meeting of the Foreign Ministers of the member-States of the Arab League in Cairo to try and dissuade Nuri from his intention and to try and establish a common Arab foreign policy based on neutrality. (It is not known whether any of the Foreign Ministers were impolite enough to point out to their hosts that the terms of the Anglo-Egyptian Agreement signed a few weeks before were incompatible with Egyptian neutrality. It was in fact already apparent that Abdul Nasr had no intention of observing the spirit of this Agreement.)

The vast majority of educated Arabs were emotionally neutral in the cold war between East and West. On the one hand the whole nationalist tradition of the previous twenty-five years was uncompromisingly opposed to the idea of any renewed alliance with the West in which the Arabs would at best be junior partners and at worst expendable instruments in a quarrel over the course of which they had no control and over the outcome of which they had little direct interest. On the other hand, this same nationalist tradition had no illusions about the status of a Soviet satellite and had no desire to exchange one imperialist master for another. The idea of a Third Force therefore had considerable attractions, and it was not unnatural for Abdul Nasr, seeking a means of re-establishing Egypt's lost primacy in Arab affairs, and newly released (as he saw it) from the bonds which had tied Egypt to the requirements of British foreign policy, should see himself as the foremost protagonist in the Arab world of what he was subsequently to describe as a policy of 'positive neutrality'. In this he was encouraged both by the example of Nehru, who was pursuing a similar policy among the countries of SE Asia, and by the attitude of Soviet Russia, whose crescent influence in the Arab world was largely due to the fact that her immediate interests in the Middle East—the denial to the West of military establishments in the Middle East—coincided with, while the Western policy of alliances (sometimes bearing a distinct resemblance to shotgun marriages) clashed with, Arab nationalist sentiments. (For this reason pro-Russian feelings in the Middle East were by no means confined to left wing politicians.)

There was a good deal of sense in the doctrine of 'positive

neutrality' as applied to the Arab world. The danger from communism was no longer the danger of military invasion (whatever may have been the case seven years before). The dangers to be apprehended, and the dangers which actually existed, were those of internal disruption arising from Russian propaganda and Russian subversion generally, and subordination to Russia arising from economic penetration. Military pacts directed against Russia, so far from protecting countries against, exposed them to, these dangers in that Russian subversive activity was primarily designed to offset Western influence. From the Arab point of view the only advantage to be derived from a military pact was any economic aid which might accrue from such a pact. The inevitable effect on the Arab world of the Western policy of offering economic aid 'with strings'—that is to say, economic aid made conditional on a military and political alignment with the West —was to divide, or rather to exacerbate and perpetuate the existing divisions in the Arab world. And inevitably, the result of such divisions so perpetuated was first, to commit the West to the support of the 'collaborationist' Arab governments, not against Russia, but against their 'neutralist' Arab neighbours and, later, to identify collaboration, in the minds of Arab nationalists, with reaction, corruption and treason. Such a policy on the part of the West might have been all very well had it been possible to recruit a majority of the Arab nations into the Western camp and had economic aid been sufficiently generous, and sufficiently well-directed and well-administered to enable collaborating Arab governments both to appease nationalist sentiment and to counter communist penetration. Egypt was the key. If Egypt had been won over to a policy of military alliance and political collaboration with the West, the combination of Egypt and Iraq would probably have been sufficient to make that policy viable. Failure to win Egypt over to the policy of collaboration can be seen in retrospect to have ensured the failure of that policy.

But Egyptian advocacy of neutralism in the Arab world was one thing; attempted Egyptian domination of the Arab world was quite another. By the end of 1954 Abdul Nasr was committed to the one, but had not as yet seriously embarked on the other.

The year 1955 has been described as a watershed in the history of the Egyptian military regime. At the beginning of 1955 Abdul Nasr's policy was, on the whole, one of conciliation towards Great Britain and Iraq, and of moderation towards Israel. In November 1954 he had received a loan of forty million dollars from the United States for development purposes. To judge by the controlled Egyptian press, the most important matter in the minds of the regime was the High Dam, the successful pursuit of which would have seemed to demand a conciliatory rather than a turbulent foreign policy. By the end of 1955 Abdul Nasr had burnt his boats, and was already well advanced on the road to Suez. The Arab world was divided into two hostile camps, the 'imperialist' camp led from Baghdad, relying on Western arms and support, and the 'popular' camp led from Cairo and relying on Soviet arms and support. The rivalry between the two camps expressed itself in the classic form of a struggle for the control of the Fertile Crescent and the Arabian Peninsula—the middle land lying between the Nile and the Euphrates. This struggle took the form, not of open warfare, but of propaganda and attempted subversion. One aspect of this struggle was mounting Arab hostility towards Israel. Anti-Israeli zeal was a compulsory attitude for any aspirant to the favour of the inhabitants of the Fertile Crescent. The Israeli-Egyptian frontier which, at the end of 1954 had been the most peaceful, was, at the end of 1955, the most turbulent of Israel's troubled frontiers. The determination to free himself from the system of arms rationing by which the Western Powers tried to damp down the fires of war between Israel and the Arab States was the immediate reason for Abdul Nasr's arms deal with Czechoslovakia in September 1955. This arms deal, which was of greater symbolic significance than it was of practical importance, marked the beginning of Abdul Nasr's imperialist adventure in the Middle East. It was at the same time a gesture of defiance towards the West, a threat to Israel and a statement of intention addressed to the rest of the Arab world.

Two events during the first four months of 1955 served as precipitants. In January a mutual defence agreement was arrived at between Turkey and Iraq. The Iraqi Government invited other Arab States to join. Egypt called a meeting in Cairo of the members of the Arab Collective Security Pact (which had been signed in 1950 by all the independent Arab States as a gesture of solidarity against Israel) which Iraq refused to attend. The Egyptian attitude of condemnation was supported by Syria, Saudi Arabia and Yemen. At the end of March the British Government announced their adherence to the Turco-Iraq Agreement which was known henceforth as the Baghdad Pact.[2] This marked a fundamental change in British Middle East policy. Previously this had been based on the assumption of a friendly or subservient Egypt and on the existence of the Canal Zone base. The loss of the Canal Zone base as a result of the 1954 Agreement (for nobody really believed in the viability of the 're-activation' of the Base as provided for in the Agreement) presented the British Government with the choice between acquiescence in Arab neutrality (with all the dangers inherent in an attempt to practise neutrality in an unpoliced power vacuum) and a renewed attempt, based on existing British relationships with Iraq and Jordan, to isolate as much of the Arab world as possible from Egypt and to attract it towards an understanding with the West. Although Abdul Nasr was of course free to join, and was pressingly invited to join, the Baghdad Pact, British adherence to the Pact was a challenge to the Egyptian conception of Arab neutrality and was taken by Abdul Nasr as such. The Baghdad Pact also underlined the popular identification between British imperialism and reaction and, by contrast, made it easy for Abdul Nasr to identify himself in the eyes of the Arab world with freedom and progress. This was to be of immense advantage to him in the coming struggle for power.

The second precipitating event was in February 1955, when a fairly heavy and entirely successful raid was made by Israeli forces on Egyptian military positions in the Gaza Strip.[3] The avowed object of this Israeli raid was to put a stop to the pin-pricking forays continually being made into Israeli territory from the Gaza Strip. These forays were not carried out or even or-

ganized by the Egyptian military forces and were amateurish
affairs carried out by refugee young men and connived at by the
Egyptian administration in the Gaza Strip. The Israeli raid compelled Abdul Nasr to take a much more active anti-Israeli line.
In the light of his pan-Arab ambitions he could not possibly risk
getting a reputation for softness towards Israel. From that time
onward, commando raids into Israeli territory from the Gaza
Strip were relatively lethal affairs organized by the Egyptian
army.

At this time Egypt and the other Arab States relied for their
supplies of arms and ammunition entirely on the West. Although
general trading contacts between Egypt and the Iron Curtain
countries were developing apace, Egypt had neither requested nor
been offered arms supplies by these countries. Under the terms of
the Tripartite Agreement of 1950, by which the United States,
Great Britain and France proclaimed their intention of keeping
the peace between Israel and the Arab States, arms supplies by
these countries both to Israel and the Arab States had been
rationed in such a way as to minimize the prospect of any large-
scale attack by one party on the other. It was well understood by
all concerned that any attempt to circumvent this rationing by
obtaining arms from elsewhere would be regarded by the signa-
tories of the Tripartite Agreement as a provocative act on the part
both of the supplying country and of the country supplied.

The announcement, in September 1955, that the military
regime in Egypt had concluded with Czechoslovakia a contract
for the supply of unspecified quantities of arms and ammunition
produced a diplomatic furore. There was talk, by those fond of
metaphor, about matches and powder magazines. Abdul Nasr
took the view that Egypt, as a sovereign State, had the right to
buy arms where she liked and that, moreover, the agreement with
Czechoslovakia had been forced on her as the result of an attempted Western conspiracy to deny to the Arabs the arms necessary to defend them against Israeli aggression.

The arms agreement with Czechoslovakia greatly raised Abdul
Nasr's prestige in the Arab world, mainly, one suspects, because

G

of his attribution of previous Arab military incompetence, not to any deficiencies in the Arabs themselves but to the military disabilities imposed on them by the West. It is not quite clear whether, in concluding this agreement, Abdul Nasr was seriously contemplating an offensive war against Israel or whether he merely intended the agreement to be a gesture of defiance towards the West and as a means of rallying Arab support to himself. The most important immediate effect of the arms deal was its effect on American official opinion. Up to this time, American policy in the Middle East had tended to regard Egypt, in her relations with Great Britain, as a 'nation rightly struggling to be free'. They had helped by diplomatic pressure to hustle the British out of the Canal Zone. Mainly out of deference to Egyptian opinion, they had declined to join the Baghdad Pact although the idea had emanated from the State Department in the first place. But the arms deal caused a considerable revulsion of feeling in the State Department which was to have momentous consequences. What was merely a logical development of, was seen as a radical departure from, previous Egyptian policy. Egypt was now regarded as a potential, if not as an actual, Soviet satellite. In view of Egypt's crescent hostility towards Israel, this view was naturally encouraged by Zionist propagandists in the United States who, since the advent of the Republican Administration, had been less assiduously listened to than formerly.

An important influence in shaping Abdul Nasr's ambitions was his attendance, in April 1955, at the Bandoeng Conference, preceded by the conclusion of an Indo-Egyptian Treaty of Friendship which proclaimed India's support for Egypt's policy of neutrality. The Bandoeng Conference gave Abdul Nasr a renewed confidence both in himself and in his policies. It enabled him to see Arab nationalism as part of the general Afro-Asian movement to contract out of the cold war. It assured him of the sympathy of many statesmen and peoples in what he was now beginning to regard as his coming struggle to gain the allegiance of the Arab peoples for his policy of unity and neutrality.

By the autumn of 1955 Egypt had, under Abdul Nasr's leadership, become almost entirely committed to a policy which, by giving a popular content to Arab nationalism, and by identifying it with neutralism and anti-imperialism, aimed at an Egyptian hegemony over the Arab world, and in consequence, involved a struggle for power in the Arab world against Great Britain and her remaining Arab allies.

Before describing the course of the struggle we must take a look at the configuration of the field of battle as it appeared towards the end of 1955, assess the magnitude of the stakes involved and examine the relative strength of the principal protagonists.

CHAPTER SEVEN

The Arab World in 1955

The six years which separated the end of the Palestine war from Abdul Nasr's arms agreement with Czechoslovakia had brought a number of changes to the Arab world. Some of its greatest personalities had disappeared, either by assassination, natural death, exile or political oblivion. Abdul Aziz ibn Saud had died in 1952 and with him the predominant and, on the whole, stabilizing influence which Saudi Arabia, out of all proportion to its population and intrinsic importance, had been able to exercise in the Arab world. Abdullah of Jordan had been assassinated in 1950 by Palestine Arab fanatics. Riad Solh, Prime Minister of Lebanon, had likewise been assassinated by those who believed him to be capable of taking himself, and of persuading others to take, a realistic view about Palestine. Haj Amin al Husaini, morally if not legally responsible for the murders of Abdullah and of Riad Solh and of many others, having led the Palestine Arab cause to disaster, was nursing his rancours in a suburban villa outside Cairo. Faruq was in exile. Nahas, profiting by that lack of vindictiveness which is one of the attractive features of the Egyptian military regime, was living at home in peaceful obscurity. Of the elder Arab statesmen, only Nuri as Said remained in the plenitude of his power. Sometimes as Prime Minister in the foreground, sometimes as *eminence grise* in the background, he had, by an adroit manipulation of the processes of parliamentary democracy, reinforced by the intelligent use of older methods inherited from the Ottoman Empire, contrived to build up an apparently strong and stable administration in Iraq which, with the aid of increasing oil revenues, was designed to perpetuate landowning privilege without exacerbating popular discontent. But Nuri had no illusions about either the strength or the ability of the Iraq over which he ruled. He knew that British power had been required to impose the Hashemite dynasty on Iraq and to protect that dynasty, first from the ambitions of ibn Saud, then from the popular rising of Rashid Áli. Like the Vichy Government during the German occupation, the regime in Iraq was rooted in and had so far been maintained by British influence. Now that British influence was on the wane Nuri, like Laval before him, knew that Great Britain could, or would, neither support him against external nor protect him against internal enemies. But he knew also that it was too late either for himself or for the regime to abandon the British connection and to seek to compound with popular forces inside or outside Iraq. And so, like Laval, he had no alternative but to continue trying to strengthen what he knew to be a lost cause in the hope that thereby he might, against all the omens, convert it into a winning one.

The Hashemite Kingdom of the Jordan had graduated from being a patriarchal State on the east bank of the Jordan to being a parliamentary democracy situated on both sides of the Jordan, with Palestine Arabs from the west bank now outnumbering the old Transjordanian population—mostly Beduin and peasants—on the east bank. In spite of its territorial gains, Jordan had suffered more than any other country from the effects of the Palestine war, from which it inherited a long and vulnerable frontier with Israel, a large and mainly refugee population from the Arab rump of Palestine, and the bitter enmity of all her Arab neighbours. Most of the refugee population, being Husaini supporters and being exposed to the anti-Hashemite propaganda emanating from all the surrounding Arab countries, were bitterly opposed to the existing regime in Jordan and represented a dangerous fifth column inside that country. The enmity which

Abdullah had aroused among his fellow Arab rulers both prevented that peace with Israel which Abdullah wanted and led to Abdullah's murder at the instigation of Haj Amin because he had wanted it. Abdullah was succeeded by his son Tallal who, after a reign of a few months, during which a new and more liberal constitution was promulgated, was forced on account of mental illness to abdicate his throne in favour of his son Husain, then a boy of 17, who was destined to become a considerable figure in the Arab world. With a young and inexperienced king, with a new and relatively liberal constitution, with a hopelessly unviable economy and with a newly acquired and unassimilated population which was both discontented and disloyal, Jordan was an obvious first choice for that propaganda and subversion which were to be Abdul Nasr's principal weapons in his attempt to win the allegiance of the inhabitants of the Fertile Crescent.

In Syria the parliamentary regime, dominated by the National Bloc, had been overthrown a few months after the Palestine war as the result of a military coup by Colonel Husni Zaim. Within a few months both Zaim and his supplanter, Hinnawi, had themselves been overthrown. There followed four years of dictatorial, progressive but unpopular rule by Colonel Adib Shishakli. This came to an end in February 1954 as the result of yet another army revolt and Syria returned to parliamentary rule. In foreign affairs Shishakli had, on the whole, followed the National Bloc policy of a close alignment with Egypt and Saudi Arabia and a refusal to accept any kind of alliance with the West. In domestic affairs he instituted a certain number of social reforms and encouraged industrialization by tariffs which involved, *inter alia*, a dissolution of the Customs Union between Syria and Lebanon which both countries had inherited from the French Mandate. The effect of the five years' interlude of military rule had been to break the previous quasi-monopoly of rule enjoyed by the National Bloc. When elections were held after Shishakli's departure, a Chamber consisting mostly of Independents was returned. This led to a series of precarious coalition governments, revealing Syria's normal condition of political instability which,

up to that time, had been masked, first by the dominance of the
National Bloc and, later, by Shishakli's dictatorship. But, as
usual in Syria, political instability was combined with that intellectual activity which has always made Syria the philosophical
centre of Arab nationalism. In the September 1954 elections the
Baath Socialist Party returned sixteen members to the Chamber.
The Baath Socialist Party was an amalgamation of the Baath
Party formed in 1950 by a group of young Syrian intellectuals
headed by Michel Aflak, and the Syrian Socialist Party, led by
Akram Hourani, another young Syrian intellectual. The Baath
(as the amalgamation was usually called) was soon to become of
considerable importance both as a political party in Syria and as a
political influence among Arab intellectuals all over the Fertile
Crescent and beyond. The Baathists could be regarded as the
legitimate heirs of the pioneers of Arab nationalism in nineteenth-
century Syria. Like them, they turned to Arab nationalism
because there was no principle of unity or of nationality resident
in a truncated and divided Syria. Like them they faithfully reflected the current political and intellectual attitudes of the young
middle class Arab intelligentsia. The nineteenth-century nationalists had been pro-Western and liberal with a belief in parliamentary institutions and an almost total lack of interest in social
reform. The Baathists were anti-Western socialists, who believed
in a mild totalitarianism as the only means of implementing those
social reforms which formed the basis of their beliefs. The nineteenth century nationalists, over-estimating the influence of
Western European liberalism as applied to the countries of the
Levant, had looked towards Western Europe for salvation. The
Baathists, making a similar over-estimate of Abdul Nasr's radicalism, began, after 1954, to look for salvation towards Cairo.
Closely allied with the Baath was a radical group in the army, led
by Abdul Hamid Sarraj, subsequently, and temporarily, to become Abdul Nasr's principal henchman in Syria, which shared
the Baath's political attitudes on a less intellectual and more
authoritarian level. Behind this potentially 'fellow-travelling'
alliance lurked an influential communist party, led by Khaled

Bikdash, which, in Syria alone of all the countries in the Arab world, was allowed freedom of activity. Largely owing to the influence of Bikdash, the coming struggle for power in Syria, to be impotently presided over by Shukry Kuwatly, the doyen of the National Bloc, elected President in 1955, was to be, not between Cairo and the West, but between Cairo and Moscow. Paradoxically, the influence of Moscow was increased, not by the apparently fellow-travelling activities of the left-wing groups and parties, but by independent magnates like Khaled al Azm who, immersed in parochialism, viewed the cultivation of relationships with Moscow as a means of retaining popular support in face of the challenge offered by the left-wing groups The only notable opposition to these leftist tendencies expressed, not in domestic legislation, but in international attitudes in which pashas competed with middle class intellectuals in expressions of detestation for the West, admiration for Abdul Nasr and respect for the Soviet Union, came from the Syrian Popular Party (PPS), the dispossessed heirs of the Arab nationalist tradition and the outmoded adherents of a united Syria. The PPS had fallen on evil days. Left isolated by the defeat of European fascism, they found themselves fighting a losing battle against more fashionable ideologies. In 1949 their leader, Anton Saade, had been arrested in Syria and handed over by Husni Zaim to the Lebanese Government who executed him for plotting against the independence of Lebanon. Under Shishakli, who was an old member of the PPS, they enjoyed more tolerance and began to look towards Nuri's Iraq as the possible future nucleus of a united Syria. With the restoration of parliamentary life, they formed a more or less permanent opposition to a series of coalition governments which became more and more leftist in complexion and composition.

During the immediate post-war years Lebanon had been remarkably free from the tensions and disturbances which had afflicted other Arab countries. Under the pliable manipulation of the Maronite President Bishara Khoury, who was in office from 1943 to 1952, and of the Sunni Moslem Riad Solh, who was Prime Minister for most of the time between 1943 and his assassination in 1951, Lebanon had been able to achieve the three essential pre-requisites for a continued independent existence—neutralism between East and West in the cold war, neutralism between the competing Arab blocs and a state of equilibrium between Moslems and Christians in Lebanon itself. This triple balancing feat was achieved at the expense of administrative efficiency and social reform. In 1952, rising discontent, and the usual accusations of 'corruption', led to the resignation of Bishara Khoury from the Presidency and to his replacement by Camille Chamoun, with a fashionable reformist programme. Any fears which may have been entertained by the merchant classes of Lebanon that the new regime might be infected by the leftist ideas becoming current in the Arab world were soon dispelled and successive Lebanese Governments continued to perform the necessary triple balancing act, undistracted either by clamant threats of revolution or by imperious demands for social reform, until the summer of 1958, when the whole complicated tight rope system on which Lebanese politics were poised, came crashing to the ground.

By 1955 Israel was firmly established behind the armistice boundary lines negotiated during the first half of 1949. There had been no peace treaties, no resettlement of Arab refugees, no arrangements regarding Arab funds and property. There was continual raiding on three of Israel's four land frontiers, and the United Nations Truce Commission was kept busy investigating charges and allocating responsibility. The failure to effect a settlement was almost entirely due to an unanimous Arab refusal to recognize that any settlement had to have regard to the unpalatable fact that the Arab States had been soundly beaten in a war which they themselves had started with the avowed object of nullifying a scheme of partition adopted by a United Nations Assembly Resolution. The continued Arab insistence that all Arab refugees should be given the choice between returning to, and receiving compensation for the loss of, their homes was quite unrealistic in the circumstances, particularly when accompanied by expressions of intention to exterminate Israel as part of the bargain. The future prospect of an Arab victory over Israel be-

came part of the Arab mythos, and not the least part of the attrac-
tion which Abdul Nasr held for Arab nationalists was the belief
that Egyptian domination of the Fertile Crescent in the name of
Arab nationalism was the only way in which this apotheosis was
likely to be achieved.

The death of Abdul Aziz ibn Saud in the autumn of 1952 had
removed a natural leader from the Arab world and had put an
end to the previous influence which Saudi Arabia, as a result of
its ruler's personality and prestige, had been able to exercise over
the Arab world. It had also removed one of the two remaining
friendly links (the other being Nuri as Said) between the Arab
world and the West. The importance of this 'bridge' between the
neutralist part of the Arab world—Egypt, Saudi Arabia and
Syria—and the West was not fully appreciated until after it had
disappeared. Abdul Aziz ibn Saud was succeeded by his eldest
son who assumed the title of King Saud. The previous control
which his father had exercised over the members of his family
and the administration of his kingdom now lapsed entirely. The
respect which his father's qualities had generated for the Ruling
House was dissipated almost overnight. The personal extravagance of the royal family soon brought the State to near bankruptcy in spite of ever-increasing oil revenues. In foreign affairs
King Saud continued his father's close connections with Egypt
and with Syria. But now that ibn Saud was dead, Egypt and not
Saudi Arabia was the senior partner. Saudi Arabia was gradually
relegated from the centre to the periphery of Arab affairs. Seldom
can a moral and material patrimony have been more rapidly
dispersed.

In 1949, before ibn Saud's death, British relations with Saudi
Arabia had been disturbed by the Buraimi dispute. Buraimi is an
oasis believed (probably erroneously) to contain oil deposits. It is
situated in south-east Arabia near where the boundaries of Saudi
Arabia, the British-protected Sheikhdom of Abu Dhabi and the
Sultanate of Muskat meet. Ibn Saud claimed the whole oasis. His
claim was resisted by Great Britain on behalf of the Sheikh of
Abu Dhabi and the Sultan of Muskat. In 1955, after attempts at

arbitration had broken down, the whole of the oasis was occupied by British-officered troops of the Sheikh of Abu Dhabi and the Sultan of Muskat. For this reason, and from that date, the Saudi Government's normal ties of friendship with Egypt were strengthened by a common hostility towards 'British imperialism'.

Yeman is one of the few countries, and perhaps the only remaining country in the world, whose Ruling House has successfully defied the onset, not only of the twentieth but also of the nineteenth century. Its internal regime is one of total and unenlightened despotism perpetuated by an almost complete absence of education and maintained by a barbarous system of punishments. Its foreign policy had in the main followed that of Saudi Arabia, but tended to diverge after the death of ibn Saud had removed the necessity for compliance. The main preoccupation of successive Imams has been the pursuit of Yeman's claim to Aden Colony and the Western Protectorates by a course of guerrilla warfare, bribery and intrigue which has never, however, exceeded the dimensions of a minor nuisance to the British authorities in Aden. In 1955, for the better pursuit of these claims, Yeman followed the lead given, first by Egypt and then by Saudi Arabia, and started obtaining imports of arms from and developing trade relations with the Soviet Bloc.

Strung along the southern and eastern shores of the Arabian Peninsula from Aden in the south-west to Kuwait in the north-east, is a chain of British protected Principalities and Sheikhdoms which, in 1955, represented the last remnants of the British Empire in the Arab world.

Aden is a British Crown Colony which had been occupied by the British in 1838 as a coaling station on the route to India. Forming the Colony's immediate hinterland are the Aden Western Protectorates, consisting of a number of petty Arab Sheikhdoms under British protection and forming both a buffer and a bone of contention between Aden Colony and Yeman. To the east of Aden and stretching along the south coast of Arabia to the borders of Dhofar, in the area known as the Hadhramut, are more Arab Sheikhdoms, rather larger in size than those in the

Western Protectorates, which are also under British protection and grouped under the name of the Eastern Protectorates. Eastward again, and occupying the whole of the south-east corner of the Peninsula, between the Indian Ocean and the Persian Gulf, is the Sultanate of Oman and Muskat, with which is incorporated the Principality of Dhofar, an independent sovereign State in alliance with Great Britain. North of the Sultanate, on the west coast of the Persian Gulf, there is a string of British-protected Sheikhdoms consisting (a) of the seven tiny Sheikhdoms on the Trucial Coast between Muskat and Qatar, (b) of the Sheikhdom of Qatar comprising the peninsula of that name, (c) of the Bahrain group of islands immediately to the north of Qatar, and (d) of Kuwait, at the north-west corner of the Persian Gulf, contiguous with Iraq and separated from Qatar by the Saudi Arabian coastal province of al-Hasa. All these Sheikhdoms had been occupied by and had accepted protection from Great Britain during the course of the nineteenth century. Generally, the terms of the Protectorate Treaties left the Sheikhs in control of the domestic affairs of their Sheikhdoms and conferred on Great Britain the conduct of their foreign policy and the responsibility for their defence. In 1955 this responsibility was exercised by the presence of British naval, military and air forces at Aden and Bahrain and by the existence of Royal Air Force stations in the Eastern Protectorates and on the Trucial Coast.

The original reason for the imposition of British Protectorates on to these Sheikhdoms had arisen out of the necessity for protecting the Indian sea route and, to a lesser extent, the overland route to India by way of the Euphrates and the Persian Gulf, from the attacks of pirates. Their importance to Great Britain in 1955 derived almost entirely from the oil deposits which had been found to exist all round the shores of the Persian Gulf and from the growing importance of these oil deposits to the British and Western European industrial economies. This question of oil was the dominant consideration for the British Government in their approach to Abdul Nasr's Egyptian imperialism.

The first major discovery of oil in the Persian Gulf was in 1908, when oil was discovered at Mesjid-as-Suleiman in Persia and near the north-east corner of the Persian Gulf, by the d'Arcy Concession, a British company which had, in 1901, been granted a sixty-year concession to search for and to produce oil in southern Persia. In 1909 this concession was taken over by the Anglo-Persian Oil Company and commercial production started at Mesjid-as-Suleiman in 1912. In 1914 the British Government acquired a controlling interest in the Anglo-Persian Oil Company, in view of the importance which the British Admiralty attached to this production as a means of refuelling the British Navy which, at about this time, began to build warships using oil fuel instead of coal. The Mesopotamian campaign during the 1914-18 war was, in part, regarded by the British Government as a necessary measure for the defence of the Persian oilfields. After the war the British Government's insistence on the inclusion of the Vilayet of Mosul in the British Mandated territory of Iraq (an insistence which had important consequences in that it made it impossible for the British Government to resist the French counter-claim to extend their Mandated territory to include the interior of Syria) was principally motivated by the existence of an oil concession, and the believed existence of oil deposits, in the Vilayet of Mosul.

This concession had been granted by the Ottoman Government before the war to a British company called the Turkish Petroleum Company, of which the moving spirit was an Armenian *négotiant* named Gulbenkian. After a period of complicated international bargaining this concession was, as a result of the peace settlement allocating the concessionary area to Iraq, transferred to the Iraq Petroleum Company, formed for the purpose of taking over the concession and of which the shares were held as follows: 23¾ per cent each by the Anglo-Persian Oil Company, the Royal-Dutch Shell Group, the Compagnie Française des Petroles and a consortium of American oil companies, and 5 per cent by Mr Gulbenkian. Oil from this concession was first discovered in 1927 at Kirkuk and by 1934 this oil was being exported from Iraq via two twelve-inch pipelines having their

terminals on the Mediterranean coast at Tripoli in the French
Mandated territory of Lebanon and at Haifa in the British Mandated territory of Palestine respectively.

Meanwhile there had been an active process of concession hunt-
ing in which the American oil companies were becoming more
and more interested, on the west coast of the Persian Gulf. In 1930
the Standard Oil Company of California acquired, from a British
syndicate, a concession which had been granted to the latter in
Bahrain. The Bahrain Petroleum Company was formed (in which,
in 1936, the Texas Oil Company bought a 50 per cent share from
Standard of California) and oil was discovered in 1932. In 1933
the Arabian-American Oil Company, a consortium consisting of
four major American oil companies (Standard of New Jersey,
Standard of California, Texas and Socony Mobiloil) obtained from
the Saudi Arabian Government a concession covering the whole
of the eastern areas of Saudi Arabia. Commercial production
started in 1938 from oilfields discovered in al-Hasa province on
the coast of the Persian Gulf. In 1934 a concession covering the
Sheikhdom of Kuwait was granted to the Kuwait Oil Company,
owned fifty-fifty by the Anglo-Persian Oil Company and the
(American) Gulf Oil Company. During the 1930s other concessions were granted to subsidiaries of the Iraq Petroleum Company
in Qatar, in Muskat and on the Trucial Coast. There was, however, no commercial production in Kuwait or in these other concessions until after the Second World War.

In 1938 total production from the Middle East oilfields
amounted to 335,000 barrels[1] per day out of a total world production of 5,559,000 barrels per day. By 1955 Middle East production had risen to 3,480,000 barrels per day out of a total world
production of 17,519,000 barrels per day. In 1938 Western
Europe consumed 710,000 barrels of oil products per day of which
most came from the Western hemisphere; in 1955 Western
Europe consumed 2,570,000 barrels of oil products per day, of
which three-quarters came from the Middle East.

In 1955 Western Europe's requirements of Middle East oil,
nearly all of which was imported into the consuming countries

as crude, was transported to Western Europe, as to about 40 per cent by a series of pipelines terminating on the Mediterranean coast at Saida and Tripoli in Lebanon, and at Banias in Syria, and as to about 60 per cent by tanker through the Suez Canal. Control of Egypt and Syria therefore conferred control of all those routes by which Middle East oil reached Western Europe.

By the beginning of the 1950s the question of the security of Middle East oil supplies had become one of the British Government's main preoccupations in view of the increasing importance of these supplies to the industrial economy of Great Britain in particular and of Western Europe in general. There were two principal areas of concern. First, the security of the concessionary areas themselves. Secondly, the security of the transport routes between the concessionary areas and the Western European markets. This preoccupation was to some extent shared by the US Government whose nationals owned nearly two-thirds of the oil produced in the Middle East. (In 1956 the US share of oil production in the Middle East amounted to about two million barrels a day as compared to the Anglo-Dutch share of about one million barrels per day.) But the concern of the US Government was considerably less than that of the British Government since Middle East oil production was not yet a vital factor in US domestic consumption.

From 1949 onwards Iraqi refusal to have Iraqi oil transported by the Haifa pipeline through the State of Israel was a reminder of what might be in store. This particular prohibition was not serious as it was not difficult to substitute the capacity of the Haifa line by doubling the line running through Syria and Lebanon to Tripoli and by building a new line running through Syria to Banias. Much more serious was the expropriation of the Anglo-Iranian Oil Company (as it was then called) by the Iranian Government in 1951. At that time Iranian production amounted to nearly one-half of total Middle East production and accounted for considerably more than one-half of total British-owned production in the Middle East. It was significant, in the light of after events, that the Conservative Opposition in the British House of

Commons pressed the Labour Government, which was in office in 1951, to use armed force to prevent this expropriation and criticized them vehemently for their refusal to do so.

The loss of Persian production was rapidly made good by increased production from the phenomenally rich Kuwait oilfields, which had come into production a few years previously. Inability to market and so derive an income from the oil resources which they had so precipitately nationalized led to the downfall of the reformist and popular Iranian Government led by Dr Musaddiq, which had been responsible for the expropriation. The eclipse of Musaddiq in 1953 and the return to power of a military government paved the way for a new Agreement under which the oil industry remained, in form, nationalized but under which the exploration, production, refining and marketing of oil in what was known as the Agreement Area in southern Persia was 'farmed out' to an international consortium of oil companies in which British Petroleum (the old Anglo-Persian Oil Company) had a 40 per cent share, American oil companies a 40 per cent share between them (representing a handsome dividend in return for the part which American diplomacy had played in the expropriation of the Anglo-Iranian), Royal Dutch Shell 14 per cent, and Compagnie Française des Petroles 6 per cent. The most important modification in the terms of exploitation agreed with the new consortium was that the Iranian Government was to receive a 50 per cent share in the nett profits of the oil operation. This was in accordance with what had now become the general pattern of profit sharing in the Middle East as between producer country and concessionary company. This 'fifty-fifty deal' had been initiated by Aramco in 1950, in respect of their Saudi Arabian concession and had gradually been extended to all the other concessions in and around the Gulf. (The offer of a fifty-fifty share of profits had been made to the Iranian Government by the Anglo-Iranian and had been refused by the Iranian Government in the course of the negotiations which finally broke down and led to expropriation.)

With the renewal of production, refining and international

marketing in Iran in 1954, all had ended happily, particularly for the Americans who had, at British expense, greatly increased their already preponderant share of Middle East oil. But the writing was on the wall. It could be interpreted in two ways by the governments of the oil producing countries. They could interpret the Iranian incident either as showing that the result of expropriation was national bankruptcy in that partnership with the Western oil companies was necessary in order to enable the oil to be sold, or as showing that they could 'get away with' anything up to and including expropriation without provoking military intervention.

The Iranian incident could also be interpreted in two ways by the Western Powers. It could be interpreted either as a sign that economic pressure would bring the expropriating country to heel or as a warning that military force must, if necessary, be used to check any further attempt to disrupt the flow of Middle East oil whether by interference with its production or with its transport. In the circumstances, it is not surprising that the Americans, who had gained substantially from the Iranian incident, tended to interpret the writing in the former way, and the British, who had lost as much as, and more than, the Americans had gained, in the latter way.

As a result of the increasing importance attached by the British Government to the continued free flow of oil from the Middle East, the previous British aim of trying to promote Arab unity as a means of preventing communist penetration was, once the prospect of a British-sponsored Arab unity had disappeared after the Palestine war, gradually replaced by a policy which aimed at the perpetuation of Arab disunity in order to avoid the danger lest Middle East oil supplies, and/or the channels by which Middle East oil was transported to Europe, should be subjected to the control of a single and potentially hostile Power, whether or not such a Power were communist-controlled. The evolution of this policy, and its coincidence with the evolution of Abdul Nasr's pan-Arab ambitions, are the keys to the understanding of events in the Middle East during 1956.

H

Perhaps the most important thing which had happened to the Arab world since 1948 was that it had greatly increased in size. 'The Arab world' is not an objective and fixed area inhabited by people speaking the same language; it is a subjective concept and consists at any given time of all those people who are conscious of their common Arabism. In this sense, an area greater in size and in population than the whole of Arabic-speaking Asia had, by 1956, been added to the 'Arab world'. Of the countries of what had formerly been French North Africa, the Kingdom of Morocco attained sovereign independence in November 1955, with the return of Mohammed V from exile and the termination of the French Protectorate. The Republic of Tunisia achieved sovereign independence in March 1956 as the result of an Agreement between the French and Tunisian Governments. (Tunisia had achieved autonomy within the French Empire in 1955.) Algeria, flanked by Morocco on the west and by Tunisia on the east, with a population of some nine million indigenous Moslems and one million French-descended *colons*, remained under French rule, being technically part of metropolitan France.

The history of French North Africa since the Second World War had been not unlike the history of the Fertile Crescent after the First World War, with Algeria taking the place of Palestine. Continual nationalist agitation and violence had resulted in the attainment of sovereign independence by Morocco and Tunisia, with the prospect of future friendly relationships with France, had not these prospects been bedevilled by the situation in Algeria, where even the distant prospect of independence seemed inhibited by the presence of about a million French-descended *colons*, who had powerful political backing in France and who were determined that Algeria should remain part of France. For years Algeria had been in an endemic state of insurrection, with an organized national resistance movement (Front de Libération Nationale or FLN) which later, in 1958, formed a 'provisional government in exile'. As in Palestine, the struggles of this national resistance movement excited popular sympathies in, but not much practical help from, the Arab world, bedevilled French relations with the independent Arab Governments, provided Arab nationalist propagandists with another stick with which to beat the West, and gave 'collaborationist' Arab governments and individuals another reason for embarrassment in their relations with the West.

Between Tunisia and Egypt lay Libya. This ex-Italian colony had been governed by a British Military Administration for a number of years while there had been an interminable process of wrangling about its subsequent disposal. Eventually, in 1952, it was proclaimed by the United Nations as an independent sovereign State entitled the United Kingdom of Libya, ruled over by King Idris al Senussi and consisting of the three territories of Tripolitania, Cyrenaica and the Fezzan. The new State entered into treaty relationship with Great Britain, providing for the presence of a British military and air force in Libya; there is also a large American airbase just outside Tripoli.

The three newly-independent States joined the Arab League, although without undue precipitation, after their elevation to independence. But, for various reasons, the attractions of Arabism were not so strong in the west as they were in the east of the Arab world. All the States of the Maghrib had a firm national tradition and none of them were artificial creations like Syria or Jordan, whose nationalists were forced to seek in Arabism a viable principle of unity which they were unable to find within their own national boundaries. None of them suffered from the population pressure of Egypt, which drove Egyptian Governments, of whatever political persuasion, to use Arabism as a cloak for Egyptian expansion. Both in Morocco and in Tunisia, the new leaders and their governments—Mohammed V and the Istiqlal Party in Morocco and Habib Bourguiba and the Neo-Dustour in Tunisia —had been closely associated with the struggle for independence and were therefore much less vulnerable to subversive propaganda —appealing to peoples over the heads of rulers—which became the main stock-in-trade of Cairo-inspired Arab nationalist propaganda. But Algeria in the west, like Palestine in the east, appeared to present a powerful argument for Arab unity in that it could be and was represented that only by means of such unity could sufficient pressure be exercised—on France and the United Nations over Algeria, on Israel and the United Nations over Palestine—to secure the 'liberation' of these countries.

The entry of the Maghrib into the orbit of Arab nationalism brought about a subtle change in the relations between Egypt and the rest of the Arab world. Previously Egypt had been on the periphery, with the centre of the Arab world still located in the Fertile Crescent. Now she was in the geographical centre, with the Maghrib on one side and the Fertile Crescent and the Arabian Peninsula on the other, extending like wings from the Egyptian head and body in Cairo and on the Nile.

The adherence to the Arab League and the admission to the United Nations of the newly-independent States of the Maghrib meant a potentially large increase of Arab influence in the councils of the nations, and a potentially large increase in power to any State which might succeed in imposing a hegemony over the Arab world. But it also meant a larger area of potential dissension among the Arabs and a larger potential opposition to any such hegemony. And it also committed Abdul Nasr to enmity with France over Algeria.

Algeria, like Palestine, was an immediate asset for the idea of Arab nationalism in that it pointed the necessity for unity and underlined the wickedness of Western imperialism. But, also like Palestine, it was an ultimate liability for this idea in that any constructive action was almost certain to cause dissension and in that failure to take constructive action would, in course of time, discredit the whole concept of Arab nationalism.

In the autumn of 1955 the Middle East was on the verge of a struggle for power. On the one side was Abdul Nasr who, with a programme of Arab unity, neutralism, anti-imperialism and social reform, aimed at achieving a system of satellite States in the Arab world, dedicated to the same policies. On the other side were Great Britain, France, Israel and Iraq, all of them opposed to the ambitions of Abdul Nasr but most of them also opposed to the ambitions and aspirations of the others. Great Britain was concerned to prevent any hegemony—other than her own—in the Arab world, lest such hegemony should endanger oil investments and oil supplies; France was concerned to prevent extraneous support for the Algerian rebels; Israel was concerned for her continued existence and Iraq was concerned both for the security of her oil exports, on which the economy of the country depended, and for the continued existence of the Hashemite regime.

In this coming struggle Abdul Nasr had the support of the Soviet Bloc from outside the Arab world and that of Syria and Saudi Arabia inside the Arab world, as well as increasing popular support in almost all Arab countries, where he was beginning to be regarded by the various legal and illegal, overt and covert oppositions as a potential Cavour or Garibaldi, as a potential liberator from a variety of foreign and domestic tyrants, from a variety of social and economic disabilities. His chances of success depended on the propagandist use he would be able to make of his fourfold programme—unity, neutralism, anti-imperialism and social reform—for the incitement of masses and the subversion of governments. In this matter he was to receive some unexpected, and unintended, assistance from Great Britain and France.

Any assistance by the West would have to be achieved indirectly—by a strengthening of the popular appeal exercised by, and of the coercive forces at the disposal of, those Middle East institutions which Abdul Nasr was endeavouring to subvert. The days in which the Western Powers could successfully impose their will by direct force of arms on militarily defenceless countries were over, a fact which the Governments of Great Britain and France were shortly to discover.

CHAPTER EIGHT

Arab Nationalist Propaganda

The Arab nationalism preached from Cairo in the 1950s was very different in content and in methods of dissemination from that furtively discussed in Syrian cafés at the turn of the century and from that proclaimed in Palestine mosques in the 1930s. Self-determination had been achieved. Now the cry was for unity. Pan-Islam was *vieux jeu*. Now the cry was for social reform. The Syrian nationalism at the first Arab Congress in Paris in 1913 had been an argument addressed mainly to intellectuals; the pan-Islamic nationalism of Haj Amin had been incitement to violence addressed mainly to the masses; the Arab nationalism disseminated from Cairo in the fifties consisted of that amalgam of argument and emotion—perfected in Great Britain by papers like the *Daily Express*—which is particularly likely to appeal to an emergent, but frustrated, middle class.

The argument was a simple one. Arab unity already existed. From the shores of the Atlantic to the shores of the Persian Gulf, from the Taurus Mountains to the Indian Ocean, all Arabs were brothers. The fact that this unity had not been achieved in practice was due to 'imperialism' which, wishing to divide the Arab world for its own sinister purposes, was continually weaving plots to prevent the consummation of Arab unity. The original 'imperialist' plot had of course been the military occupation of the whole area. When the Arabs, by their own efforts, had achieved a state of technical independence, which should have led automatically to unity, this independence was limited, and this unity frustrated, by imperialist efforts to continue enslaving the Arabs. Examples of this attempted enslavement were, the creation of the State of Israel, and the employment of Arab 'opportunists' and 'reactionaries'—people like Nuri as Said, King Husain of Jordan, President Bourguiba, President Chamoun, General Qasim, and anybody else who, for the time being, happened to be in opposition to the policies of Abdul Nasr.

According to this argument, since imperialism is the only obstacle to Arab unity, imperialism must necessarily remain active until or unless Arab unity has been achieved. Every setback on the road to Arab unity has to be interpreted in terms of imperialist sabotage. At various times, such widely differing institutions as the Neo-Dustour in Tunisia, the Communist Party in Iraq and the Moslem Brotherhood in Egypt have all been denounced as 'agents of imperialism'.

What is this Arab nationalism which, like the Will of God, already exists, but which remains largely inoperative owing to the wickedness of man? *Qawmia arabiya* is the Arabic term for it and it signifies something like 'the conscious sense of being an Arab'. This *qawmia* has to be distinguished from *wataniya* or patriotism, which means loyalty to a particular State. This may and, according to the argument, does, in countries like Egypt, co-exist with and supplement *qawmia* but may also, and sometimes is, abused and twisted by imperialists and reactionaries, in countries like Jordan and Iraq and Lebanon, to become the antithesis of *qawmia*.

Abdul Nasr has, himself, several times defined an Arab as a person speaking Arabic as his or her mother-tongue. According to Abdul Nasr's argument, the fact of being an Arab, according to this definition, automatically imbues a person with a conscious sense of being an Arab. This implies a certain set of aspirations and beliefs which, unless they have been perverted by imperialist or reactionary influences, coincide with the aspirations felt and the beliefs held by Abdul Nasr himself and preached by Egyptian propagandists. It is not a matter of educating people in Arabism.

It is a matter of liberating, and bringing to the surface, that feeling of and belief in Arabism which is the birthright of every Arab but which has, in many cases, been overlaid by insincere feelings and erroneous beliefs implanted in them by the enemies of Arabism.

The secret of Arab nationalist, and the secret of most successful, propaganda is to convince people that the ideas which you are presenting to them are their own natural and inherited beliefs, and that any opposing ideas are alien in origin, predatory in design and calculated, by persuading people to ignore their birthright, to deprive them of it. Such propaganda is presented, not as an attempted conversion to new ideas, but a revelation of what is there already. It is analogous to Roman Catholic and to communist propaganda, which presents Roman Catholicism or communism as the revelation of an objective Truth which has been there all the time and as an exposure of error which clouds objective Truth. It imposes the necessity for continual denunciations of rather than attempted reconciliation with any deviation from whatever is presented as the existing, immutable Truth. In such a context compromise is the beginning of treason for the student, the beginning of defeat for the master because, in such a context, compromise is, not an adjustment with reality but a denial of Truth.

In the Palestine war the Egyptians had demonstrated their military incompetence. In the Suez campaign it was to be demonstrated that neither the military regime nor supplies of Czech or Russian arms had done anything to repair this incompetence. But in the propaganda field, in which the struggle for the control of the Middle East was about to be fought, the Egyptians showed a remarkable and, up to a point, effective virtuosity.

Cairo is easily the largest city in the Arab world. Culturally, intellectually and technically, it can command resources far superior to those at the command of any other Arab city. In no field is this superiority more marked than in the field of those mass communication media—newspapers, films and radio—which are the principal vehicles of propaganda. The advantage conferred by a common language, spoken, read and written, from Casablanca to Baghdad, from Aleppo to Khartum, is of course enormous. All these advantages were reinforced by the increasing demand for, and the increasing presence of, Egyptian schoolteachers, engineers and other technicians in the neighbouring Arab countries, who were short of all those varieties of intellectual manpower of which Egypt had a surplus. Self-interest and national pride combined to make these people willing propagandists, in the Arab countries where they worked, of Egyptian imperialism disguised as Arab nationalism.

But the real strength of Egyptian propaganda lay, not so much in the fact that it was technically efficient as in the fact that its content was both emotionally satisfying and based on a substratum of truth. Arabs of all classes resented the prospect of being involved in a third world war over issues in which they felt no interest and over the conduct of which they would have no control. There really was a case for believing that 'feudalism' was allied with Western imperialism for the preservation of the privileges of both, and that the combination of the two did perpetuate social injustice at home and involve the Arab peoples in foreign quarrels abroad. There were of course arguments on the other side, but these arguments were seldom, if ever, heard from Arab sources and the Cairo propaganda for unity and neutrality as a means of resisting imperialism and of bringing about social reform had an undeniable appeal both to the heart and to the head. The strength of this appeal enabled it to be presented, not as an arguable thesis, but as a self-evident truth. There was also a temptation to believe, and a feeling of gratitude towards those who continually asserted, that the existence of Israel, the Arab defeat at the hands of Israel and the subsequent Arab failure to reverse the results of that defeat were all due, not to any Arab deficiencies, but to imperialist machinations designed to perpetuate imperialist interference and Arab disunity. The particular strength of the Egyptian propaganda about Israel was that the case for regarding the whole Israel business as an imperialist plot—and in this belief all Arabs were united—was congruent with the rest of the

Egyptian case, whereas it was not congruent with any case based on collaboration with imperialism. For the Egyptian case was that the whole Israel business was not an aberration in British policy which the British had come to regret and had tried (however ineffectually) to remedy, but part and parcel of a consistent imperialist policy which, *inter alia*, included the unsuccessful British attempts to remain in the Canal Zone and the successful British attempt to inveigle Iraq into the Baghdad Pact.

The 'imperialist plot' legend to explain the Arab defeat in Palestine is obviously comparable with the German 'stab in the back' legend to explain Germany's defeat in 1918. It was not invented by Abdul Nasr, any more than the 'stab in the back' legend was invented by Hitler. But it was utilized by Abdul Nasr as the keystone of his propaganda arch in that it gave coherence and stability to the structure as a whole. The existence of Israel could be pointed to as a living proof that imperialism had been able to exploit Arab 'feudalism' and Arab dissensions to create in Israel a bridgehead with which to attempt imperialist control of and to perpetuate imperialist interference in the Arab world. The only remedy was unity, social reform and a refusal to collaborate in imperialist military plans which were directed, not against the myth of communist aggression, but against the reality of Arab nationalism.

None of this was new in content. Egyptian propagandists had been saying the same thing about imperialism, about neutralism, about Israel, about unity, and even about social reform, for years. But the military regime succeeded in introducing a note of sincerity, of efficiency and of urgency into the whole business. After all, they could point to some achievement, brought about by themselves, in the directions indicated. They had got the British out of the Canal Zone and the Sudan. They had got rid of Faruq and his entourage. They had done something about land reform. But it was not until the regime looked as if it might do something about Israel that their propaganda really began to 'take' in the Arab world.

It is at this point that one begins to notice a subtle difference between the old and the new, a difference which, more than anything else, illustrates the nature of the impact which Abdul Nasr has had on the Arab world. In this respect the importance of 'nasserism' was not that it created but that it expressed and publicized a change which was beginning to take place in the Arab outlook. Previously, the Arab case, as presented to themselves and to the outside world about Israel and imperialism generally was based on the assumption that the Arabs, as a noble, peace-loving and guileless, but technically backward people, fond of their traditional ways and shrinking from the rude impact of Western materialism, had been exploited by and should be protected from, the exponents of this materialism in the shape of Zionists, oil companies and the like. This was the case developed by Haj Amin before the Peel Commission and the case which had captivated British Arabophiles for generations. This concept of Arabism, although consciously repudiated by nearly all Arabs, had an immense unconscious influence on Arab diplomatic attitudes and on Arab propaganda and was to a large extent the reflection of Arab social conventions. It was still part of the nobleness of life to approach matters circuitously, to take things slowly and not to get one's hands dirty. The greatest, the most enduring and perhaps an almost entirely unconscious achievement of the Egyptian propaganda machine is the massive contribution which it has made towards discrediting that image of picturesque, aristocratic indolence which for too long and for too many Arabs, continued to be the symbol of civilization and the good life. Hard work in oilfields, factories, and hospitals began to acquire the same social status as picturesque idling in government offices over innumerable cups of coffee. In their attitude towards Israel Arabs began to think, not in terms of being protected from but of being able to compete with Israel. This shift from an aristocratic to a bourgeois society had of course been going on for some time in the Arab world, but it was the Egyptian military regime, and all the publicity given to its lean young officers tearing about in bush shirts, to its eager technicians reclaiming lands in the western desert, to its pioneering young doctors and nurses in remote clinics in Upper Egypt, which really destroyed the old picturesque images of procrastination, formal politeness, genteel venality and interminable coffee drinking.

One of the features of Abdul Nasr's Arab nationalist propaganda, as preached from Cairo, and later from Damascus, was its relative lack of Islamic religious content and its entire absence of Moslem fanaticism. This was no doubt, and in part, a gesture towards the non-Moslem communities in the Arab world who had to be wooed into an acceptance of the principle of Arab unity. But it was also, and perhaps mainly, a tacit recognition of the connection which exists, and which has been noted by nearly all outside observers, between Islam and that lack of social and technical progress which has made Arabs a prey to 'imperialism'. No Arab leader with any pretensions to being a social reformer could possibly afford to make overmuch use of pan-Islam. Although Abdul Nasr in his book *The Philosophy of the Revolution* mentioned Islam as one of the three 'circles' (the other two being the Arab and the African 'circles') of which Egypt was the centre, he has never shown any enthusiasm for pan-Islam. A common neutrality shared with India and Yugoslavia has proved a much closer political bond than a common religion shared with Pakistan and Turkey. On the other hand Abdul Nasr has not, either in his acts in Egypt or in his propaganda addressed to the Arab world, shown anything like the uncompromising secularism of Ataturk. The suppression of the Moslem Brotherhood in Egypt was for political and not for religious reasons. The abolition in Egypt of the Sharia Courts and the reform of the Awqaf[1] were both overdue social reforms (like, for example, the setting up of the Ecclesiastical Commissioners and abolition of ecclesiastical jurisdiction in England during the nineteenth century) and not attacks on Islam as such. One suspects that Abdul Nasr regards Islam in much the same light as a modern English Prime Minister might regard Christianity—as a dignified appendage to the Arab way of life, as something to be given lip service to, as a creed whose moderate adherents must not needlessly be antagonized, as a stick with which to beat communism, but by no means as something which should be allowed to decide or even to influence policy.

The official, as distinct from the well-informed, Western world has, for the last fifty years, tended greatly to overestimate the influence of Islam among the Arab peoples and particularly among the educated Arab peoples. On the whole there has, over the last fifty years, been more agnosticism in thought, and more outward neglect of religious observances in practice in the Arab Moslem world among educated people, than there has been in the Western European Christian world. And Islamic modernism has been no more successful, and perhaps less successful, than Christian modernism in reversing the trend. In the relative secularity of its approach (which does not prevent occasional readings from the Quran any more than the secularism of the BBC prevents occasional religious broadcasts) Egyptian propaganda reflects an existing trend rather than encouraging a new one. But, as in other matters, so in the matter of religion, this reflection has had a powerful, if unconscious, influence in making fashionable an attitude which previously had been merely habitual.

Although Abdul Nasr's Arab nationalist propaganda did much to destroy, in the minds both of the Arabs themselves and in the minds of the outside world, those social and religious conventions which had contributed so much to the social and technical backwardness of the Arabs, and although this propaganda was certainly subversive of existing governments in many Arab countries, it was not revolutionary propaganda in the twentieth century sense. That is to say, it advocated changes in the political alignment (to be brought about by violence if necessary) but not changes in the social order. 'Feudalism' was only attacked in those Arab countries, e.g. Iraq, where feudalism was equated with imperialism, and not in those Arab countries, e.g. Saudi Arabia, where an extremely reactionary social order was not so equated. Private property, as such, was never attacked. Communism was never given the slightest encouragement, either by word or deed. In Egypt the Communist Party was always severely repressed and no attempt was made to use the Communist Parties in other Arab countries as agents of Egyptian propaganda. There seems to have been an early realization that, if Western imperialism was the present, communism was the probable future enemy of Arab nationalism. Similarly, the communists appear to have realized that Arab nationalism, and neither Islam nor the Baghdad Pact, was the most effective prophylactic against communism. But, until the Iraq coup, anti-communism was never an important plank in the Egyptian propaganda platform. This was partly due to the desirability of keeping on friendly terms with Russia (although this did not prevent the continued persecution of Egyptian communists) and partly no doubt due to Abdul Nasr's estimate that communism was not an immediately important rival to Arab nationalism. Later, if it became necessary (as it did), the epithet 'imperialist' could be broadened to include communists, since imperialism, in the Egyptian propagandist vocabulary, is a generic term used to denote any influence operating in opposition to the interests of the Egyptian Government. Although Abdul Nasr probably underrated the influence of communism until after the revolution in Iraq, he owed a lot of the support which he received in the Arab world as a whole, and particularly in Syria and Iraq, to conservative Arabs, who had no enthusiasm whatever either for Arab nationalism or for Egyptian domination, but who regarded these things as a lesser evil than communism and who regarded support for Abdul Nasr as a form of insurance.

Generally, Egyptian propaganda, like Egyptian policy, was, in intention politically subversive and socially reformist. But, since it was politically subversive, it often, in effect, although unwillingly and unwittingly, encouraged those socially subversive forces which it was trying to control and to contain.

CHAPTER NINE

Suez

———◆◆◆◆———

As has been indicated, the struggle for power to which Abdul Nasr had, by the end of 1955, become almost committed, was essentially a struggle for the attainment of Egyptian hegemony in the Arab world. In this respect Abdul Nasr's ambitions were a continuation of the ambitions cherished, not only by his immediate predecessors, but by almost all the rulers of an independent Egypt since the beginning of historical time. Nor was the use of Arab nationalism as a cloak for Egyptian penetration peculiar to Abdul Nasr. It had been used over a hundred years before by Mohamed Ali; it had dictated Egypt's Arab League policy for the previous ten years and had determined Egypt's disastrous incursion into the Palestine war. The neutralism, and its corollary, the anti-imperialism, to which Abdul Nasr sought to convert or to persuade the other Arab States, had been an integral part of Egyptian policy, at all events since the Wafd Government had abrogated the 1936 treaty and refused the offer of a regional defence pact in October 1951. The difference was that the military regime succeeded in obtaining popular support both inside and outside Egypt for what had previously been a more or less dilettante exercise on the part of the Palace and of the Wafd. This popular support was obtained primarily as a result of the nature of the regime. The Egyptian revolution had much the same effect on the Arab world as the French revolution had on Western Europe. Like the French revolution it had put an end in fact to the

rule of the Egyptian Royal House and to the political privileges
of the Pashas and had, in appearance, ushered in a new social
order based on the three pillars of social reform, anti-imperialism
and technological achievement. To the frustrated middle classes
of Syria, Iraq, Jordan, Arabia and the Persian Gulf—army officers,
government officials, professional men, students—the Egyptian
revolution must have seemed like the beginning of a new age. The
linking of Arab nationalism with those reforms which they
wished to see brought about in their own countries gave to Arab
nationalism a dynamic which it had not previously possessed for
them, having been associated in their minds with dynastic ambitions, national humiliations, imperialist plots and rotund oratory.
Instead of being seen as an attempt to divert popular resentment
from the social and political *status quo*, Arab nationalism, in the
hands of Abdul Nasr, and as a result of the circumstances of the
Egyptian revolution, became an instrument for the reforming of
the *status quo*. Instead of being seen as an additional piece of
pomp and circumstance for the glorification of existing rulers, it
became a means by which allegiance to these rulers could be
superseded by a higher form of patriotism.

Such references as have been made to 'Egyptian imperialism'
must be qualified by an acknowledgment of the extent to which
this imperialism was spontaneously welcomed by the people to
whom it was directed, and the extent to which the nationalist
emotions in the Arabic-speaking countries were transferred to
the support of what, to Western ideas, might seem the substitu-
tion of one form of imperialism for another. On the other hand,
all Arab nationalist enthusiasm was not immediately and automatically transferred to Abdul Nasr as soon as he unfurled his
banner. The governments of the various Arab States and Sheikhdoms were not entirely separatist creations or the obedient
creatures of Western imperialism. Nor were they entirely without popular support deriving from dynastic, historical and racial
loyalties. Nor of course were they without the means to repress
internal disaffection, whether spontaneous or whether generated
from outside. In so far as these means depended on foreign assis-

tance Abdul Nasr could be, and was, regarded by the generality of the Arab world as a potential liberator; in so far as they depended on indigenous resources—whether of force or of prestige or of popular backing—Abdul Nasr could be, and was, plausibly represented as a potential invader and as an actual disturber of the peace. The extent to which Nasserism was resisted by indigenous means was to determine the course of Egypt's imperial adventure.

The effect of the Egyptian revolution on the Arab world has been compared with that of the French revolution on Western Europe. But the Egyptian revolution was neither challenged by force of arms by the 'dynasts' of Arabia, nor were the dynasts of Arabia challenged on the field of battle by the Egyptian revolutionary forces. Abdul Nasr's struggle for power was conditioned on the one hand by the Arab military weakness which prevented any Arab State from altering the territorial *status quo* in the Middle East itself and on the other hand by the rivalry of the Great Powers which inhibited them from imposing on the Middle East, either separately or collectively, any alteration in the territorial *status quo*. The weapons used on each side therefore, apart from the Suez aberration, were limited to extensions of diplomacy such as propaganda, bribery, sabotage, attempted assassination, the imprisonment and torture of those political opponents who were get-at-able, and the systematic vilification of those who were not. Even so, the delicate international web within which the politics and economics of the Middle East lay so precariously suspended imposed a certain economy in the use of these paradiplomatic weapons.

Although, for propaganda purposes, Abdul Nasr made little or no distinction between Great Britain and the United States in his references to 'Western imperialism', it was important for him to avoid the creation of anything like a united Anglo-American front in the Middle East. The extrusion of British influence in the Middle East had been assisted—one might almost say caused— by the absence of such a united front and by the existence of strong American support for local nationalism against British

I

'colonialism'. (The American word of abuse to denote what the Egyptians meant by 'imperialism'.) Every successive British withdrawal from the Middle East had been, if not brought about, at least hastened, by the United States. British withdrawal from Palestine was hastened by American support for, accompanied by a refusal to assist in implementing, a pro-Zionist policy in Palestine. The expulsion of the Anglo-Iranian Oil Company from Iran, and its eventual replacement by an international consortium with a 40 per cent American interest, was hastened by American diplomatic support for the Musaddiq Government. The British withdrawal from the Canal Zone was hastened by American diplomatic support first for the Wafdist and later for the military Government in their negotiations with the British Government. Later, and almost entirely as a result of Abdul Nasr's objections, the United States refused to join the Baghdad Pact, although this Pact had been regarded by the Americans themselves as an integral part of the American-inspired defence system for the Middle East. Apart from the American attitude over the Palestine question, which could be ascribed solely to electoral considerations, this American policy of associating themselves with local nationalism against British imperialism, in so far as it was not attributable to atavism derived from memories of the War of Independence, could reasonably be interpreted as an indication of American willingness to acquiesce in Arab neutralism beneath the umbrella of the American alliance with Turkey and Persia, as being a preferable alternative to that Arab hostility which would be provoked by an attempt at continued Western control. Such a policy, although at variance with US policy in Southern Europe and in SE Asia, and although vitiated even in the Middle East by the presence of American Air Force bases in Libya and Saudi Arabia, might have been successful if it had been consistently pursued and if some attempt had been made to associate the British Government with it. But, in the same way as British policy towards the French position in the Levant States after the Second World War, American acquiescence in Arab neutralism seems merely to have been a tactical move to replace British by American influence in the Middle

East and not a genuine and coherent strategy based on a belief in the congruence of Arab neutrality with Western interests.

In the light of past events Abdul Nasr might, in the summer of 1955, reasonably have calculated on a continued American benevolence towards his designs, particularly so long as those designs were being pursued with the acquiescence and financial support of Saudi Arabia. (One of the principal weaknesses of US policy in the Middle East after 1952 was the continued attempt to pivot this policy round Saudi Arabia. This was not unreasonable while King Abdul Aziz had been alive. But after his death Saudi Arabia sank to the status of an occasionally rebellious Egyptian satellite. American policy makers never seemed to have been able to appreciate this.) This continued benevolence was particularly necessary for two reasons. First, the continued erosion of British influence in those places where it was still effective would be greatly facilitated by a continuance of the previous American 'anti-colonial' attitude towards the exercise of such influence. Secondly, Egypt's economy, and particularly the High Dam scheme, imperatively demanded financial assistance which could only come, in the measure required, from the United States.

It seems probable that the American reaction to Abdul Nasr's Czechoslovak arms deal in September 1955 was very much more unfavourable than anything which Abdul Nasr had expected. In retrospect it can be seen that the exaggerated enthusiasm with which this deal was greeted in the Arab world was, from the point of view of Abdul Nasr's ultimate ambitions, more than offset by the equally exaggerated alarm with which it was greeted in Washington. What was seen in Cairo and Damascus, and to some extent in Riadh, Baghdad and Beirut, as a gesture of Arab liberation from the trammels imposed on them by the West, was seen in Washington, and to some extent in London and Paris, as a sign of Egyptian subservience to Moscow. It was Abdul Nasr's Rubicon. Like most Rubicons, its symbolic significance was probably unappreciated at the time by the person crossing it. But from that time onwards events marched inexorably towards their climax, a year later, on the Suez Canal.

The signature of the Baghdad Pact in March 1955 revived, in its sharpest form, the age-old rivalry between the Nile and the Euphrates. And this rivalry, as always, took the form of a struggle for the control of the Fertile Crescent. But the struggle was to be one involving not military but psychological warfare.

The two countries of the Fertile Crescent in the front line of this psychological warfare were Syria and Jordan, one of which was precariously in the neutralist and the other, even more precariously, in the collaborationist, camp. A year previously Syria had, as a result of a military revolt, put an end to nearly five years of military dictatorship and had returned to a constitutional regime which was distinguished by the normal Syrian degree of instability. The coalition government was closely aligned with Egypt in a policy of neutrality, but there were strong, clandestine pro-Iraqi elements both in parliament and in the army. Iraqi intrigues and propaganda were active and the possibility of a pro-Iraqi coup, or even of an Iraqi invasion (if sufficient provocation were offered or manufactured) was by no means an impossibility, since Iraq was perennially and justifiably anxious about the security of the oil pipelines which passed through Syrian territory to convey Iraqi oil to the Mediterranean. Any successful pro-Iraqi coup or Iraqi invasion would clearly have been a great blow to Abdul Nasr's ambitions.

In Jordan the position was reversed, in that there was a 'collaborationist' government in treaty relation with, and dependent on a subsidy from, Great Britain. This government was harassed by intrigues from Saudi Arabia, by propaganda from Egypt and by a vociferously critical Arab nationalist opposition which manifested itself both in parliament and on the streets. Jordan, with a hopelessly unviable economy, with a long frontier with Israel to defend, with hostile Arab States on her northern and southern borders, and with a majority of her population consisting of discontented and part-destitute Palestine refugees, was even more inherently unstable than Syria and an obvious mark for subversion.

In December 1955, Taufiq Abu Huda, the Prime Minister of

Jordan, whether actuated by the hope of increased subsidies or by the prospect of more effective protection from Jordan's Arab friends and Israeli enemies, made private enquiries of the British Government about the implications of Jordan joining the Baghdad Pact. The consequent despatch of General Templer, the British Chief of the Imperial General Staff, to Amman for consultations was the signal for a Cabinet crisis and for countrywide rioting, resulting in a change of government and an official announcement that Jordan would not be joining the Baghdad Pact. Three months later, in March 1956, King Husain, under strong popular pressure, summarily dismissed General Glubb, the British Commander-in-Chief of the Jordan Army, together with such few British officers as still remained in the Jordan service. From then until the time of Suez Jordan was slowly sucked into the Egyptian orbit. In June parliament was dissolved, and in October elections were held resulting in a large nationalist majority which took office, under the premiership of Suleiman Nabulsi, pledged to the abrogation of the Anglo-Jordanian Treaty. Two days after the Nabulsi Government had assumed office, the Jordan army became incorporated into a Joint Military Command consisting of the armies of Egypt, Syria and Jordan, under an Egyptian Commander in Chief.

These events in Jordan, combined with an uninterrupted pro-Egyptian alignment in Syria, and the continued subservience of the spendthrift King Saud, made Abdul Nasr an observed figure among the malcontents of the Arab world—'characters in search of a hero'. Jordan had been regarded as a bastion and Glubb as a symbol of continuing British influence in the Middle East. The fall of that bastion and the abrupt disappearance of that symbol had a profound effect in Iraq, in Kuwait, in Bahrain, where opposition to the collaborationist regimes became identified with Arab nationalism, just as support of the existing regimes had been identified long since with imperialism. Even in the Maghrib Abdul Nasr was beginning to be seen as a symbol of liberation. Arms and money were being given by Egypt to the Algerian rebels. Egyptian aid and comfort was being given to those nationalist

elements who had not reconciled themselves with the 'collaborationist' regime of Habib Bourguiba. Almost everybody in the
Arab world who had a grievance, real or imagined, against any
regime not entirely in sympathy with the aims and ambitions of
Abdul Nasr found a ready hearing in Cairo. In Egypt itself Abdul
Nasr had been steadily consolidating his position. In May 1956
the last British troops left Egypt. In June a republican Constitution was promulgated in which Egypt was declared to be part of
'the Arab nation'. This Constitution was inaugurated by a
referendum in which the people of Egypt (including, for the first
time, women) had to vote 'yes' or 'no' both to the Constitution
and to the nomination of Abdul Nasr as President. There was a
99 per cent affirmative answer to both questions.

But in this process of making friends and influencing people,
Abdul Nasr was also making enemies and alarming people. The
British were becoming increasingly disturbed at the loss of Jordan,
at growing Egyptian influence in Syria athwart the Iraq Petroleum Company pipeline routes to the Mediterranean, at the
growing isolation of Iraq from the rest of the Arab world under
the impact of Egyptian propaganda, and at the effect of that
propaganda on the young Arab nationalists of the Persian Gulf.
The Israelis, knowing that their continued safety lay in the
hitherto endemic state of Arab disunity which had prevented
any combined military operations against her frontiers, and
watching the tightening grip of Egyptian influence, first in Syria
and then in Jordan, saw themselves being encircled by a potentially united Arab Federation. The French, always hostile to
and contemptuous of Arab nationalism, were becoming increasingly furious at the assistance being given by the Egyptian
Government to the Algerian rebels.[1] The US State Department,
always hypersensitive on the subject of communism, lent a ready
ear to information, much of it exaggerated, and some of it from
Zionist sources, about the extent of Russian and Czech arms
shipments to Egypt and about the extent of Russian influence in
Egypt. An extremely formidable combination of forces was beginning to build up in opposition to Abdul Nasr's designs.

For Abdul Nasr there was no retreat. Almost imperceptibly he had become a world figure. In the West he was an *enfant terrible*; in the East, one of the Tito-Nehru-Abdul Nasr triumvirate which sought to lead the newly independent nations of Asia and Africa down a middle road which led neither to Moscow nor Washington; in the Arab world, a hero to whom millions were beginning to look for some act of desperate defiance which would imbue Arab nationalism with a feeling of self-respect and of renewed hope. 'Characters in search of a hero.' In that phrase Abdul Nasr betrays his consciousness of and sensitiveness towards the pressures which were egging him on. These pressures had compelled him, in 1955, to react spectacularly to the Israeli attack on Gaza and to fling a gesture of defiance to the 'imperialists' and of confidence to Arab nationalists in the form of the Czech arms deal. Given these mounting pressures, it was clear that any public rebuff administered to Abdul Nasr would, with almost mathematical certainty, produce another resounding gesture as a means of preserving his credit with the Arab world.

Side by side with his Arab nationalist propaganda addressed to the Arab world, Abdul Nasr had, on the home front, been developing the idea of the High Dam which had, for the previous two years, been presented to the people of Egypt as the principal means by which Egypt's perennial and worsening land-hunger would be relieved. The High Dam was not a new idea any more than was Egyptian-sponsored Arab nationalism. For the previous twenty years at least the idea of a heightened dam at Aswan which would greatly increase the amount of stored water, and so enable a great increase in Egypt's cultivable area, had been a matter of continual but ineffective study. Nothing had been done about it, an omission which could conveniently be laid at the door of British imperialism. In addition to providing increased water storage, the various plans for the heightened dam provided for the generation of hydro-electric power, for the manufacture of nitrogenous fertilizer and for the establishment of a steel industry from the iron pyrites found in the neighbourhood of Aswan. The High Dam was the magnum opus which every

Egyptian Government, in its more optimistic moments, had dreamed of composing. It was almost inevitable that the military regime should have taken it up. It was likewise almost inevitable that such a scheme should be benevolently viewed by Western governments, who were accustomed to believe that economic development was a prophylactic against communism and that reasonable political behaviour was likely to be encouraged by the need of loans for such economic development. To the British Government, the High Dam scheme represented the Dr Jekyll side of Abdul Nasr. To the State Department the question of a loan, whether to the Egyptian or to any other government, was still a diplomatic bargaining weapon, a gift to be bestowed or witheld according to the recipient's behaviour.

The loan required was very large, and one which only a potential troublemaker would be able to command. Up to a point Abdul Nasr's past troublemaking had paid dividends. The immediate Anglo-American reaction to the Czech arms deal had been an increased willingness to help with the High Dam, with the presumable object of encouraging the Dr Jekyll side of Abdul Nasr's character. In February 1956 a provisional agreement was announced between the Egyptian Government and the World Bank by which the latter agreed to lend the Egyptian Government 200 million dollars towards the cost of the construction of the High Dam on condition that the American and British Governments would between them lend Egypt 70 million dollars for the same purpose. As part of the agreement the Egyptian Government undertook to find the equivalent of 900 million dollars in local currency for local services in connection with the construction of the dam. In addition, the various loans were made dependent on agreements with the Sudan, Ethiopia and Uganda over the division of Nile waters between these countries and Egypt.

At this point everybody concerned started to overplay their hands. Abdul Nasr, possibly fearing the extent of his provisional commitment to the West, appears to have sounded Russia about the possibility of participating in the finances of the dam. There was a strong minority opinion in the State Department which deplored the policy of attempting to wean Abdul Nasr from Russia by means of a loan from which the customary strings had been removed. Abdul Nasr's approach to Russia, together with apparently reliable information to the effect that Russia would not be willing to finance the dam in the event of no loan being forthcoming from the West, converted this minority into a majority. At the same time Congress was becoming annoyed with Abdul Nasr, first because its China lobby was annoyed at Egypt's recognition of communist China in the spring of 1955 (a step which, it was felt, nobody in the queue for an American loan ought to be allowed to take with impunity), and secondly because its Israel lobby was becoming alarmed at the reported build-up of Czech and Russian arms in Egypt.

The British Government, always sceptical about the Dr Jekyll side of Abdul Nasr's character, was disagreeably impressed by the fact that Abdul Nasr had made no serious attempt to negotiate with the Sudan or the other Nilotic countries about the High Dam, and came to the, probably correct, conclusion that Abdul Nasr had, for the time being, lost all interest in the High Dam and was entirely absorbed in his pan-Arab adventure.

In July 1956, immediately after the Referendum which elected him President, Abdul Nasr went to a meeting at Brioni with Tito and Nehru, where all three reaffirmed their faith in 'positive neutrality'. On his return to Cairo he learned that the US Government had withdrawn its provisional offer of a loan for the High Dam on the ground that Egypt's financial position had deteriorated, since the provisional offer had been made, to an extent which made the Egyptian economy unable to bear the Egyptian share of finance under the terms of the provisional agreement. (The implication was that the financial deterioration was the result of over-spending on arms from behind the Iron Curtain.) The British Government and the World Bank followed the lead of the US Government. Abdul Nasr's reaction was immediate. In a public speech on 24 July he promised the Egyptian people that the dam would be financed without Western assistance. Two days later, in the course of a speech in which, for the first time, he displayed his talent as a rabble-rousing orator, he announced the nationalization of the Suez Canal Company, stating that the revenues from the Canal would be sufficient to finance the construction of the High Dam. Even as he was speaking, 'vesting day' was being forcibly inaugurated in Ismailia by soldiers with fixed bayonets.

The act of nationalization produced a wave of enthusiasm throughout the Arab world comparable to, but greater than, the enthusiasm which, nearly a year before, had greeted Abdul Nasr's arms deal with Czechoslovakia. He had done something which, privately, very few intelligent Arabs considered wise, but which no intelligent Arab was prepared publicly to criticize, let alone denounce. As in the case of the Czech arms deal, the allies of the West were compelled, by the force of local public opinion, half-heartedly to applaud actions aimed directly at their ally and indirectly at themselves.

On all sides the realities of the situation were completely submerged beneath a flood of emotion. For the British, and particularly for the British Conservatives, the Suez Canal—the 'imperial life line'—had an emotive significance far exceeding its (undoubtedly considerable) importance to the British economy, which lay in its being the principal channel for the transport of oil to Great Britain from the Persian Gulf. For the French, who had built, and who had, up to the time of nationalization, administered the Canal, it also had an almost religious significance over and above its economic and financial importance to them. For the Egyptians it was both an assertion of Egypt's sovereign right to do what she liked on territory which, up to four months previously, had been occupied by British troops, and an assertion of Egypt's ability to return blow for blow in any argument which might develop with the West. For the Arab world as a whole, it was one more act of defiance, one more piece of vicarious satisfaction to set against twenty years of frustration and humiliation. There was a note of hysteria both in the Anglo-French anger and in the Arab enthusiasm.

In this super-heated emotional atmosphere Great Britain and France claimed that Abdul Nasr's action was a breach both of the 1888 Suez Canal Convention[2] and of Egypt's commitments under the Suez Canal Company's Concession.[3] Egyptian assets in Great Britain and France were immediately blocked and all Egypt's sterling and franc operations put under exchange control. On 30 July Eden[4] told the House of Commons that Great Britain was strengthening her military forces in Cyprus as a precautionary measure and insisted that vital British interests demanded that the Canal should be put under international control.

In view of Abdul Nasr's actual policy and obvious ambitions, and in view of the way in which the act of nationalization had been carried out, there was, superficially, some justification for the Anglo-French alarm. Three-quarters of Western Europe's oil supplies came from the Persian Gulf. Of this three-quarters, two-thirds, or about sixty-seven million tons per annum, came through the Suez Canal, and the remaining third was pumped to the Mediterranean through pipelines which passed through Syria, a country in close alliance with Egypt. Apart from the extra cost, there were not enough tankers afloat to maintain the existing flow of oil from the Persian Gulf round the Cape route. Therefore Abdul Nasr stood between Western Europe and a raw material vital for the Western European economy. He had in his hands a blackmailing weapon of immense power which could only be neutralized by the use of armed force. Everything in Abdul Nasr's past record suggested that he had every intention of using that blackmailing weapon, trusting that Great Power rivalries and UN Resolutions would prevent the application of the only effective sanction. Furthermore, there was good reason to suppose that Abdul Nasr's ambitions extended to the control, not merely of the transport lanes, but of the oil itself, and that the nationalization of the Suez Canal had to be viewed together with the Egyptian subversion of Jordan, and Egyptian intrigue and propaganda in Iraq and the Persian Gulf, as part of a grand design for obtaining control of the sources of Middle East oil as a preliminary to playing a game of power politics between Russia and the West. Colour was certainly given to these possibilities by Abdul Nasr's Hitlerian technique of invoking a spurious reasonableness in support of his worst outrages. Just as, when Hitler sent his troops into the Rhineland, he was only reoccupying what was already German territory, so Abdul Nasr, when he nationalized the Suez Canal, was only treating an Egyptian public utility in the same way as the British had already treated their railways and coal mines.

But what were the realities of the situation? Abdul Nasr's control of the Suez Canal had been secured, not by the nationalization of July 1956, but by the Anglo-Egyptian Agreement of July 1954. In the same way previous British control of the Suez Canal had been secured, not by Disraeli's pantomimic gesture in 1875 but by the British occupation of Egypt in 1882. The act of nationalization was not a breach of the 1888 Convention, in which it was specifically stipulated that the Convention was not co-terminous with the Suez Canal Company's Concession. It was an act analogous to the Iranian nationalization of the Anglo-Iranian Oil Company in 1951, in that it was a sovereign act arbitrarily cutting short a Concession granted by a sovereign State to a foreign Company. Such an act was only doubtfully in breach of international law, provided that it was an act, not of confiscation, but of nationalization against compensation. So long as the 1888 Convention, providing for freedom of passage, was secured, the act of nationalization was a matter which only concerned the Government of Egypt on the one hand and the shareholders of the Canal Company on the other. (Curiously enough, the British Government were shareholders both in the Suez Canal Company and in the Anglo-Iranian Oil Company, but it was something far more atavistic than outraged equity which made British Tories scream for paratroops at Abadan and actually use paratroops at Port Said.)

In fact, the 1888 Convention had been repeatedly breached since the Palestine war when Egypt (with the connivance of Great Britain up to the time of the evacuation of British troops from the Canal Zone) had, in defiance of a UN Security Council

Resolution, denied right of passage to Israeli ships and Israeli cargoes transiting the Canal. The right time to have invoked the 1888 Convention was not when Abdul Nasr nationalized the Canal but when Faruq denied it to Israel. After nationalization, Abdul Nasr, possibly because he was slightly alarmed at the furore which he had created, was scrupulously careful not to breach the Convention (other than by continuing to deny the Canal to Israeli shipping) in spite of the payment of Canal dues by British and French ships into blocked accounts and in spite of the extremely provocative behaviour of the Suez Canal Company, which did its best to discourage its pilots from working for the nationalized Canal Administration, with the avowed intention of bringing traffic through the Canal to a standstill. (This display of 'canalmanship' was unsuccessful in that the nationalized Administration had little difficulty in recruiting sufficient pilots to replace those who had left; it appeared that the mysteries surrounding the art of navigation through the Canal had been greatly exaggerated.)

By the end of July, four days after nationalization, Abdul Nasr's action, and the Anglo-French reaction to it, had stirred up a first-class international crisis. Dulles, the US Secretary of State, flew to London and persuaded the British Government to convene a Conference of all those nations whose ships used, or whose trade depended on, the continued free use of the Canal. Representatives of 22 out of the 24 nations invited (Egypt and Greece had been invited but had refused, Egypt for obvious reasons, Greece in a fit of pique connected with Cyprus) attended, and 18 of them agreed to a Resolution calling for the creation of a Suez Canal Board which provided for international control of the Canal. This plan was presented to Abdul Nasr by a delegation from the Conference headed by Menzies, the Australian Prime Minister. Abdul Nasr would have none of this Resolution, stating that its implementation would be a derogation from Egyptian sovereignty. Instead, he reiterated his intention of observing the 1888 Convention, of developing the Canal to meet future requirements, of keeping tolls equitable, and of operating the Canal efficiently.

(Part of the suspicion with which Abdul Nasr's pledges about the Canal were greeted in Europe derived from his earlier boast that the revenues from the Canal would be used to finance the High Dam. This was held to imply both that the tolls would be raised and that no compensation would be paid. In 1955, the dividend paid to shareholders of the Canal Company, after putting aside about £6 millions for capital works and contingencies, amounted to £10 millions. Assuming a continuation of existing tolls and existing traffic, and assuming a continuation of the policy of self-financing of capital additions, Abdul Nasr would have had about £10 millions a year out of which to pay equitable compensation—amounting under the terms of the Concession to a capital sum of about £22 millions, excluding any consideration for cutting short the Concession—to the Canal Company shareholders and to finance the High Dam. In the event Abdul Nasr not only had to find finance for the dam elsewhere, but also had to get a World Bank loan to finance capital improvements to the Suez Canal, the nett income from the Canal presumably having been merged in Egypt's general revenue.)

The British and French Governments were now convinced that a 'showdown' with Abdul Nasr was necessary and were determined to use the Suez Canal nationalization as the occasion for trying to associate USA with the application of sanctions. In the Users' Conference in August, Dulles had associated himself wholeheartedly with the idea of international control which Abdul Nasr had rejected. After the Conference had failed, Great Britain and France tried to associate USA with a Suez Canal Users' Association (SCUA) which, according to Anglo-French intentions, would be used as an instrument for imposing international control of the Canal on Egypt, if necessary by force of arms. But the State Department had already 'gone off the boil'. The comparative reasonableness of Abdul Nasr's behaviour since the act of nationalization, combined with the violent attitudes displayed, both in public and in private, by some British and French Ministers, had reawakened all the old suspicions of Anglo-French 'colonialism'. After Eden who, speaking in the

House of Common on 12 September, had seemed to imply that SCUA would be used, with American consent, to impose international control of the Canal on Egypt, Dulles made it clear in Washington that US ships would not be permitted to 'shoot their way through the Canal'. This appeared to be almost the precise opposite of what the British Prime Minister had implied. Abdul Nasr must have heaved a sigh of relief. There was no longer a united front between Washington, London and Paris.

By the time the Security Council met on 5 October the Suez Canal nationalization was no longer a burning international issue. For over two months the nationalized Canal had been working efficiently and without incident. There had been no accidents due to inexperienced pilotage, no delays due to inefficient administration, no discrimination (except against Israel) and no increases in tolls. In this relaxed atmosphere, the Secretary General was able to bring the Foreign Ministers of Great Britain, France and Egypt together to discuss an amicable settlement. But Great Britain and France continued to insist upon, and Egypt to object to, international control. A proposal embodying international control was submitted to the Security Council by Great Britain and France and vetoed by Russia. It was at this point, on 29 October, that Israeli forces crossed the Egyptian border into Sinai.

The Israeli invasion was only accidentally concerned with the dispute over the nationalization of the Canal. Ever since Israel's attack in force on Gaza in February 1955 the Egyptians, operating from the Gaza Strip, had been making commando raids in increasing force and with increasing frequency deep into Israeli territory. In addition the Egyptians had been building up a considerable concentration of arms, equipment and ammunition in the Sinai Peninsula, and were attempting to interfere with Israeli shipping transiting the Gulf of Aqaba on their way to and from Elath, the new port which the Israelis had established at the head of the Gulf of Aqaba and through which, denied the use of the Suez Canal, they were developing an increasing trade with the countries of SE Asia. Against this background, the announcement, on 26 October, of the grouping of the armies of Egypt, Syria and Jordan into a Joint Command under an Egyptian Commander-in-Chief appeared to presage an almost immediate Egyptian-inspired attack on Israel from three sides. The object of the Israeli invasion of Sinai was to forestall this.

It is doubtful whether, in fact, Abdul Nasr seriously intended to invade Israel. He was certainly threatening Israel both by his propaganda and by his actions. But he was probably under no illusions about the real strength of his army which, under his regime, had been developed as a political rather than as a military machine. (For example, the principal qualification of the C.-in-C., Abdul Hakim Amer, for his job was his friendship with and his loyalty to Abdul Nasr; he had no pretensions to being a military commander.) An unsuccessful war with Israel would have brought his flimsy imperial structure crashing to the ground. And it now appeared that this was exactly what, by his continual provocations, he had blundered into. But, by a strange irony, he was to be saved, if not from destruction, certainly from deflation, by the very two nations which were seeking most urgently to deflate him.

The story of the Anglo-French intervention has often been told. Even now it is impossible to piece together a coherent story of what really happened. There is no doubt that the French knew in advance about the Israeli attack and that they assisted the Israelis with aerial support. There is no doubt that the French, knowing British sensitivity to any overt partiality for the Israelis versus the Arabs, had concealed from their British allies their knowledge of Israeli invasion plans and their own intention of assisting them. It seems probable that the Israeli invasion genuinely took the British Government by surprise and that they seized on it, without overmuch thought, as a convenient pretext for reoccupying the Canal Zone. Military preparations for this reoccupation had been going on ever since the act of nationalization, three months before, and Abdul Nasr's circumspect behaviour since nationalization was probably influenced by his knowledge of these military preparations. But the negotiations in

London and, later, at the Security Council, while they produced no immediate threat from Abdul Nasr to justify armed intervention, certainly, in the eyes of the British and French Governments, produced no guarantee from Abul Nasr sufficient to justify halting the preparations for armed intervention. It was probably hoped either to scare Abdul Nasr in a climbdown or to provoke him to some action which would provide a clear justification for the use of force. But Abdul Nasr refused either to be scared or provoked. From the time that Dulles, in the middle of September, announced that American ships would not be allowed to shoot their way through the Canal, the practicability of successful armed intervention had passed. But the British and French Governments, with memories of crises twenty years before, when a world war might have been averted by a little firmness with an incipient aggressor, felt that a dispersal of their military concentrations would immediately result in some further act of aggression by Abdul Nasr, thus necessitating an immediate reconcentration. The implications of such a feeling were obvious. (It is now clear that the Anglo-French appreciation of the situation was vitiated by an over-estimate of Egyptian military strength almost as gross as the British over-estimate of Arab military strength in 1948.)

To Eden and his fire-eating Tories the Israeli invasion must have seemed almost like an answer to prayer. But as a pretext for intervention it lacked certain advantages. If the original stated reason for intervention[5]—the need to separate the combatants and to safeguard passage through the Suez Canal—was to be validated, an immediate landing in force was necessary as soon as Egypt had rejected the Anglo-French demand (addressed to both sides) to withdraw ten kilometres from the Canal. But the plans for intervention were based on the transport of a landing force from Malta which would take several days to arrive. Assuming the probability of Egyptian resistance, it was deemed impracticable to occupy the Canal Zone by parachute landings from Cyprus unless this landing were preceded by the 'strafing' of Egyptian airfields and followed up within forty-eight hours by a

K

landing from the sea. As a result the campaign took a course which might have been especially designed to serve the interests and to heighten the prestige of Gamal Abdul Nasr.

For some forty-eight hours after the expiry of the Anglo-French ultimatum, Egyptian airfields were efficiently 'strafed' by British and French fighters and fighter bombers and inefficiently assailed by some incredibly inept propaganda emanating from the Sharq al Adna broadcasting station in Cyprus, which had been taken over by the British Government from its commercial owners for this grotesque purpose.

This broadcast propaganda, on the one hand calling on the Egyptian people to get rid of Abdul Nasr because he was a source of inconvenience to the British, and on the other hand attempting to frighten them with what was in store for them if they did not do so, seemed, like other British actions at the time, nicely contrived to serve Abdul Nasr's and to defeat British purposes to the maximum possible extent. It was the sort of stuff which used to be written on leaflets addressed to rebel tribesmen on the NW frontier and dropped by RAF planes as a preliminary to punitive raids on their villages. It illustrated that aspect of the Suez adventure which for the time being rallied the whole Arab world behind Abdul Nasr, which destroyed forever any real prospect of an Anglo-Arab *rapprochement*, which imperilled the whole prospect of co-operation between East and West, and which did for communism in the Middle East what years of communist propaganda had been unable to achieve.

The significance of Suez for future relationships between the Arabs and the West was not that it was an act of aggression by two powerful countries on a weak one; it was not even that it was an act of aggression which failed ignominiously and humiliated the aggressor in the eyes of the intended victim; it was not even that it was an act of aggression which appeared to have been jointly planned with the Israelis; there had after all been considerable provocation, and it is always easier to forgive when it is the other fellow who has been humiliated. These things could have been forgiven and forgotten as the acts of governments and

not of peoples. But what could never be forgiven or forgotten was
the unconscious revelation by the British, in their propaganda
and in the attitude taken up by most of the members of the
British Government, that they regarded the whole affair, not as a
quarrel between equals, but as the attempted chastisement of a
black servant by his white master. It was abundantly apparent to
the whole Arab world that the British attitude would have been
quite different had they been dealing with, say, Denmark. It is
not surprising that, after Suez, there should have been a tremendous revulsion of feeling on the part of pro-Western Arabs, a
feeling which went far beyond the political disappointment to
which they had become accustomed. Before Suez it was not altogether nonsense to assert, as was often asserted by British politicians and others, that there was a considerable fund of goodwill
existing towards Great Britain in the Arab world, which would
become apparent once political differences had been straightened
out. Suez destroyed that fund of goodwill by making it appear
that collaborationist Arabs were not merely traitors bought by
British gold, but dupes deceived by British hypocrisy. To be
accused of being a betrayer is bad enough; to be convicted of
having been betrayed is infinitely worse.

Hardly less important than this open humiliation inflicted on
actual, and secret humiliation inflicted on potential, friends of
the West was the confirmation which the Anglo-French action
seemed to provide of the validity of what had appeared to many
Arabs as the anti-imperialist excesses of Egyptian propaganda. In
the light of the Suez action it really did appear that the creation
of Israel had been a Western plot for the purpose of securing a
bridgehead in the Arab world from which attacks could be
launched on the Arab world. It really did appear that 'imperialism' was not just a term of abuse to label something of which
Abdul Nasr did not happen to approve, but that it was an active,
evil force, seeking to suppress any manifestation of independence
among the Arab nations. To the Egyptian propagandist the
Anglo-French aggression must have appeared in much the same
light as a miracle to a faith healer—as an event lending an air of

verisimilitude to an otherwise unconvincing story. The whole sinister world of imperialist plots aimed at the frustration of Arab aspirations, of secret agents working night and day to seduce and deceive Arab 'opportunists', of Western statesmen endlessly plotting against Arab independence, seemed to come to life. The fact that the forces of darkness concentrated their attacks on Abdul Nasr was proof enough that Abdul Nasr was the principal champion of the children of light.

A determined and ruthless attack against the Suez Canal Zone, whether from the air or from the sea, would probably not have been vigorously resisted by the Egyptian forces, and would have faced the United Nations and the world at large with a *fait accompli*. It would have forestalled the blocking of the Suez Canal. It might have led to Abdul Nasr's overthrow in Egypt. But surprise was deliberately eschewed. Twelve hours elapsed between the expiry of the ultimatum and the beginning of the bombing. Forty-eight hours elapsed between the beginning of the bombing and the landing of the first paratroops. Another forty-eight hours elapsed between the landing of the first paratroops and the first sea landing. During all this time opposition to the Anglo-French assault had been steadily building up. The Egyptians blocked the Canal by sinking a number of ships in the fairway. In Syria, one of the Iraq Petroleum Company's pumping stations was blown up, thus cutting off the flow of oil through the pipeline. Egypt, Syria and Saudi Arabia broke off diplomatic relations with Great Britain and France; Iraq, Sudan and Jordan with France only. Jordan refused to allow her bases to be used by the British, under the Anglo-Jordanian Treaty, for operations against Egypt. Mildly impressive as these acts were as a demonstration of Arab solidarity, only one, the cutting off of the flow of IPC oil through Syria, was of any serious inconvenience to the British and French in that, combined with the blocking of the Suez Canal, it disrupted the supply of Middle East oil to Western Europe. None had any effect in checking the rather leisurely progress of the Anglo-French assault. (The Israeli advance, after enveloping and destroying the Egyptian forces in Sinai, and having thus achieved its principal purpose, had halted along a line approximately ten kilometres from the Suez Canal in accordance with the terms of the Anglo-French ultimatum.) Much more important was the hostile reaction of the non-Arab world, which exceeded anything which the British and French Governments could possibly have expected. Within a few days of the start of the operation, this reaction had reached an intensity which, probably for the first time in history, forced the abandonment of an attack by a Great Power upon a small one. The British decision to evacuate Egypt (followed by a reluctant French decision to evacuate as well) was taken immediately after the capture of Port Said by sea-borne invaders and before the initial object of the expedition, the occupation of the Suez Canal along its entire length, had been achieved. It was taken as a result of the operation of four converging pressures, of unequal strength, and could only have been defied by a government even more divorced from reality than was the British Government of the day.

The least immediately important of these pressures was the Russian threat to attack London with rocket missiles and the Russian promise to send volunteers to fight in Egypt. Only slightly more important was the attitude of the British Labour Opposition which, after some initial hesitation, condemned the whole operation. (The importance of this lack of unanimity on the eve of what might have been a major war was minimized by the fact that public opinion in Great Britain was almost certainly heavily in favour of the Government in this matter.) Considerably more important was the vote in the UN Assembly on 2 November, three days after the expiry of the ultimatum and three days before the sea landing at Port Said, which, by sixty-four votes to five, condemned the Anglo-French action and called for a cease fire. But the really decisive factor was the attitude of the United States Government which, after having voted with the majority in the UN Assembly Resolution on 2 November, appears to have made it quite plain to the British Government that every pressure short of, and perhaps even including, armed force, would be used against Great Britain and France if the Assembly

Resolution were not promptly complied with. Even so, it appears that a section of the British Cabinet, led by Macmillan (Eden was now virtually *hors de combat* as the result of a nervous break-down), preferred the probability of national ruin to the certainty of Tory humiliation. But the pressure of reality, and the warnings of the City of London (to whose counsel, both wise and foolish, a Tory government is always sensitive), prevailed. Eden resigned and Macmillan, rather surprisingly, succeeded him. Butler, who was usually regarded as being next in succession to Eden, was apparently unacceptable to the majority of Tories as the result of an alleged lack of enthusiasm for the Suez expedition.

It would be naïve to suppose that this collective resistance to aggression had been dictated by any considerations of inter-national morality. The Russians, estimating correctly that American disapproval would bring the operation to a premature end anyway, and wanting themselves to pose to the Arabs as their rescuers (which they did very successfully), gave great publicity to a threat and to a promise which they knew they would not have to fulfil. The Americans, who had no vital interest in the Suez Canal and who, in view of their control of the Panama Canal, had no violent prejudice in favour of internationalization, regarded communism as the real enemy in the Middle East and regarded Arab nationalism as a potential ally against com-munism. They were by no means disposed to encourage communism by conniving at an attack on Egypt which they regarded as being inspired by predatory Anglo-French imperial interests. In the course of a few weeks the rapidly swinging pendulum at the State Department, which oscillated between the extremes of regarding Abdul Nasr as a crypto-communist and as a bulwark against communism, and which at one end of the swing had precipitated the crisis by cancelling the provisional offer of a loan for the High Dam, had now swung right over to the opposite extreme. The adverse UN Assembly vote had been secured automatically as a result of the strange and almost unpre-cedented spectacle of USA and USSR taking the same side in an international dispute.

In the eyes of the Arab world the fact that Abdul Nasr had suffered a resounding military defeat at the hands of the Israelis was masked by the fact that he had won an equally resounding diplomatic victory against the 'imperialists'. (Even the fact of military defeat was plausibly explained by the fiction that he had voluntarily pulled the bulk of his army back from Sinai across the Suez Canal in order to face the impending Anglo-French attack. In fact, the bulk of his army in Sinai had been enveloped and destroyed in the first few hours of the fighting and before the despatch of the Anglo-French ultimatum.) In the eyes of the rest of the world Abdul Nasr's high-handed (to put it at its lowest) action in nationalizing the Suez Canal literally at the point of the bayonet and without previous warning or negotiation, and his generally aggressive behaviour towards Israel during the previous several months, was effectively masked as the result of Egypt having become the first nation to have been rescued from aggression by United Nations action. For some months Abdul Nasr was a kind of UN mascot and, by a judicious moderation, both in word and deed, appropriate to the victim of an aggression, he was able to extract the maximum of advantage from his position. Under pressure from the UN Assembly which was, in this unprecedented situation, acting as an executive body through the agency of the Secretary General, Great Britain, France and Israel were compelled unconditionally to withdraw from Egyptian territory, handing over their positions to the units of the United Nations Emergency Force (UNEF) which, with Egyptian permission, had already started to arrive in Egypt. The Israelis, victors in a lightning campaign which had ended before the UN Resolution had been debated, tried before withdrawal to insist (a) that Egypt should not return to the Gaza Strip and (b) that Egypt should renounce the belligerent rights by which she had justified her denial of the Suez Canal and her attempted denial of the Gulf of Aqaba to Israeli shipping. But, for the time being, there was no limit to the complaisance of the UN towards their only effective protégée. The US Government made a veiled threat of economic sanctions against Israel in the event of their not evacuating

Egyptian territory. Under protest, Israel withdrew from Sinai and from the Gaza Strip and the border was policed (and at the end of 1959 was still being policed) by a United Nations force.

Looking back, it appears that at this point Abdul Nasr was at the height of his career. He had carried his point over the Suez Canal in face of initial objections from nearly all the Powers, including USA, and in the face of armed intervention by Great Britain and France. The Canal had been nationalized; there was no more question of international control; the damage which Egypt had done to the Canal at the time of the invasion was to be repaired at the expense of UN and the British and French were to take no part in the repairs. Abdul Nasr had been able to use UN as an instrument, not only to repair the Canal, but to secure the unconditional withdrawal of British, French and Israeli troops from Egyptian territory. He had seized without effective protest and without payment all the British bases in the Canal Zone which, under the 1954 Agreement, had been placed in the care of civilian contractors. He had, without effective protest, sequestrated all British and French property in Egypt. In the Arab world Saudi Arabia, Syria and Jordan seemed to have been reduced to the position of Egyptian satellites. The separation of Jordan from the Western Bloc seemed to be confirmed by an agreement arrived at on 19 January, 1957, by which Saudi Arabia and Egypt agreed to pay £5 million each and Syria £2½ million annually to Jordan in order to enable Jordan to forgo the British subsidy and so set her free to terminate the Anglo-Jordanian Treaty. The Treaty was in fact terminated in March 1957, after some negotiation, and the British agreed to evacuate their forces from Jordan within six months. (In the event the promised subsidy was not paid by the three Arab States except for a few instalments from Saudi Arabia.) There seemed a real possibility of some form of economic and political union between Egypt, Syria and Jordan. Popular feeing in the rest of the Arab world was strongly pro-Abdul Nasr. As an indication of the strength of this popular feeling, there was virtually no openly expressed criticism of Abdul Nasr at all in the Arab world, although there were many private misgivings. Nasserite Arab nationalism was, for the moment, a force which could not easily have been withstood, if there had been the means and the opportunity thoroughly to exploit it.

But Abdul Nasr's triumph over the Suez Canal and his conversion of a military defeat into a diplomatic victory, had only been made possible as the result of a momentary and, as it were, freakish phenomenon. Russia, who had no particular interest in the Suez Canal, and who naturally supported any action of Abdul Nasr's likely to embarrass the West, had supported the act of nationalization and condemned the Anglo-French intervention. The American reaction to this intervention, which was mainly dictated by the fear lest this intervention be used by the Russians as an excuse for their own military intervention in the Middle East, paradoxically and temporarily aligned USA with USSR against Great Britain and France. But the Russians, by their dramatic threat of reprisals against Great Britain, and by their romantic promise of volunteers to fight in Egypt, had succeeded in convincing the Arab world that it was they and not the Americans who had been instrumental in bringing the Anglo-French invasion to an end.

CHAPTER TEN

The Eisenhower Doctrine

It has already been noted that American policy in the Middle East was dictated almost entirely by the desire to avoid communist penetration. It must have seemed to the State Department that the two most conspicuous results of Suez in the Middle East were a strengthening of Russian influence, as evinced, *inter alia*, by Russian loans to and the presence of Russian trade missions in Syria, and a weakening of British influence, as evinced, *inter alia*, by the growing isolation of Iraq from the rest of the Arab world and the growing hostility to the Baghdad Pact in the Arab world. After Suez it must have seemed urgently necessary to the State Department to strengthen anti-communist defences in the Middle East. So long as it had been possible to identify Arab neutralism with 'anti-colonialism' it had been benevolently regarded. After Suez, with 'colonialism' in ruins, Arab neutralism lost its 'anti-colonial' attractions and became less benevolently regarded. The American policy which became known as the Eisenhower Doctrine was an attempt to achieve what the British had failed to achieve in the Baghdad Pact—a weaning of the Arab world away from neutralism and into the Western camp.

The Eisenhower Doctrine, like the Baghdad Pact, was directed, in fact and in intention, against communism, in appearance and in effect against Egyptian imperialism. It was first enunciated in a message by President Eisenhower to Congress on 5 January, 1957. In this message the President stressed the economic and strategic importance of the Middle East and asked for funds designed to assist in the development of economic strength for the purpose of maintaining the independence of Middle Eastern countries and for authority to use US forces 'to secure and protect the territorial integrity and political independence of such nations requesting such aid against overt aggression from any nation controlled by international communism.' Congress agreed with the President and voted 200 million dollars for economic assistance to Middle Eastern countries.

The first fruits of the Eisenhower Doctrine and the first diplomatic setback suffered by Abdul Nasr since Suez were in connection with freedom of navigation through the Gulf of Aqaba. At the head of the Gulf of Aqaba, as well as the Jordanian port of Aqaba, was the newly-constructed Israeli port of Elath. As a result of the denial of passage through the Suez Canal, Elath had been developed by the Israelis as a channel for their growing trade with the countries of SE Asia. On the assumption of the continued denial of the Suez Canal, which Israel could not, by her own means, open to Israeli shipping and cargoes, freedom of navigation through the Gulf of Aqaba to and from Elath was obviously vital to Israel's trade. When compelled, under the threat of US sanctions, to withdraw unconditionally from Egyptian territory, the Israelis had, under protest, evacuated Sharm as Sheikh, at the entrance to the Gulf of Aqaba on the Egyptian side from which an Egyptian force could, with suitable artillery, command the narrow entrance to the Gulf of Aqaba. The Israelis privately made it clear, both in Washington and in London, that, while they were compelled reluctantly and temporarily to acquiesce in the continued denial of the Suez Canal to them, they would, if necessary in defiance of the UN, resist with force any Egyptian or Saudi attempt to blockade the Gulf of Aqaba. The eastern shore at the entrance to the Gulf of Aqaba was Saudi territory and any effective blockade would involve joint action by Egyptian and Saudi forces. The fact that no Egyptian attempt was made to blockade the Gulf of Aqaba by remounting gun emplacements at Sharm as Sheikh was almost certainly due, first to knowledge of the Israeli threat and to an intimation from UN that they could expect no assistance in the event of their provoking Israel into carrying out this threat, and secondly, to the disinclination of King Saud to co-operate in carrying out the blockade.

It so happened that King Saud spent most of January 1957 in USA on a State visit. His presence in USA, his close connections with American oil interests, and his perennial need for money owing to his own and his family's personal extravagance, all made it inevitable that he should be exposed to the blandishments of the Eisenhower Doctrine. It is possible that he was already becoming alarmed at his growing subordination to Abdul Nasr, and at the increasing influence of Egyptian 'liberalism' among the more educated of his own people. It is certain that he could afford neither seriously to quarrel with America nor openly to oppose the prevailing current of Arab nationalism. Faced with a not unfamiliar necessity for equivocation, he agreed to an increase in the size of the Dhahran air base (the existence of which was in any case a denial of that neutralism to which he was officially dedicated) in return for a promise of military aid, vociferously denounced international communism, and appeared cautiously to approve the Eisenhower Doctrine. On his return home, although continuing to give verbal support to the policies of Abdul Nasr, and although reiterating the Arab claim to regard the Gulf of Aqaba as territorial water and not as an international waterway (the legal basis of the Arab claim to blockade the Gulf of Aqaba was that it was territorial water shared between Egypt and Saudi Arabia) he did nothing to assist Egypt to enforce that claim. Moreover, in his visits to Baghdad in May, and to Amman in June (after King Husain's successful coup in April), he showed an increasing tendency to try and redress the balance of power in the Arab world between the 'neutralists' and the 'collaborationists'.

President Chamoun of Lebanon was much less equivocal in his support of the Eisenhower Doctrine. For reasons quite unconnected with international communism, the Lebanese Government was particularly anxious to counter that growing Egyptian influence in the Arab world which was regarded, particularly by Lebanese Christians, as a threat to Lebanese independence. Syria was virtually an Egyptian satellite and exercised a powerful attractive influence on a number of Lebanese Moslems, who traditionally looked for support towards some powerful Moslem nation in the same way as Lebanese Christians traditionally looked for support towards Western Europe. For the previous thirteen years Lebanese independence had been safeguarded by a tacit self-denying ordinance on the part of both Christian and Moslem leaders who both refrained from leaning too far either westwards or eastwards respectively in accordance with their traditional instincts. This balance had been preserved as the result of an even balance of power between Moslems and Christians, represented for most of the time by the Christian President, Bishara Khoury, and the Moslem Prime Minister, Riad Solh. The balance was upset by the assassination of Riad Solh in 1951 and by the disgrace and resignation of Bishara Khoury in 1952. No comparable Moslem statesman existed in Lebanon to balance the authority wielded by Camille Chamoun, Bishara Khoury's successor[1], and the vulnerability of Lebanese Moslems to Egyptian propaganda was increased by the feeling that, within Lebanon, the preponderant power wielded by Chamoun loaded the dice unfairly against the Moslems. The promulgation of the Eisenhower Doctrine seemed to Chamoun and to his (mainly Christian) advisers a suitable opportunity for offsetting the pressure of Egyptian influence. Charles Malik, the Lebanese Foreign Minister, left for Washington in January 1957, soon after the Eisenhower Doctrine had been promulgated. Shortly afterwards, the Lebanese Government invited an envoy from President Eisenhower to visit Lebanon and, in March, announced their adherence to the Eisenhower Doctrine, receiving in return promises of American military and economic aid. This policy was approved by the Lebanese Parliament early in April with seven abstentions and one dissentient. In June, general elections, preceded and accompanied by a barrage of Egyptian, Syrian and Soviet propaganda, denouncing the Lebanese Government as 'imperialist hirelings' were held and resulted, as general elections in Lebanon usually did, in a decisive majority for the Government.

By this time the Eisenhower Doctrine had produced even more impressive results in Jordan. For the first few months after Suez the Government of Suleiman Nabulsi moved closer and closer to the Egyptian orbit. As has already been related, the Anglo-Jordanian Treaty was terminated in March and arrangements made for the withdrawal of British troops within six months and for the replacement of the British subsidy by subventions from Egypt, Saudi Arabia and Syria. In January the Jordan Government had denounced the Eisenhower Doctrine and forgone an American loan in consequence. In February Jordan successfully insisted on the withdrawal of Iraqi troops who had entered Jordan at the time of Suez, representing that, as a result of the Joint Military Command established in October 1956, all troops in Jordan should be under Egyptian command. Although Iraqi troops were withdrawn, Syrian troops stayed. It only seemed a matter of weeks before the declaration of a political union between Egypt, Syria and Jordan. This pro-Egyptian orientation by Nabulsi was, very clumsily, accompanied by a rather ostentatious complaisance towards Soviet propaganda and by a decision to establish, for the first time, diplomatic relations with USSR. This proposal gave Husain, whose throne was clearly in danger as a result of his Prime Minister's policy, the opportunity for a counter attack in which he would be able to rely on American support. On 10 April Nabulsi was dismissed, but the King was unable to form an alternative government. Disorders broke out. Abu Nawar, who had succeeded Glubb as Commander-in-Chief, attempted to start an army revolt against Husain, but the majority of the army stood firm for the King and Abu Nawar fled to Syria. For some days the situation hung in the balance. Prompt action by the Syrian army would have gained the day for Arab nationalism. But, as always, the Syrians, vociferous in propaganda and fertile in intrigue, wilted before the prospect of decisive action. Iraq and Saudi Arabia forestalled Syria by moving troops into Jordan, ostensibly to prevent an Israeli invasion, actually to prevent a Syrian occupation (which might well have led to an Israeli occupation of the west bank). On 24 April President Eisenhower declared that the territorial integrity and independence of Jordan was a vital American interest, and moved the Sixth Fleet to Beirut. This was decisive encouragement for Husain and for his supporters in Jordan. Martial law was declared, Amman occupied by loyalist troops, political parties dissolved, a new government of Independents formed under the premiership of Samir Rifai and the decision to open diplomatic relations with Russia cancelled. Within a few days order was restored, Husain firmly established on what had appeared to be a tottering throne, and Nabulsi put in gaol. The fact that this had been achieved almost entirely as the result of American intervention by remote control was delicately minimized by the new government which, while accepting American aid to the tune of ten million dollars, announced that Jordan was not committed to the support of the Eisenhower Doctrine.

By May 1957 it seemed that the Eisenhower Doctrine had brought to an end that isolation from the rest of the Arab world which had been imposed on Iraq as a result of the Baghdad Pact. The Suez affair had embarrassed the Iraqi Government in many respects. The blowing up of the IPC pumping station and pipeline in Syria and the consequent delay—imposed by Syria—in repairing it, had seriously affected Iraqi oil exports and, in consequence, Iraqi revenues. The relationship with Great Britain in the Baghdad Pact had come under more than usually heavy fire from the other Arab countries and, within Iraq, had made the Baghdad Pact policy even more unpopular than it had been before. All this did not prevent the Iraqi Government from re-insuring the Baghdad Pact by adherence to the Eisenhower Doctrine in concert with Turkey and Pakistan. In May King Saud, who, in April, had joined with Iraq in sending troops to Jordan in order to forestall a Syrian occupation, paid a state visit to Baghdad, thus publicly signalizing the end, for the time being, of his term of subservience to Egypt. In June, this visit to Baghdad was followed by a state visit to Amman. The old Saudi-Hashemite hatchet had apparently been buried—an impressive but unintended result of

Abdul Nasr's Arab unity propaganda. In the communiqués which followed these two meetings nothing impolite was said about Abdul Nasr or about Arab unity. The usual polite noises were made about positive neutrality, independence, the Algerian patriots, the Palestine refugees and the Arab League. The Baghdad communiqué made a reference to 'subversive ideologies'. But the Amman communiqué actually referred slightingly to the Baghdad Pact and mentioned with approval Jordan's alliance with Egypt and Syria against Israel, the 'common enemy'. But, beneath these kind words, there lurked an unmistakable challenge to Abdul Nasr—and to Syria. The dynasts of Arabia had forgotten their old differences and were uniting against the new order in the Arab world as represented by the republican governments in Cairo and Damascus. The immediate problem before Abdul Nasr was no longer that of isolating Iraq or of subverting Jordan. He now had to save Syria, his only remaining ally, from the complicated pressures which were now threatening that country.

The modern State of Syria is an artificial creation carved out of that geographical region which has from time immemorial been known as Syria and which comprises roughly the modern States of Lebanon, Jordan, Syria, Israel, and part of Turkey. A further complication is added by the fact that the modern State of Syria includes a large stretch of territory east of the Euphrates, known as the Jezireh which, historically, is not part of Syria but part of the geographical region known from time immemorial as Mesopotamia. On the one hand, Lebanon, Jordan, Israel and the Sanjak of Alexandretta are regarded by Syria as temporary and illegitimate subtractions from Syria's rightful area of sovereignty. On the other hand, the Jezireh is regarded by Iraq as a temporary and illegitimate subtraction from Iraq's rightful area of sovereignty.

To make matters worse, these subtractions have not had the advantage of leaving the 'rump' of Syria as a homogeneous unit. On the contrary there were within the State of Syria, at least two separatist movements—that of the Druzes in the south and that of the Alawites in the west—whose demands ranged from complete independence to increased regional autonomy, intense regional rivalry between the two great cities of Damascus and Aleppo, and endemic insubordination towards the central government on the part of the Beduin tribal leaders, whose status approximated to that of the 'robber barons' in mediaeval Europe. There was no sense of loyalty towards the Syrian State as such. There was a wider loyalty towards Arabism, which was regarded as more or less synonymous with a Greater Syria; there was a narrower loyalty towards the city, the tribe, the region, or the religion. A man could regard himself as an Arab and as a Damascene; he could regard himself as an Arab and a Druze, an Arab and a member of the Aneizeh tribes. He found it difficult to regard himself primarily as a Syrian. In fact, the only people habitually known as Syrians are Lebanese living in West Africa or South America.

The fact that these truncations from an ideal and a notional Syria had been brought about, not by revolt, but by an arbitrary partition on the part of the Western Powers, added a particular spice of bitterness to the situation. Lebanon had been carved out of Syria by France during the period of the Mandate. This French creation consisted of an area more than twice as big as the old and mainly Christian Sanjak of Mount Lebanon, which had enjoyed a semi-autonomy in Ottoman times, and included the three ports of Tripoli, Beirut and Saida. The Sanjak of Alexandretta, which had been part of the French mandated territory of Syria until 1938, had then been ceded by France to Turkey, this depriving Syria of yet another port. In the south, Transjordan had been cut off by the British to provide for her lines of imperial communication and to provide a throne for Abdullah, her Hashemite protégé. Finally, and much the worst cut of all, Palestine, including the ports of Haifa and Jaffa and the Holy City of Jerusalem, had been subtracted from the Syrian homeland in order to provide a national home for the Jews. Under these circumstances the Governments of Israel, Jordan and Lebanon were regarded, not merely as rebel administrations who had reneged from their true allegiance, but as imperialist puppets who had connived with

L

Great Britain and France in the creation of so many separatist regimes. The feeling of outrage induced by what was regarded as a deliberate Western policy of subsidising and supporting a series of artificial separatist movements as a means of destroying Arab nationalism, explains two of the salient features in Syrian policy since the war—extreme suspicion of the West and endemic hostility towards all her neighbours. But the very factors which had to some extent justified and to a great extent facilitated previous truncations—religious differences, local rivalries and so on—not only inhibited any serious prospect of restoring what was merely a notional unity, but threatened the State of Syria with the prospect of total dissolution. It might indeed have been plausibly argued that such a process of dissolution was both a logical extension of the fragmentation which had already taken place and a necessary preliminary to putting the pieces together again in some form of federation. For the State of Syria, as it stood, was neither strong enough to enable it to impose, nor weak enough to compel it to abjure, a forcible reunion. As a result Syrian policy towards her neighbours consisted of an ineffective aggressiveness, which irritated without intimidating. Occasional consciousness of this neurotic inadequacy led sometimes to internal upheavals and sometimes to ostentatious advances, made either to Moscow or to Cairo, or to both simultaneously, with the object of offsetting that isolation and protecting themselves against those reprisals to which their bad neighbour policies continually exposed them.

Against this background, it was only to be expected that the Syrian contribution to the Palestine war had been marked by a maximum of invective and a minimum of effective hostility, and that the Syrian reaction to defeat had been marked by an immediate revulsion from the National Bloc Government nominally responsible for it. This Government, which had been in power in Syria since 1943, owed its original elevation to and its subsequent retention of power to its success in ridding Syria of French rule. After the end of 1945, when this process of liberation was completed, those centrifugal forces, which are particularly strong in Syria, began inevitably to work against the National Bloc, until the Palestine disaster gave it the *coup de grâce*. The military regime which succeeded the constitutional, ineffective, and rather corrupt National Bloc administration, after a few confused months during which two would-be military dictators came and went, gave Syria nearly four years of strong, relatively efficient and relatively honest rule under Colonel Adib Shishakli. Colonel Shishakli's term of power in many respects foreshadowed that of Colonel Abdul Nasr. Like Abdul Nasr, he tried first to rule through a civilian façade and later through a military puppet, Colonel Silo. Like Abdul Nasr, he eventually (in 1952) assumed the appearance as well as the reality of power, becoming both President and Prime Minister. Like Abdul Nasr, Shishakli pursued a policy of moderate reform at home and neutralism abroad. Unlike Abdul Nasr he was unable either to retain the loyalty of the Syrian army or to enlist the enthusiasm of the Syrian people. In 1954 he was dismissed and fled the country as the result of a successful military coup against his regime. Constitutional life was restored, political parties resumed their activity and elections were held in September 1954. These elections returned a Chamber consisting mainly of Independents. The two older parties, the National Bloc and the Syrian Popular Party, returned about forty members between them, and the Baath Socialists returned 16 members.

Shishakli had bequeathed to Syria a more or less coherent domestic and foreign policy, consisting of moderate reform at home and close co-operation with Egypt in a neutralist policy abroad. But his fall deprived Syria of any authoritative direction in the pursuit of these policies. Deprived of this authoritative direction, domestic reform tended to degenerate into left-wing attitudinizing and neutralism into alignment with Russia. The general tendency was to follow the Abdul Nasr line but always to pursue it a little further than Abdul Nasr himself. For the first year of its existence the restored constitutional regime pursued a reasonably coherent domestic policy and a policy of alliance with, without involving subordination to, Egypt abroad. The process of subordination to Egypt can be said to date from the election of Shukri Kuwatli, the veteran National Bloc leader, to the Presidency in August 1955. Kuwatli, who, since the death of Abdul Aziz ibn Saud in 1952, had been like a monkey deprived of his organ-grinder, was all too obviously prepared to serve Gamal Abdul Nasr in lieu of his dead master. By the time of Suez this process of subordination had brought Syria to the verge of a federal union with Egypt, and the Syrian army was already part of a joint Egyptian-Syrian-Jordanian force under Egyptian command. But there were already signs that this passive subordination was developing, not so much into an independent policy to the left of Abdul Nasr, as into a caricature of the policies of Abdul Nasr. To vary the simile, the monkey had jumped off the top of the barrel-organ and, still attached to it by its chain, was gesturing and capering some yards ahead of it.

The blowing up of the IPC pumping station at the time of Suez was not so much a calculated action designed to assist Abdul Nasr in his struggle with the West as an automatic reaction of anger against the West. It was not done by the direction of the Government; it was done by an army commander on his own responsibility. At the time it was done, the President was on a state visit to Moscow, where he appears to have concluded an agreement for the supply of Soviet arms to Syria.

The increasingly pro-Egyptian and pro-Soviet orientation of Syrian policy, combined with the continual delays imposed by the Syrian Government on the repair of the IPC pumping station, were causing considerable anxiety to the Iraqi Government. This anxiety was shared within Syria by the Popular Party which, traditionally, supported a policy of friendship with Iraq against the traditional National Bloc line of friendship with Saudi Arabia and Egypt. Since the return to constitutional life, the Popular Party had come to represent the right-wing pro-Iraqi opposition to the prevalent and increasingly left-wing pro-Egyptian tendency represented by a majority of the army, by the Baath and by the President. In December 1956 the Government announced that they had discovered an Iraqi plot against Syrian independence which implicated leading members of the Popular Party.

The discovery of this plot greatly weakened the Popular Party and led to the reconstitution of the Government on lines which confirmed and intensified the pro-Soviet and pro-Egyptian orientation of Syrian policy. The first act of the new Government was to denounce the Eisenhower Doctrine which had just been promulgated. In March 1957 the contract for a government oil refinery at Homs was awarded to a Czech firm in spite of a more favourable American tender. From that time on commercial contacts with Iron Curtain countries steadily increased and, in August 1957, an agreement was signed in Moscow by which Syria was to receive an unspecified amount of financial and technical aid on apparently very easy terms.

This increasing and ostentatious commerce with Russia and her satellites was less a matter of deliberate policy than the result of an auction for popularity within Syria between the Baath on the one hand and various Independent politicians on the other.

The Baath was a reincarnation of that traditional Arab nationalism which had come to birth among the Syrian students and intellectuals during the nineteenth century. It was founded in 1950 by a certain Michel Aflak, and for some time enjoyed the patronage of Colonel Shishakli. In 1953 it amalgamated with the Syrian Socialist Party under the the leadership of Akram Hourani. The combined party was known as the Baath Socialist Party. They advocated social reform at home and neutralism and pan-Arabism abroad. In their advocacy of such policies they may fairly claim to have anticipated the policies later developed by Abdul Nasr. But, as always with Syrian nationalists, the development of their policies had to await the advent of a suitable champion from outside Syria. They must have viewed the rise of Abdul Nasr with an almost messianic enthusiasm; they certainly viewed the increasingly pro-Egyptian alignment of Syrian policy with satisfaction. From the middle of 1956 the Baath were increasingly represented in the various coalition governments which succeeded one another in Syria.

The rising power of the socially reformist and middle-class Baath was by no means welcome to the mainly wealthy and

socially reactionary Independent politicians who, however, had
the sense to realize that social reaction was out of fashion and
that the increasing power of the Baath could only be combated
by outbidding the Baath in popular favour. It occurred to Khaled
al Azm, the most powerful of the Independents, a rich landowner,
a member of the leading family of Damascus and an unsuccessful
candidate for the Presidency in 1954, that this popular favour
could be achieved and the Baath flank neatly turned by diverting
popular enthusiasm from the prospect of social reform—which
had its inconveniences for Khaled al Azm and his friends—to the
prospect of financial assistance from Russia which, since Suez,
had been regarded with much the same feeling of affection and
respect in the Arab world as had been accorded to the United
States after the announcement of President Wilson's Fourteen
Points forty years before. In terms of domestic politics this was an
intelligent calculation. The Baath, although they feared and dis-
trusted communism and Russia, could not publicly oppose a pro-
Russian alignment at a time when Russia had succeeded in getting
herself regarded as a champion of Arab freedom. Neither could
Abdul Nasr. And so there appeared to be a great deal more indigenous enthusiasm than there really was for the Syrian Government's increasing intimacy with Russia.

This ostentatious and, in some ways, rather grotesque flirta-
tion was viewed with a good deal of alarm both inside and outside
Syria. The State Department, as always assessing events in the
Middle East exclusively in terms of the cold war, seems to have
assumed that events in Syria represented Russian reaction to the
success of the Eisenhower Doctrine in Jordan, Lebanon and Saudi
Arabia and that it had become a case of a cold war struggle between USSR and USA for the control of the Fertile Crescent. The
Iraqi Government, still furious at Syrian action over the IPC
pumping station, and perennially alarmed at Syrian hostility to
the Baghdad Pact, would undoubtedly have welcomed a British
or an American invitation to intervene in Syria. Turkey, with
sufficient American encouragement, would probably have been
prepared to move into northern Syria. Jordan, with similar en-

couragement, would probably have been prepared to move into southern Syria. In fact, the Syrians, with their customary ineptitude, had manoeuvred themselves into a position in which they were faced with the possibility of an invasion from three of their neighbours, which they could not resist and which they could only prevent by an appeal to Russia for protection, which protection, if extended, might possibly result in a third world war.

(It is inappropriate to refer to the 'Syrian Government' as having been responsible for any action during this period. For some months Khaled al Azm on the one hand, and the Baath on the other, although both included in the Government, had been acting independently of and often in opposition to one another. Similarly, the army, the real power in the country, had been acting quite independently either of the Baath or of Khaled al Azm. Under the pressure of threatened invasion the Baath and the army tended to draw nearer to each other and nearer to Abdul Nasr, whom both Baath and army were beginning to regard as the potential saviour of Syria.)

Abdul Nasr himself must have been irritated almost past bearing by the antics of his Syrian allies, whose excesses had exposed them to the possibility of an invasion in which he would have been unable to assist them and which, if it had taken place, would have consummated the ruin of his pan-Arab policy, already shaken by the defection of Saudi Arabia and Jordan. As had happened a year before, he was rescued unexpectedly and unintentionally by the US Government. Most of the public and official alarm in the West about the alleged Russian penetration of Syria had been created as the result of a visit to the Middle East by Loy Henderson of the State Department in August 1957. On Henderson's return to Washington, Dulles declared that other Middle East States had expressed apprehension about communist influence in Syria and Eisenhower made a statement in which he expressed a fear lest international communism should drive Syria into acts of aggression against her neighbours. (This was naïve; in so far as there was any danger of aggression it was a danger of American-inspired aggression against Syria by her neighbours and not Russian-inspired aggression by Syria against her neighbours.)

These two statements nullified most of what had been achieved by the Eisenhower Doctrine during the previous six months. Russia was able once more to pose as the champion of Arab independence by sending Notes to Great Britain, France and the United States warning them against interference in Syria. (At about this time three members of the US Embassy in Damascus were expelled from Syria on a charge of plotting against Syrian independence in concert with France and Israel.) Iraq, Lebanon and Jordan felt compelled to rebut an implied suggestion of complicity with Western imperialism by a declaration of support for Syrian independence. Abdul Nasr was able to rehabilitate his waning prestige in the Fertile Crescent by sending a small body of Egyptian troops to assist Syria against the threat of a Turkish invasion which, if it had ever been contemplated at all, had certainly, as a result of the Russian attitude, been abandoned before ever Abdul Nasr's troops landed in Syria.

In much the same way as the Suez invasion, the Eisenhower Doctrine could now plausibly be represented to the Arab world as a concerted and organized Western plot against Arab independence; it could plausibly be argued that the communist threat, as applied to the Middle East, was a mere excuse for Western intervention and that those Arab Governments who associated themselves in alliances with the West were themselves conniving at attacks on Arab independence; it could reasonably be represented that there was nothing much to choose between the French, the British and the Americans; that the Americans, with their superior resources, had simply taken over from the British and French; and that the common aim of all three was to make the Arab countries the instruments of their policies and the servants of their economies.

The principal immediate effect of the Syrian crisis was to destroy such reputation as USA still had among the Arabs for honesty of purpose. Henceforward USA was, in the minds of the generality of Arabs, identified with Great Britain and France as an imperialist power. They simply could not believe that alarmist utterances by Eisenhower and Dulles about Syria were due to a genuine over-estimate of the extent of communist penetration of Syria. They assumed that these utterances were part of a deep-laid plot to encourage Syria's 'collaborationist' neighbours to partition Syria between themselves. They assumed that references to the possibility of Syria attacking her neighbours was an example of the well-worn aggressor's technique of attributing aggressive intentions to the country one is about to attack oneself. More importantly perhaps, and certainly more unfortunately, the generality of Arabs became convinced that communism, as applied by Western imperialists to the Middle East, was nothing but a smear word designed to discredit and to justify attacks on Arab nationalism, in the same way that communism, in the USA, had been used as a smear world by Senator MacCarthy and his associates to discredit and to encourage and justify attacks on American liberals.

Although the Americans had undoubtedly, but probably quite genuinely, over-estimated the extent of communist influence in Syria, there was equally no doubt that communist influence in Syria was increasing and that conditions in Syria were such as to encourage its further increase. There was a small, but relatively strong and relatively united communist party in Syria, which was allowed complete freedom of manoeuvre and propaganda, and whose leader, Khaled Bikdash, easily the ablest and most experienced of Arab communists, was expert at exploiting domestic rivalries and jealousies in the interests of communism. There was a tremendous and growing admiration for Russia among nearly all sections of the community; this admiration was due partly to the ingrained Syrian nationalist habit of looking for a champion outside Syria; partly to a feeling of superiority to Egypt which made it less unpalatable to look towards Moscow rather than towards Cairo for such a hero, and partly to a general feeling that, in the crisis of 1957, as in the crisis of 1956, Russia had, by her timely diplomatic interventions, saved the Arabs from being attacked by the West. There was great governmental instability. No one party was able to form a government, and each successive government was a precarious coalition with its various components trying to outbid each other in popular favour by the extravagance of its left-wing attitudes. The Popular Party which, paradoxically, was the only Party which did not participate in this auction, was in opposition and many of its members were either in prison or in exile as a result of being suspected of connivance with Iraq for the overthrow of Syrian independence. To be openly anti-Russian almost exposed a person to the suspicion of treason.

In this precarious situation the army, in Syria as elsewhere in the Arab world the one potential stabilizing influence, was known to be divided and to contain many communist sympathizers. It was also too inefficient to constitute the slightest disincentive to invasion from outside. (Eisenhower's conception of Syria as a potential aggressor was entirely grotesque; the intention was certainly there, as always, but, as always, the means were entirely lacking.) But for some months before the Syrian crisis there had been a growing *rapprochement* between the Baath Party and a strong faction in the Syrian army led by a certain Colonel Abdul Hamid Sarraj, who was Head of the Syrian Army Intelligence Service. This *rapprochement*, which was based on a common support for the neutralism of Abdul Nasr was, in spite of the suspicion with which it was viewed by the West, the one stabilizing force in Syrian politics, in that it was anti-Communist, authoritarian and reformist—Sarraj and his army group contributing the first two attributes and the Baath the third. In a country where notables like Khaled al Azm were irresponsibly flirting with Moscow, where an active communist party stood ready to exploit the discontents of workers and peasants, where religious, racial, tribal and political minorities were constantly intriguing, some with hostile foreign Powers, against the central government, the emergence of such a relatively responsible combination was almost a necessary condition of the continued existence of any effective central government at all.

By the time of the Syrian crisis it was becoming apparent that Syria would be unable much longer to sustain an independent national existence. The lack of any general sentiment of national entity and the weakness of the central government seemed to present Syria with an inexorable choice between a further and probably final partition on the one hand and some sort of federation into a larger Arab nationalist unity on the other. Since the great preponderance of political opinion in Syria was anti-Western and anti-'collaborationist', such a federation could only be with Egypt, in spite of the geographical disadvantages of such a federation. The possibility had been in the air for some time and as early as July 1956 the Syrian Government of the day had announced its intention of negotiating a federal union with Egypt. But there were many difficulties in the way. Abdul Nasr himself was unenthusiastic, probably realizing that such a federation would retard instead of advancing the cause of Arab unity among Syria's Arab neighbours (which eventually proved to be the case). It was also appreciated, by those Syrian politicians who retained a sense of reality, that Syria would be very much the junior partner in such a federation which would, as was eventually the case, reduce Syria to the status of an Egyptian colony. But after the Syrian crisis, and in face of Syria's increasing isolation from her Arab neighbours, and in face of increasing communist influence in Syria, both Abdul Nasr and a growing body of Arab nationalists in Syria began unenthusiastically to accommodate themselves to the view that nothing short of a federal union between Egypt and Syria could save the cause of Arab nationalism in the Fertile Crescent. In Syria the case for such a union was energetically sponsored by the Sarraj-Baath combination. The practicability of such a union depended on the popular support which the Baath could command from the people and on the authority which Sarraj wielded over the army. For it was necessary that such a union should appear to be consummated as a result of the unanimous wish of the Syrian people. Anything which had the appearance of a shot gun marriage would have precipitated that dissolution which union was designed to prevent.

The fact that federation, when eventually it came about in

February 1958 (five months after the Syrian crisis) was an immediate and sensational success in the Arab world—it was greeted with an enthusiasm comparable to that which had been evoked by the Czechoslovak arms deal and by the nationalization of the Suez Canal—was principally due to the influence of the Baath. (In passing, and since Abdul Nasr's career does, on a small scale, bear some resemblance to the career of Adolph Hitler, it may not be altogether fanciful to compare the Czechoslovak arms deal to Hitler's announcement of Germany's rearmament in defiance of the Treaty of Versailles, the nationalization of the Suez Canal to Hitler's march into the Rhineland, and the federal union with Syria to the Austrian Anschluss.)

By this time the influence of the Baath had extended all over the Fertile Crescent. It had gained supporters and adherents in Lebanon, Jordan, Iraq and in the Sheikhdoms of the Persian Gulf. Its influence lay not so much in its political organization, which was weak, as in its ideology. This ideology, confused and imprecise as it was, exactly mirrored the confused imprecision of Arab nationalist middle-class youth, who wished to be assured that there was a viable third alternative to communism and Western imperialism, that social amelioration was a principal object and inevitable consequence of political reform, that freedom would be the inevitable result of revolution and that unity was the sovereign remedy for all the humiliations from which the Arabs had suffered for so long.

The ideology of the Baath mirrored these aspirations; the Arab nationalist policies of Abdul Nasr held the promise of realizing them. It is hardly surprising that the federal union between Egypt and Syria appeared, in the eyes of the generality of Arab nationalists, to be the first instalment of that Arab unity for which they had waited for so long, instead of being an almost desperate expedient to keep the concept of Arab unity alive.

The act of union was almost unanimously confirmed by referenda taken in the two countries. The results of these referenda were endorsed by the almost unanimous applause of the rest of the Arab world. As with Abdul Nasr's earlier coups, even those governments or individuals who were either dubious of its wisdom or alarmed at its implications had perforce either to remain silent or join in the applause.

In comparison with the union of Egypt and Syria into the 'United Arab Republic'—a union only made slightly less impressive by the addition of Yeman which joined the union as a kind of country member—the union between Iraq and Jordan, announced a few days later, was received with very little éclat and greeted with very little enthusiasm either in Iraq or Jordan. Although polite messages were exchanged between Cairo and Damascus on the one hand and Baghdad and Amman on the other, the union between Iraq and Jordan was clearly intended as a counterblast to the United Arab Republic, as an assertion of Hashemite as against Nasserite unity. As such it did Abdul Nasr the service of underlining the progressive aspect of Nasserite unity as opposed to the reactionary nature of Hashemite unity, and did the West the disservice of underlining the popular identification between collaboration and social reaction.

Two things soon became apparent. First, that the Iraq-Jordan union was nothing but a façade. It could have been made a useful reality if the two armies had been welded together into a single fighting unit and if the financial and territorial resources of Iraq had been made available for the settlement of the Palestine refugees in Jordan and for the relief of the Jordan economy generally. But any sharing of Iraqi oil revenues with, or any acceptance of immigration from, a country with which she had just become formally united, would have been quite unacceptable to Iraq. Secondly, that Abdul Nasr had regained that initiative in the Fertile Crescent which he had lost for several months as a result of the operation of the Eisenhower Doctrine on Saudi Arabia, Jordan and Lebanon. During these months Syria had become isolated through being surrounded by a ring of hostile 'collaborationist' States. Now the tables were turned and Lebanon and Jordan were facing isolation. This was not due to any shift in the balance of military power. What was being fought was a psychological and not a military war, and it was psychological and not military changes that counted. Up to a point the Eisenhower Doctrine had been successful and up to that point the initiative had passed away from Arab nationalism. Then, as it appeared to the Arabs, the Americans failed to accomplish in Syria what they had succeeded in accomplishing in Jordan and Lebanon, and to some extent in Saudi Arabia. One failure, or what appeared to the Arabs to be a failure, was enough to cost them the initiative. (For virtually all Arabs, whatever their political sympathies, saw the Eisenhower Doctrine, not as a proposal for insurance against communism but as an American campaign against Abdul Nasr. And the union with Syria, which was seen by virtually all Arabs as a successful counter-attack by Abdul Nasr on the Eisenhower Doctrine, was enough to give the initiative back to Abdul Nasr.)

In appearance the Syrian crisis had disabled American power for effective intervention in the Arab world as decisively as the Suez crisis had disabled the British and French from such effective intervention. But appearances are sometimes deceptive. The ineffectiveness of Anglo-French intervention in the autumn of 1956 had been entirely due to American opposition. The ineffectiveness, or rather the unwisdom, of American action over Syria had been largely due to lack of consultation and co-operation between the State Department and the Foreign Office. By the end of 1957 lessons had been learnt and bridges had been built both in London and in Washington. From the beginning of 1958 Abdul Nasr was to have to reckon with an unusual degree of Anglo-American solidarity in opposition to his pan-Arab ambitions. It is perhaps ironical that this united opposition should have begun to manifest itself at a time when Abdul Nasr himself was beginning, as a result of his Syrian experiences, to take the danger of communist penetration seriously. Before the end of the year he was to take it more seriously still.

CHAPTER ELEVEN

Civil War in Lebanon

————◆◆◆◆————

'The United Arab Republic.' The title was well chosen for its evocative effect on Syria's neighbours. In its unity, in its Arabism, and in its republicanism it constituted a reproach both to the separatism and to the lack of enthusiasm for Arabism characteristic of the Lebanese Government and to the reactionary Hashemite rule over Iraq and Jordan. And at the same time as it constituted a reproach to the rulers it constituted an incitement to the ruled. The formation of the UAR was an open threat to the continued independent existence of Jordan, Lebanon and Iraq and was recognized as such by the governments of these countries. But at the same time as it represented a threat to the governments, it represented a promise to many of the peoples of these countries.

The Republic of Lebanon was a French creation, carved out of the territory allotted to France at San Remo under the Mandate for Syria. The historic Lebanon was included within the boundaries of the autonomous Sanjak of Lebanon, which had been imposed on the Ottoman Empire in 1864 as a result of European intervention after a massacre of Lebanese Christians. It consisted of Mount Lebanon, from Jebel Akbar in the north to Jebel Amil in the south, and was inhabited almost entirely by Maronite Christians and Druzes. Instead of reconstituting this autonomous Sanjak (which had been abolished by the Ottomans at the beginning of the First World War) under some form of autonomous

government, the French created the 'Grand Liban', which included the three ports of Beirut, Saida and Tripoli and extended
inland as far as the summits of the Anti-Lebanon so as to include
not only the whole of the Lebanon range, but the fertile plateau
of the Bq'a as well. Thus Lebanon, instead of being a small
Christian-Druze enclave, was enlarged to include a population
of about a million people, of whom about half were Moslems.

When Lebanon achieved national independence in 1943 her
main problem, both in domestic and in foreign affairs, was to
keep an even balance between the interests and the aspirations of
her Christian and Moslem citizens. In this matter, domestic and
foreign considerations were inextricably intertwined. The
Lebanese Moslems, feeling themselves at a disadvantage in
Lebanon as a result of the superior energy, enterprise and education of the Lebanese Christians, tended to react to this inferiority
by seeking closer Lebanese ties with, or even for the absorption of
Lebanon into, a larger Moslem Arab union. The Lebanese
Christians, resentful at the prospect of such absorption, yet fearing to provoke it, wished at the same time to pursue a policy of
friendship towards the member States of the Arab League and to
strengthen their contacts with the West, regarding these contacts
as a necessary insurance against the possibility of Moslem aggression from outside Lebanon. Although relations with Syria were
consistently and increasingly difficult, any serious clash between
Moslems and Christians had been successfully avoided until after
the Suez crisis. This had been principally due to the fact that,
until the advent of Abdul Nasr's pan-Arabism, there had been no
movement of Moslem Arab policy outside Lebanon sufficiently
attractive to seduce Lebanese Moslems from their allegiance to a
State which, by comparison with other Arab States, was relatively
prosperous, relatively stable and relatively free from confessional
or political tyranny or discrimination. Beneath the surface, most
Lebanese Christians (to whom, privately, the word Arab was
almost a term of abuse and certainly a term of denigration) had an
arrogant contempt for their less gifted Moslem neighbours; most
Lebanese Moslems nursed a smouldering resentment at the

superior economic status of and at the arrogant assumption of superiority by most Lebanese Christians. But these passions were kept under control by the businesslike common sense of the leaders of the two communities who realized that Lebanon's position as a bridge between the Arab world and the West was an immensely advantageous one, both economically and politically, to both Moslems and Christians, and who appreciated that this position could only be maintained so long as there was an amicable *modus vivendi* between Moslems and Christians in Lebanon.

In the aftermath of Suez it became clear that this *modus vivendi* was being threatened by the attractive force which the concept of Arab unity was exercizing, not only on the Lebanese Moslem masses, but on their leaders as well. The Lebanese Christians, who were determined to ensure that what they regarded (with considerable justification) as their superior civilization should not be engulfed in the fanatical obscuranticism (as they saw it) of pan-Arabism, looked instinctively to the West. A state of tension developed which, in the event, was nearly to pull Lebanon apart. Unfortunately, internal political circumstances were not propitious. Camille Chamoun, the Maronite Christian President, who had succeeded Bishara Khoury, was a man of strongly European sympathies who barely concealed his distaste for pan-Arabism. All the really influential Moslem leaders had recently gone into opposition (the previous Prime Minister, Abdallah Yafi, had resigned with his government after the President had refused to break off diplomatic relations with Great Britain and France at the time of Suez); the new Moslem Prime Minister, Sami Solh, was a man of small account and quite unable, in an admittedly difficult situation, to keep the ship steering a safe middle course between the Scylla of pan-Arabism and the Charybdis of the Eisenhower Doctrine—a task at which his murdered cousin, Riad Solh, would have been particularly adept. He could exercise no effective control either on the Christian President or on his Moslem opponents. The Lebanese Government, acting under the strong influence of their Christian Foreign Minister, Charles Malik, who was particularly obnoxious to Arab nationalists for

M

his well-known and frequently-expressed Western sympathies, subscribed, with perhaps unnecessary precipitancy, to the Eisenhower Doctrine.

For a time the apparent success of the Eisenhower Doctrine had the effect of reducing the attractive force of Arab nationalism on the Lebanese Moslems. But after the formation of the UAR had restored the initiative to Abdul Nasr, the full blast of Arab unity propaganda was turned on to Lebanon. Adherence to the Eisenhower Doctrine was branded as treason against Arabism. Denunciations of the Lebanese, Iraqi and Jordanian Governments from Cairo and Damascus now became quite uninhibited. Diplomatic relations were broken off between Lebanon and UAR and between Jordan and UAR. The Government of the United Arab Republic was now quite openly determined to absorb, first Lebanon and Jordan and, later, Iraq, by the organization of internal revolutions in these countries. The technique was Hitlerian; the means, fortunately, were only Egyptian.

Revolutions cannot be brought about by means of propaganda, however skilful, or bribery, however well distributed. When it comes to the point, guns have to be turned on to the regime which it is desired to overthrow. Physical invasion was impracticable, both because it would almost certainly provoke outside intervention and because neither the Egyptian nor the Syrian armies were capable of any such martial exercise—such military resources as they had were principally concentrated on the Israeli frontier. (The Israelis were, at this time, the chief, although unacknowledged, guarantors of Lebanese and Jordanian independence.) In Iraq and Jordan the army held the key to the situation. Unless and until the Iraqi and Jordanian armies could be successfully subverted, revolution in these countries was impracticable, however ardent the masses might be for Arab unity and however grievous the oppressions from which Abdul Nasr's supporters were suffering. In Lebanon the situation was different. The split between Chamounites and Nasserites (as it is convenient to call the opposing factions) was more or less on confessional lines. The Lebanese army, recruited about equally from Moslems and

Christians, was about equally divided in its sympathies. This meant that the Lebanese army was not a factor in the situation. It could be used neither for subverting nor for sustaining the authority of the government. Because of this limitation it was possible to resort to methods which were not possible in Jordan or in Iraq. The Syrian authorities organized large-scale smuggling of arms and ammunition over the Syro-Lebanon frontier. By the beginning of summer 1958 the Lebanese Moslems, under the leadership of Sa'eb Salem, an ex-Minister, were in open rebellion against the Lebanese Government which was defended, not by the Lebanese army which, under the command of General Shihab, the future President, was to preserve an intact and prudent neutrality throughout the struggle, but by organized bands of Christian guerrilla fighters, spearheaded by the Phalange, the Christian Youth Movement, led by Pierre Gemeyel, another ex-Minister.

Outwardly, it was a domestic insurrection, and as such it was presented to the outside world both by the rebels themselves and by the UAR propaganda machine, which took the line that the Lebanese Moslems were in the front line of the endemic Arab struggle against Western imperialism, in this instance represented by President Chamoun and the Moslem 'traitor' Sami Solh. But no objective observers, with the apparent exception of the UN observation team which came to Lebanon later to control the Syro-Lebanese frontier (mainly, it must be added, by remote control from the Riviera Hotel in Beirut), had any doubt about the reality. The rebellion had been fomented, and was being supported and sustained, by the United Arab Republic from over the Syrian border; it had as its object the overthrow of the Lebanese Government and the putting into power of a government which would incorporate Lebanon into the UAR.

Throughout the crisis President Chamoun had been assured of the support of both the American and British Governments, and had also been in close touch with the Iraqi Government. He was not inclined to compromise with the rebels and was not encouraged by the British and American Governments to do so.

Indeed, it seemed that the rebels would have been satisfied with nothing short of a government which would have been acceptable to, and which would have turned Lebanon into a satellite of, the United Arab Republic.

In the middle of July, Chamoun sent a message to the Iraqi Government asking for an Iraqi armoured brigade to be despatched to the Iraqi-Syrian frontier as a diversion. (This request may have been in response to an offer of help from the Iraqi Government.) It was to have momentous consequences. By what was to be almost, if not quite, the last official act of his life, Nuri as Said unwittingly precipitated the Iraq revolution and all its still unpredictable consequences. He himself was soon to die horribly, but he had the posthumous satisfaction of achieving, further along the chain of events which started with his own death, the frustration and then the extinction of Abdul Nasr's ambitions for the hegemony of the Arab world.

The Iraqi armoured brigade which was ordered to proceed to the Syrian frontier was commanded by Brigadier Abdul Karim Qasim. Instead of proceeding to the Syrian frontier, it stopped in Baghdad en route and, on 18 July, overthrew the Government. This coup, unlike the Egyptian military coup six years before, was accompanied by much violence and bloodshed, in the course of which the young King Feisal, his uncle Abdulillah, the ex-Regent (and probably the most hated man in Iraq), and Nuri as Said, the Prime Minister, were murdered, and the British Embassy sacked. When, after two or three days of rioting, looting and murder, order was more or less restored, General Qasim emerged as the head of a revolutionary government composed partly of army officers and partly of civilians who were known to have been in opposition to the Nuri regime. The prisons were opened to liberate hundreds, or perhaps thousands, of political prisoners, including a number of communists, and to receive in exchange a number of ex-Ministers and others identified with the previous regime.

In the outside world the coup was generally regarded as being another triumph for Abdul Nasr, and was either greeted or apprehended as such. The origins of the coup are still obscure. It seems probable that many, if not most, of the officers involved had been in communication with Abdul Nasr. It seems improbable that Abdul Nasr, or any of the officers concerned, were thinking in terms of the immediate absorption of Iraq into the UAR. It seems likely that they were thinking in terms of a very close relationship with UAR. On this assumption the situations of the regimes in Lebanon and Jordan were indeed precarious.

The effect of the coup in the West was analogous to the effect of the Suez Canal nationalization almost exactly two years before. The main difference was that the Foreign Office and the State Department were now in very close accord over the Middle East. Both governments now had to take what might have been a fateful decision. President Chamoun asked the Americans and King Husain asked the British for military assistance, the one against actual infiltration of men and arms from UAR, the other against what appeared to be a likely invasion from Iraq which was still, technically, united with Jordan. On the face of it, and in the light of the information available at the time, the decision which the two governments had to take was whether to acquiesce in the prospect of Abdul Nasr controlling the Arab world, or whether to continue to resist this prospect. The question of communist penetration, although in reality more relevant than in any previous Middle East crisis, now hardly came into consideration. The avowed enemy, both in Washington and in London, was not communism but Arab nationalism. Washington, chastened by the experiences of 1957, had now come into line with London. American troops made an unopposed landing just south of Beirut and, a few days later, British paratroops were flown into Jordan. On the whole subsequent events appeared to justify these two interventions, both of which were much criticized at the time, particularly by the Labour Opposition in Great Britain. There was no violent reaction to the landings either from Baghdad or from Cairo. One of the first acts of the revolutionary Government in Baghdad was to wash its hands of Jordan and to declare the union between the two countries at an end. Cairo confined itself to routine verbal denunciations of imperialism. Seen in retrospect it seems likely that Abdul Nasr was already worried by the course of events in Iraq, and realized that things in Baghdad were not all going his way.

Fears expressed lest the Americans might have to stay indefinitely in Lebanon to sustain Chamoun and that the British would have either to stay indefinitely in Jordan or else fly Husain out with them, were dissipated by the diplomacy of Robert Murphy and by the existence of the Israeli army.

The original intention of the American landing was to assist Chamoun to crush the forces in rebellion against the Government. But Murphy, sent from the State Department to review the situation, was quick to realize that compromise and not victory was necessary if Lebanon were to continue to have an independent existence. This compromise meant the resignation of Chamoun, whose term of office was almost over anyway, the election of a neutral President and the formation of a Government representing both rebels and loyalists. All this was a bitter pill for the more militant of Chamoun's supporters to swallow, but the damage which had been done to Lebanon's economy by the civil war was already beginning to cause misgivings among the influential business community, comprising both Moslems and Christians, and there was a considerable body of opinion in favour of 'getting back to normal'. Chamoun resigned, General Shihab, the commander-in-chief of the army, was elected President by the Chamber, and a coalition government formed under the premiership of Rashid Karami, who might have been described as a moderate rebel. The constitution of this Government undoubtedly represented too large a concession to the rebels; this, together with the kidnapping and murder of a Christian journalist by Moslems, precipitated another civil war, in which the Christians were the rebels and the Moslems the loyalists.

By this time Abdul Nasr was anxious for a settlement in Lebanon. He wanted to get the Americans out. He was probably worried by events in Iraq. He was deeply engaged in quarrels with King Saud, who had tried to bribe Abdul Hamid Sarraj to procure

CHAPTER TWELVE

Revolution in Iraq

While civil war was petering out in Lebanon the attention of the outside world was becoming focused on the confused and confusing progress of revolution in Iraq. Iraq had had previous experience of military coups since attaining independence in 1932. In 1936 General Bekr Sidqi came into power as the result of a military coup which displaced a reactionary 'landowner' government and substituted for it a short-lived authoritarian but reformist regime, which appears to have been inspired by the methods and objectives of Kemal Ataturk. This experiment came to an end as the result of another military coup ten months later. Thereafter the army interfered time and again to make and unmake governments. Sometimes this interference was on behalf of extreme nationalist groups, sometimes on behalf of the moderate nationalist group represented, *inter alia*, by Nuri as Said and Abdulillah, the Regent, who had been appointed after the death of King Ghazi in 1939 and the succession of his infant son Feisal. In March 1941, Abdulillah was exiled as a result of an extreme nationalist, anti-British and pro-Axis coup which brought Rashid Ali al Qailani into power. This regime lasted only a few weeks, and was displaced after British military intervention which restored the Regent and put a 'collaborationist' government into power. Thereafter, apart from a short period in 1947, Iraq, under the dominating and increasingly autocratic influence of Nuri as Said, became more and more committed to a collaborationist policy *vis-à-vis* the West. During the war this was a matter of necessity. After the war this policy was mainly inspired by a fear of communism. In the immediate post-war years Iraq, unlike the other Arab States, had been able to view at close quarters the Soviet attempts at subversion in Turkey and Iran; unlike the other Arab States, Iraq had a large Kurdish minority which was a potential channel for Soviet penetration. Unlike the other Arab States (except, at that time, Saudi Arabia), Iraq's economy was increasingly dependent on the exploitation of her oil resources by means of Western capital and access to Western markets and, in the years 1951-54, Iraqis had had a close-up view of the results of an extreme nationalist policy on the Iranian economy.

Until the advent of Abdul Nasr this collaborationist policy did not isolate Iraq politically from the rest of the Arab world. Relations with Syria were on the whole bad, mainly as the result of an Iraqi tendency to interfere in Syria's internal politics. The main object of this interference was to try and secure a subservient, or at all events friendly, Syria in view of the vital Iraqi interest in what was, at that time, the only channel for her oil exports to the West. Relations with Jordan were close and cordial. The old dynastic quarrel with Saudi Arabia was almost healed. There was an underlying rivalry with Egypt for leadership in the Arab League but there was no major conflict on policy. In the matter of Palestine, Iraq was impeccably nationalist, both in its actions and in its gestures. The Iraqi Government submitted to considerable temporary loss of oil revenue as a result of refusal to allow oil to be exported through the Kirkuk-Haifa pipeline; Iraq, alone of the Arab States, refused to sign an armistice with Israel (it was true that Iraq's contribution to the Palestine war was minimal and that they had no common boundary with Israel to provide a compelling reason for such an armistice); Iraq excelled all other Arab States in the barbarity of the treatment meted out to Jews resident in Iraq, nearly all of whom were despoiled of their property and expelled from Iraq. It was only after the Anglo-Egyptian Agreement, which marked the beginning of the development of Abdul Nasr's pan-Arabism, that Egypt and Iraq began to drift apart and, as a result of the increasing popularity and success of Abdul Nasr's propaganda and policy, that Iraq began to experience isolation from the rest of the Arab world.

This increasing isolation was accompanied by increasing domestic discontent. This discontent was caused by the same basic factors which had caused similar discontent in Egypt—the frustrated ambitions of a rising middle class caused by the concentration of political and, consequently, economic power between the hands of a small landowning group, the currency inflation resulting from wartime conditions which bore particularly hardly on the frustrated middle class, and the influence of subversive ideas from abroad ranging from British socialism to Russian communism. This discontent was accentuated, at the same time as the active expression of it was delayed, by the extremely and increasingly authoritarian nature of the regime. Within the framework of a constitutional monarchy, with parliamentary institutions, the regime in Iraq was in fact a dictatorship, sustained by the familiar methods of a police State. In September 1954 all political parties were dissolved by Government ordinance and, thereafter, any opposition to the Government had, perforce, to go underground.

The breach with Egypt was the culmination of continual Iraqi attempts to promote, and of continual Egyptian attempts to frustrate, various schemes for bringing about unity between the Arab countries of the Fertile Crescent. Egypt had been able successfully to use the Arab League as an instrument for defeating any such schemes of unity under any but Egyptian auspices. The Egyptian-sponsored Arab Collective Security Pact had never been a serious instrument of defence against an external enemy. From the time of its inception in 1949 to the autumn of 1954 it had been an instrument for the frustration of Hashemite-inspired schemes for the political unity of the Fertile Crescent. After the autumn of 1954, it became, in Abdul Nasr's hands, an instrument for bringing about the unity of the Fertile Crescent under Egyptian domination. It was the realization of this trend, as much as the desire for external defence, which led Iraq to strengthen its alliances outside the Arab world. The signature of the Turco-Iraq Treaty (the Baghdad Pact) in February 1955, and the subsequent adhesion to it of the British Government in April 1955, completed Iraq's breach with Egypt and with the Arab Collective Security Pact. From that time onwards there was a continual barrage of Egyptian propaganda and intrigue directed against the 'collaborationist' regime in Iraq.

As a result of this propaganda, and as a result of the undoubted unpopularity of the Western alignment among most Iraqi nationalists, domestic discontent in Iraq tended to become identified with that mixture of pan-Arabism and reformism which was the basis of Abdul Nasr's appeal to the Arab peoples. But pan-Arabism under Egyptian auspices had not the same attractions as it had in Syria or in Jordan. Syria had been the cradle of pan-Arabism because, in Syria, Arabism was an accepted principle of unity. In Jordan, which was regarded by the majority of its inhabitants as an artificial creation carved out of Syria by the British for their own purposes, no emotional significance whatever was attached to the label 'Jordanian'; the prospect of seeing Jordan merged into a larger Arab unity was a prospect, not of subordination, but of liberation. In Iraq, on the contrary, which had a definite geographical and historical entity and which, in the Kurds, had within its borders a large and powerful non-Arab minority, Iraqi nationalism was a principle of unity between Arabs and Kurds, while pan-Arabism was a principle of division between Arabs and Kurds. And to a lesser extent, since pan-Arabism was associated principally with Sunni Islam, it acted not as a principle of unity but as a principle of division between the Sunni and Shia sects. (In Iraq the Sunni Arabs and Kurds—who are Sunnis—slightly outnumber the Shias; the Shias slightly outnumber the Arab Sunnis.) In Iraq, therefore, pan-Arabism had undertones of subordination and disruptiveness which would have been incomprehensible in Syria or Jordan, and communism became a much more acceptable alternative to discontented nationalists than it was either in Syria or Jordan. For it was not difficult for communism to be represented, in terms of Iraqi nationalism, as a much more patriotic alternative to the existing regime than pan-Arabism. Thus reformist elements, both inside and outside the army, tended to become divided between pan-Arabism and communism. Since all reformist elements had been driven underground by the authoritarian nature of the regime, particularly after the suppression of political parties in September 1954, this rivalry did not become generally apparent until after the revolution in July 1958.

It was at first generally assumed in the outside world that the revolution was another Nasserite coup. The American landing in Lebanon and the British landing in Jordan were largely based on this assumption, which seemed at first to be justified by events. The officers closest to General Qasim, and particularly Colonel Abdul Salam Aref, were avowedly pan-Arab. There then occurred the complicated quarrel between Qasim and Aref. Aref's being sent to Bonn as Ambassador to Western Germany was at first regarded as arising from a personal difference between leader and henchman. But Aref's unauthorized return to Iraq, without ever having assumed his diplomatic post, and his subsequent arrest and trial, revealed the existence of much deeper differences. It became apparent that Aref was a member, and perhaps the leader, of a pan-Arab group of Iraqi army officers who, in their desire for closer ties with, and perhaps subordination to, the UAR were in opposition both to Qasim himself and to the majority of the members of the revolutionary Government. At first this apparent sign of independence was generally welcomed in the West, where the disgrace of Aref was hailed as a set-back for Abdul Nasr. But soon, out of the confusion of plots and counter-plots which hung like a smoky curtain over Baghdad, a more or less coherent pattern began to emerge. What appeared to be going on was a struggle for power between communists and pan-Arabists, with a weak Government, consisting of Qasim himself, a few neutral army officers and a handful of civilian National Democrat politicians trying to hold an even balance between the two. The precipitancy of Aref and the pan-Arabists, who tried to stampede the Government into close association with, if not actual

adhesion to the UAR, forced a probably reluctant government into
using the communists as a counterweight. Western satisfaction
at the disgrace of Colonel Aref was considerably modified when it
began to appear that communism was a likely alternative to pan-
Arabism.

The increasing influence of the Communist Party, and the
apparent inability of the Government effectively to control it,
became alarmingly apparent to foreign observers in Iraq. Communist-inspired demonstrators shouting communist slogans
paraded the streets of Basra and Baghdad. Russian technicians and
Russian arms, in unknown but probably exaggerated quantities,
were seen to be entering Iraq. The Kurdish, and supposedly pro-
communist, leader, Mullah Barzani, was permitted to return to
Iraq from his enforced exile in Soviet Russia. Another pan-Arab
plot was exposed and its alleged leader, Rashid Ali al Qailani (who
had caused the British so much trouble in 1941) was arrested.
The UAR Government, as alarmed and confused by these events
as were the State Department and the Foreign Office, took the line
that communists and imperialists had banded together to defeat
Arab nationalism. This line, absurd as it was to the Western
mind, at least, and for the time being, avoided the necessity for a
breach with Qasim, who was assumed to be the victim of and
not an accomplice in this plot. There were in fact signs that the
Iraqi Government was making some resistance to communist
demands. The Baghdad Pact had not yet been formally denounced.
(It was denounced early in 1959; it was then renamed CENTO
and remained in being minus the membership of Iraq.) Death
sentences which had been passed on various ex-Ministers of the
old regime, as well as on Colonel Aref, had not yet been executed
in spite of unceasing clamour from the communist Press and
from communist-inspired demonstrators. No members of the
Communist Party had been admitted to the Government in spite
of communist demands. It appeared that the Government's power
of resistance to the local communists was increased by Russian
reluctance to give much support to their henchmen. (Local communist parties are traditionally regarded by Moscow as being

highly expendible.) No Russian encouragement was given in public, and little, if any, appears to have been given in private, to the local Communist Party in support of their more extreme attitudes. On the contrary, the Soviet Government appears to have discouraged the Iraqi Government from acts, such as the nationalization of the Iraq Petroleum Company, which were being urged on them by the local communists. The Soviet Government in fact appeared to be anxious to avoid creating a situation which might have brought the West to seek the alliance of pan-Arabism against Iraq.

In March 1959 there was an abortive revolt in Mosul led by a group of pan-Arab officers. This revolt, although it failed ignominiously, revealed the extent of pan-Arab feeling and the extent of disloyalty to the Government which still existed in the army, and consequently revealed the Government's necessary reliance on the communists as an alternative source of support. The failure of the Mosul revolt seemed to spell the ruin of the pan-Arab cause in Iraq. But Qasim, supported by a section of the army and by the National Democrats, began to emerge as a positive entity with a definite personality. The ruin of pan-Arabism in Iraq did not automatically lead to the triumph of communism. Something was forming in the centre which was neither pan-Arab nor communist. Soon after the Mosul revolt the communists were sharply, if only verbally, rapped by Qasim for having instigated a massacre of alleged rebels in Kirkuk. A few weeks later Qasim successfully resisted further communist demands for inclusion in the Government. For months Qasim also continued to resist insistent communist demands for the execution of various 'traitors', consisting both of members of the old regime and of those convicted of being implicated in the various pan-Arab 'plots' against the regime. When in September a batch of such executions did take place, the decision appeared to be due not to communist pressure, but to Qasim's own desire to assert his authority.

During the late summer of 1959 it became apparent that the political instability of the revolutionary regime was accentuated by deepening economic chaos. The development plans inaugurated by the old regime were almost at a standstill; there was little foreign investment, owing to lack of confidence in the new regime. When, early in October, an attempt was made to assassinate Qasim, as a result of which he was severely wounded, a complete breakdown of law and order seemed imminent. But by this time a powerful 'centre' group in the army, headed by the Military Governor of Baghdad,[1] appeared to have taken hold and, by the time Qasim emerged from hospital at the end of November, Iraq appeared to be not so much on the verge of communism as in the grip of an effervescent nationalism, which was perhaps partly dictated by the necessity for diverting attention from Iraq's domestic problems. In a series of bellicose announcements Qasim, by way of celebrating his recovery from his wounds, made it clear that the new regime was now thinking specifically in terms of competing with Egypt for the control of the Fertile Crescent. (Qasim also started picking a quarrel with Iran over the Shatt-el-Arab boundary.)

Abdul Nasr's attitude towards the Iraqi revolution went through a series of interesting changes. Until Aref's disgrace the revolution was hailed in the UAR Press and on the UAR radio as an 'act of liberation', an 'imperialist defeat', and so on. When communist influence became apparent, the Qasim Government was not openly attacked but the line was taken that the communists and imperialists had banded together to intrigue against the Iraqi revolution and to destroy Iraqi independence. (This led to some public but temporary disagreement between the UAR and Soviet Russia.)[2] Abdul Nasr tried unsuccessfully to arrange a meeting with Qasim. But after the failure of the Mosul revolt a much stronger line was taken. Qasim was denounced as a communist and a destroyer of Arab unity, and all the stops in the UAR propaganda organ were pulled out in denunciation of the new regime in Iraq. An unsuccessful attempt was made to reorganize Egyptian-sponsored pan-Arabism on the basis of an anti-communist front against Iraq. In the late summer of 1959 it apparently began to be recognized in Cairo that Qasim and his Government, so far from being communist, represented the only

existing barrier in Iraq against communism. Once more, therefore, a distinction began to be made between the Iraqi Government and the communism which was threatening it. This phase
was short-lived and ended abruptly in September when there was
a furious outburst of anger from Cairo at the executions of some
of those convicted for complicity in the Mosul revolt. From then
on the communist menace, which had never been treated very
seriously in the Arab world outside the UAR, was played down
and propagandist attention concentrated on the anti-Arabist
nature of the Iraqi regime. The assassination attempt against
Qasim in October was cautiously handled, being treated as evidence of deepening chaos and incipient disintegration. Injudicious
references by King Husain to the possibility of 'rescuing' Iraq
from communism by invasion were ill-received in Cairo. The
possibility of another revolution in Iraq and the emergence of a
regime more favourable to Cairo seemed to be regarded, in Cairo
if nowhere else, as a serious possibility. Then, as Qasim recovered,
the speeches from hospital began to make it clear that the real
danger from Iraq, as far as the UAR was concerned, was not communism, but an imperialist policy, in competition with that of
the UAR, aiming at the establishment of Iraqi hegemony in the
Fertile Crescent. After fifteen months of turmoil, the classic relationship between Egypt and Iraq—competition for the control of
the lands lying between the Nile and the Euphrates—seemed to
be reasserting itself. The Egyptian reaction to this was, as might
have been expected, one of undisguised hostility. But this 'imperialist' turn in Iraqi policy was dictated by weakness rather
than strength—a move to disguise increasing discontents at home
rather than evidence of super-abundant vitality craving for expression. As far as Jordan, Syria, and to some extent Lebanon
and Saudi Arabia were concerned, the effect of Qasim's rhodo-
montades was not to strengthen the attractive power of Iraq
vis-à-vis UAR, but rather to discourage elements in those countries
which had been looking towards Qasim as an offset to the
influence of Abdul Nasr.

The British attitude towards the Iraqi revolution was, from

N

the outset, one of careful neutrality. Public regrets and reproaches for the butchery of King Feisal and of Nuri as Said were so perfunctory as to be almost indecent, considering the long-standing British relations with the old regime. The early emergence of Qasim as a rival to rather than an accomplice of Abdul Nasr was greeted with scarcely disguised glee in Whitehall. This glee was slightly mitigated by the increasing influence of communism in Iraq, but there seems to have been an early and prescient appreciation of the fact that Qasim was a barrier against rather than a harbinger of communism. Thereafter the maintenance of the Qasim regime in power seems to have become a cardinal principle of British Middle East policy. On the whole this policy seems to have justified itself. On the one hand Iraq left the Baghdad Pact. But on the other hand the Iraq Petroleum Company was not nationalized, nor were its operations seriously interfered with. No serious attempt was made by the Iraqi Government to create trouble in the British-protected Sheikhdoms of the Persian Gulf. It was in the highest degree unlikely that the revolutionary regime in Iraq could ever exert an attractive force over the Arab world comparable to that which had been exerted by Abdul Nasr. But, provided that it remained non-communist, it could exercise just sufficient attractive influence to form an insurance against the attainment of Arab hegemony by the UAR. A policy of friendship with Iraq, combined with attempts to settle outstanding differences with UAR—attempts which culminated in a renewal, at Chargé d'Affaires level, of diplomatic relations between Great Britain and UAR towards the end of November—seemed likely to bring about and to perpetuate the state of balanced and more or less stable disunity in the Arab world which seemed the best available guarantee for the continued security of Middle East oil supplies and Middle East oil investments.

The American attitude was less sophisticated. Hypersensitive, as always, to the threat of communism in the Middle East, the State Department took a more pessimistic view than the Foreign Office about the menace of communism in Iraq. Predictably, this led to a reappraisal of American relations with Abdul Nasr, which was manifested in financial assistance and in negotiations for a World Bank loan to UAR to finance capital improvements to the Suez Canal. But British and American Middle East policy did not again get seriously out of step. USA maintained diplomatic relations with Baghdad, and British relations with Cairo slowly improved. A slight British bias towards Baghdad was corrected by a slight American bias towards Cairo. Nothing in the nature of a war by proxy was allowed to develop. The lesson of Suez had been learnt both in London and in Washington.

CHAPTER THIRTEEN

The Dissolving Mirage

———————

Throughout the autumn and winter of 1958-59 Abdul Nasr's pan-Arab policies experienced a series of grievous checks. First there was the partial failure over Lebanon. Then there was the total failure, after the departure of the British, to overthrow, or even seriously to disturb, the regime in Jordan. Then, in December, there was a curious military coup in the Sudan, when the Prime Minister, Abdullah Khalil, connived at and may even have engineered the overthrow of the Constitution by a clique of army officers with the object of frustrating Egyptian intrigues both with the parliamentary opposition and with certain members of Abdullah Khalil's government. The new military regime under General Abboud remained on friendly terms with Cairo but made it clear that it would resist such attempts as might yet be made to subordinate Khartum to Cairo. Saudi Arabia, the government of which was now in the relatively capable hands of the king's brother, Feisal, assumed an uncompromisingly neutral position between Baghdad and Cairo. The Syrians were showing an irritating lack of docility towards their new masters. The Syrian army and civil service obstructed Abdul Nasr's attempts to re-establish friendly relations with Lebanon; the big landowners objected to the land reform measures imported from Egypt; the Baath was becoming disgruntled at the ever increasing extent of Egyptian control over what was now known as the 'Northern Province'. Damascenes objected to the new provincial status of the capital of the Omayyads. The Governments of Tunisia and Morocco were unenthusiastic about Abdul Nasr's sponsorship of, and encouragement of the intransigence displayed by the Algerian Government-in-exile.[1] Tunisia had even started boycotting the Arab League in protest against alleged UAR interereference in Tunisia's internal affairs.

By the beginning of 1959 Abdul Nasr was at odds with almost every other Arab government. Iraq had become his main preoccupation, and communism was linked with Western imperialism as his principal bogy. This new anti-communist line began to cause a marked change in the relationships between UAR and the other Arab States, just as the check to Abdul Nasr's ambitions administered by Iraq led to a marked change in the attitude towards the UAR adopted by the other Arab States. The recruitment of an Arab anti-communist and anti-Iraqi bloc was incompatible with a continued subversion of 'reactionary' Arab governments. Fears of a break with Russia resulting from a development of the situation with Iraq made it desirable for him to try and reestablish something like normal relations with the West. And so he began cautiously to mend the fences which he had so impetuously trodden down during the last eighteen months. But, as he had no intention of abandoning his ultimate plans, and as he regarded himself as executing a move of *reculer pour mieux sauter*, he had to move carefully in order to try and avoid alienating those reformist elements in the Arab world on which he would have to rely when the time came to move forward once more. He made agreements[2] for the desequestration of British and French property in Egypt which had been seized at the time of Suez. He ingratiated himself with the State Department by the virulence of his anti-communist utterances. He toned down the propaganda and other subversive acts which he had been directing against Jordan and Tunisia.

The response to this change of tactic was not remarkably favourable either from the West or from the Arab world. It was recognized for what it was—a change in tactic and not a change of heart. The British Government noted that anti-British propaganda from Cairo addressed to Africa and the Persian Gulf Protectorates was as virulent as before. The French noted the continued diplomatic and military support being given to the Algerian government-in-exile. Even the State Department, which found Abdul Nasr's anti-communist line almost irresistible, moved with caution. The Arab Governments were even more sceptical. They were extremely critical of Abdul Nasr's handling of the Iraq situation and were by no means inclined to subordinate themselves to Abdul Nasr in a quarrel with Iraq on the issue of a communist peril which, they considered, had in part been caused by Abdul Nasr's repeated and unsuccessful attempts to overthrow the Iraqi Government and was in part a bogy conjured up by Abdul Nasr for his own purposes.

By the spring of 1959 the Arab League had been in existence for fourteen years. The original member-States had been Egypt, Syria, Iraq, Jordan, Lebanon, Saudi Arabia and Yeman—seven in all. By 1959 this number had increased to ten as the result of the membership of four more Arab States—Sudan, Libya, Tunisia and Morocco—which had become independent since 1945, and the subtraction of one owing to the fusion of Egypt and Syria into the UAR. During its fourteen-year period of existence it had had two Secretaries-General, both Egyptians—Abdul Rahman Azzam and Abdul Khaliq Hassuna. Its headquarters had originally been established and had remained in Cairo. It had proved quite ineffective in promoting common action between its member-States in their relations either with each other or with the outside world. It had not even been an effective forum for the discussion of differences arising between its member-States. After the Palestine catastrophe it was used not for promoting unity but for concealing disunity behind a series of resolutions, unaccompanied by any sort of action, proclaiming Arab solidarity in the face of Zionism, imperialism and so on. The only really effective aspect of the League was its increasing effectiveness as an organ of Egyptian foreign policy. This had been noticeable in the pre-Abdul Nasr era when the influence of the League had been consistently directed against Hashemite-inspired attempts to bring about the unity of the Fertile Crescent. It had become much more noticeable after Abdul Nasr's accession to power, when the Secretariat of the Arab League virtually became part of the Propaganda Section of the Egyptian and, later, of the UAR Foreign Office. Signs of restiveness among the member-States at this domination began to appear during the first few months of 1959 when Abdul Nasr started trying to mobilize the League against the regime in Iraq. In April 1959 the UAR suffered an open diplomatic defeat at a meeting of the Political Committee of the Arab League held in Beirut, at the request of UAR, to discuss the situation in Iraq. At this meeting, which was not attended by any representatives from Iraq, Jordan or Tunisia, the UAR Deputy Foreign Minister, who circumvented the privacy of the sessions by having his speeches distributed in advance to the Press, made a blustering attempt to secure a majority for a Resolution condemning the Iraqi regime root and branch. Opposition to this Resolution, led by Saudi Arabia and Lebanon, was unanimous and a neutral Resolution was substituted and carried which, while condemning communism, adopted a careful neutrality between UAR and Iraq. (Even so the Sudanese delegate refused to vote for it on the ground that it was not sufficiently neutral.) Thus the UAR, in a meeting of the Arab League from which the three States most obviously in opposition to Abdul Nasr's policies were absent, found themselves in a minority of one in a matter of fundamental importance to Abdul Nasr's pan-Arab ambitions. The member-States of the Arab League had applied Abdul Nasr's neutralist doctrine to the Arab world and had declared themselves neutral as between the UAR and Iraq. Resentment at Abdul Nasr's ambitions had proved stronger than fear of communism. Pan-Arabism was recognized as Egyptian imperialism.

What were the causes behind this tremendous loss of influence over so short a period? It was only just over a year since the union with Syria had seemed to place Abdul Nasr within striking distance of dominating the Arab world. But since then Abdul Nasr had been successfully defied by the rulers of Jordan, Iraq, Tunisia and the Sudan. His friends and supporters had been imprisoned and executed in Iraq, imprisoned in Jordan, exiled from Tunisia and rendered impotent in the Sudan. He could neither protect his friends nor punish his enemies. He was able neither to beat Israel nor render any really effective aid to the Algerian rebels. His military weakness was a fatal barrier to the success of a policy based on subversion and intimidation. When it came to the point nobody had much to hope from his support, nobody had much to fear from his enmity.

In face of the diplomatic rebuff received in Beirut Abdul Nasr had two alternative courses open to him. One course was to renew and to intensify his campaign of subversion against that increasing number of Arab Governments which were now opposed to him, with the object of fomenting popular revolutions in these countries and in the hope that these popular revolutions would produce pan-Arab regimes. The other course was to abandon those methods which had caused him the enmity of his Arab neighbours (which meant abandoning, for the time being, his pan-Arab ambitions) and to concentrate on rallying conservative Arab opinion against the regime in Iraq. It seems probable that two principal considerations influenced his decision to take the second course. The first was UAR's military weakness which made it impossible to exploit any propaganda victories which he might win. The second was the fact, made apparent by events in Iraq, that communism was just as likely as pan-Arabism to be the beneficiary of a revolution in an Arab country. The Iraqi revolution had seemingly, and perhaps temporarily, converted Abdul Nasr from being a disturber to becoming an upholder of the *status quo* in the Arab world. From being an *enfant terrible* he was trying to become an elder statesman.

In August 1959 diplomatic relations were restored between UAR and Jordan. At about the same time Haj Amin al Husaini, the ex-Mufti of Jerusalem and an inveterate opponent of the Hashemite regime in Jordan who had, since the Palestine war, enjoyed asylum in Egypt, and who still cherished ideas of becoming the head of an Egyptian-sponsored Palestine government-in-exile, was expelled from Egypt and pursued to his new home in

Lebanon with precisely the same accusations as had been levelled at him by the Hashemites for the previous twenty years. Friendly relations were restored between Abdul Nasr and King Saud whom, hardly a year before, Abdul Nasr had accused of trying to procure his assassination. Earnest but unsuccessful attempts were made by Abdul Nasr to heal the breach with Habib Bourguiba, who remained sceptical of Abdul Nasr's intentions. Feelers were put out in Khartum about the conclusion of a Nile Waters Agreement in spite of Abdul Nasr's knowledge that such an agreement was only likely to be concluded at the cost of considerable Egyptian concessions to the Sudanese point of view.

In Egypt itself there were signs that the emphasis was being shifted away from pan-Arabism and back to Egyptian domestic affairs. Elections were held[3] under the new Constitution which provided for some *simulacrum* of popular representation. Popular attention was once more switched on to the High Dam, towards the construction of which a substantial loan had been received from Russia.[4] Arrangements were made to expedite the installation of television and to transfer to the prospective local television services much of that money which had previously been spent on radio broadcasts to the rest of the Arab world. Efforts were made to stimulate interest in the possibilities of domestic reform, Abdul Nasr stating in a public speech that the Egyptian revolution, so far from having been completed, had not yet begun.

This move away from pan-Arabism, and this concentration on the accomplishment of reform at home instead of on the propagation of reformism abroad, was hardly likely to be welcome to the Baath, who were already sufficiently disillusioned by the effectiveness of Egyptian control of Syria and by the ineffectiveness of Egyptian penetration elsewhere. Akram Hourani, their leader, had been created Vice-President of the Republic at the time of the formation of the UAR and had taken up his headquarters in Cairo. But he was of little account there and had never been taken seriously into Abdul Nasr's counsels. In the Syrian elections in July, strong Egyptian influence was exercised in opposition to Baathist and in favour of more right-wing candidates. The guardians of the fortress of Arab nationalism began once again to experience the all-too-familiar sensation of betrayal.[5]

Meanwhile an increasingly chauvinistic attitude was being displayed by King Husain and by his new Prime Minister, Haza Majali. In the spring King Husain had visited the United States and Great Britain and, shortly after his return, had got rid of his old Prime Minister Samir Rifai and replaced him by Haza Majali. This was generally interpreted as a bid for popular favour in Jordan, where Samir Rifai's heavy hand had not been universally popular. This change was followed by a series of processional tours about the country and by a number of oblique indications that Husain regarded himself as a possible successor to Abdul Nasr as the champion of pan-Arabism. These new ambitions were underlined in the course of a dispute which arose between Lebanon and Jordan over Palestine.

One of the principal subjects to be discussed at the forthcoming meeting of the Political Committee of the Arab League to be held at Casablanca in September was a report by Dag Hammarskjold, the Secretary General of the United Nations, on the future of the Arab refugee problem. In this report Hammarskjold had made the obviously sensible suggestion that the only ultimate solution of the problem lay in the absorption of the refugees by the Arab States to which they had emigrated and in which they were resident. This recommendation was vigorously opposed by the majority of the Arab States, and particularly by Lebanon, whose delicate confessional balance would have been upset by the absorption of the hundred thousand or so mainly Moslem refugees living in Lebanon. As an alternative Lebanon had propounded a proposal by which a Palestinian government and a Palestinian army should be formed on the rump of Palestinian soil west of Jordan which still remained in Arab hands and which had since the Palestine war, formed part of the Kingdom of Jordan.[6] This proposal revived the old question (whether an Arab Palestine should be a separate independent entity or whether it should be merged with Transjordan) which had wrecked the prospect of

Arab co-operation and which had ensured Arab defeat in the Palestine war. As was to be expected, the Jordan Government reacted strongly, pointing out that Jordan had, in fact, integrated all Palestine refugees in Jordan, that the Arab 'rump' of Palestine was an integral part of the Kingdom of Jordan and that there could be no question of the formation of a Palestine government or a Palestine army on Jordan soil. The open quarrel which developed between Lebanon and Jordan on this (entirely academic) issue was a dismal augury for the success of the Casablanca Conference and a dismal commentary on the achievement of the movement for Arab unity. The Arab States, having quarrelled about almost everything else, were now quarrelling about the only matter—Palestine—on which they had, for the past several years, been unanimous. Sterile of results as this unanimity had been, it was at least more impressive than dissension, which was certain to be equally sterile. For neither the Jordanian nor the Lebanese formula held out the least hope of settling the refugee problem, either by negotiation with or by the conquest of Israel, or indeed in any other way.

It seemed as if the reverses suffered by Abdul Nasr had put an end not only to the prospect of an Egyptian-dominated Arab unity but to any prospect of Arab unity at all. Some of the more percipient Arab politicians began to realize that such importance as the Arab States had been able to achieve in the world had been entirely due to the cold war; that the cold war was showing ominous signs of coming to an end (the meeting at Casablanca coincided with Krushchev's visit to the United States); that in default of some measure of unity the Arab States were in for some rough handling from both East and West if the cold war did come to an end; that having rejected the unity propagated by Abdul Nasr, the Arab States were even further from unity than they had ever been. To such politicians the Casablanca Conference represented the moment of truth. Nine of the ten member-States were represented at Casablanca, Iraq alone being unrepresented. No agreement was reached about anything. Lebanon and Saudi Arabia quarrelled with the UAR and Jordan about Iraq, the one side advocating strict neutrality, the other side canvassing the possibilities of intervention. Lebanon quarrelled with Jordan about Palestine. Morocco and Tunisia, not wishing to shut the door against a possible settlement between France and the Algerian Government-in-exile, quarrelled with UAR about the latter's apparent determination to exacerbate matters between the two parties. At the end of the Conference it proved impossible even to draft an agreed resolution about Palestine.

Soon after the Casablanca Conference a remarkable air of realism began gradually to become manifest in Cairo. First, with regard to Iraq. The belief that the encouragement of army revolts might lead to an Arab nationalist regime in Iraq had been tacitly abandoned after the collapse of the Mosul revolt. The belief that the rest of the Arab world might be persuaded to be led by Egypt into an anti-communist 'crusade' against Iraq was abandoned. Then, the belief, inspired by an attempt on Qasim's life, that the regime might collapse into a chaos from which an Arab nationalist regime would emerge, was reluctantly abandoned. Finally, the existence and probable persistence of a regime, which was not, and which was unlikely to become, either communist or Arab nationalist, was tacitly recognized and a realistic policy of containing it and attempting to discredit it substituted for the previous and hopeless policy of trying to overthrow it.

Secondly, with regard to Syria. After eighteen months of union, relationships between Cairo and the Northern Province had, by September 1959, become strained almost to breaking point. The Syrians, since union, had been suffering from a mixture of political interference and administrative neglect. Arab nationalist slogans had proved to be insufficiently potent charms to assuage the consequent discontent. What was needed was tighter political control—as opposed to sporadic political interference—combined with more attention to the special needs of the Syrian economy. In October 1959 Abdul Nasr took Syria under his wing, so to speak, by the appointment of Abdul Hakim Amer, C-in-C of the Army, and his closest personal associate, as Governor of the Northern Province.[7]

Thirdly, with regard to Palestine. For several months Abdul Nasr had been engaged in delicate negotiations with UN about the Danish vessel, *Inge Toft*, carrying a cargo from Israel, which had been detained at Port Said by the UAR authorities. The ship had been routed through the Canal by Israel with the specific object of drawing UN attention to the denial of passage to Israeli cargoes. (For some months after Suez Abdul Nasr, as the result of a private agreement with Hammarskjold, had allowed Israeli cargoes under a non-Israeli flag to transit the Canal. Criticism by the Arab League Boycott Committee had induced him to revert to the *status quo ante* Suez and to stop all Israeli cargoes whether carried in Israeli bottoms or not.) UAR propaganda had played the *Inge Toft* incident down, since it appeared to be jeopardizing the prospect of a World Bank loan for capital improvements to the Suez Canal;[8] but Abdul Nasr had always reacted sharply to any suggestion that a loan was dependent on a change of policy regarding the blockade of Israel. Then, in September, after it had been pointed out that by denying passage to Israeli ships and cargoes, UAR was in breach of a Security Council Resolution, Abdul Nasr made public an ingenious and apparently realistic offer. He announced that he would obey all UN Resolutions about Palestine provided that Israel did so too. In other words he would allow Israeli shipping and cargoes to use the Canal provided that Israel implemented the UN Partition Resolution (which, incidentally, the Jewish Agency had accepted and the Arab States had rejected at the time) and the Resolution about the repatriation and/or compensation of the Arab refugees. This announcement was an extremely clever diplomatic move, transferring the onus of disobedience from UAR to Israel. It was also the first occasion on which any responsible Arab leader had publicly proposed any basis of negotiation with Israel. (By implication the offer proposed the UN Partition Resolution's boundaries for Israel as an acceptable basis for an eventual peace treaty with Israel.) The offer had no immediate effects, being greeted with an embarrassed silence both by Israel and by the other Arab States.[9] But it appeared to be part of the 'new look' which Abdul Nasr was injecting into the Arab approach to international affairs.

The fourth problem which Abdul Nasr proceeded to approach with a new mind was the division of Nile waters between Egypt and the Sudan. The conventional attitude of both countries towards the question of Nile waters was such as to make any agreement between them impossible. The conventional Egyptian attitude, in so far as it acknowledged the independent status of the Sudan at all, was that any division of Nile waters must be based on the proportions laid down in the 1929 Agreement, by which Egypt got eleven parts to every one part retained by the Sudan. The conventional Sudanese attitude was that no agreement was necessary at all, since the Sudan would take whatever she wanted for herself and Egypt could have the rest. In terms of the level of realism prevailing in the Arab League, Abdul Nasr would never have negotiated the question with the Sudan at all, but would have satisfied himself with a series of gestures ascribing Sudanese recalcitrance to imperialist plots. For the only possibility of a successful outcome to such negotiation, since Egypt had not the means to impose her will on the Sudan, and since the Sudan in this matter had the means by the accident of geography to impose her will on Egypt, was a considerable and prestige-damaging Egyptian concession to the Sudanese point of view. The conclusion of a Nile Waters Agreement between UAR and the Sudan, announced at the end of October, therefore represented a considerable concession to realism on the part of the UAR Government. (Under this Agreement the Sudan's percentage share of available water was considerably increased compared with her share under the 1929 Agreement.[10]) The Agreement also greatly facilitated the prospect of additional finance from the West for the High Dam. (Part of the finance had already been advanced by Soviet Russia.)

Fifthly, relations with Great Britain, partly restored at the beginning of the year by an agreement for the de-sequestration of British property and by the reception of a British Mission to arrange this de-sequestration, were normalized by the restoration of diplomatic relations on a Chargé d'Affaires level. (This restoration was accompanied by a British agreement to the establishment of UAR Consulates in the British-protected Sheikhdoms in the Persian Gulf. From the British point of view this may have indicated, either acquiescence in Abdul Nasr's pan-Arab ambitions, or a conviction that these ambitions no longer were effective, or merely a desire to offset possible Iraqi influence in the Persian Gulf. From Abdul Nasr's point of view it represented access of prestige.)

Over Algeria Abdul Nasr was less conciliatory, but probably no less realistic. He incurred the displeasure of Tunisia and Morocco (and of course of France) by refusing to advise the Algerian government-in-exile to take de Gaulle's self-determination offer seriously. This may well have been sapient prescience on his part rather than the obstinate intransigence which it appeared at the time to be.

By the end of 1959 it could be said that if Abdul Nasr had failed to educate the Arab peoples into a sense of unity by precept, he was at least educating them into a sense of reality by example. And, by the end of 1959, the Arabs were even more in need of a sense of reality than they were of a sense of unity. The steady, and, to the Arabs, alarming amelioration of relations between East and West threatened to deprive the Arab States of that nuisance value which had been conferred on them by the cold war. The Palestine refugees were beginning to become impatient with the series of gestures which had for so long been regarded as a substitute for an Arab Palestine policy. The prospect of a long-terms buyer's market for crude oil began to disturb the complacence of those who were accustomed to regard the possession of crude oil as being in much the same lucrative category as the possession of guilty secrets.

After the Arab League had been in existence for fifteen years it was difficult to point to any matter of substance affecting the Arab States as a whole on which there had been any realistic and consistent line of policy or any effective and concerted course of action. Through all the labyrinthine corridors of Arab politics, the pursuit of unity had always led to a flight from reality. It may possibly be that the pursuit of reality may lead, not to that all-embracing unity dreamed of by the Baath and its predecessors, but to a measure of common action on certain specific subjects, analogous to what has been achieved in Western Europe over the last fifteen years.

CHAPTER FOURTEEN

The Twilight of Imperialism

———◆◆◆———

For nearly thirty-six years, from the Turkish Armistice signed at Mudros in October 1918 to the Anglo-Egyptian Agreement in July 1954, Great Britain had been the paramount Power in the Middle East, with the ability to make and unmake kings and governments, to move troops and ships and aircraft as she pleased throughout the lands and waters of the Middle East and over the air space of the countries of the Middle East. There had been defiance followed by concessions; there had been rebellions followed by appeasement; but in the last analysis the great British military establishment based on the Canal Zone had ensured British hegemony and had exacted ultimate recognition of that hegemony. British diplomats, British soldiers, British business-men even, felt, in the middle of their sometimes acrimonious nego-tiations over British ambitions, British interests and British rights, that they could, in the last resort, 'call in the troops'. Even at Abadan in 1951, it was widely felt that Great Britain had had the power effectively to intervene against the nationalist policy of Dr Musaddiq but that she had failed to use that power owing to the pusillanimity and pacificism of the Labour Government. The 'Suez Group' Tories, in their vigorous and vociferous objec-tions to the Anglo-Egyptian Agreement, showed a more prescient appreciation than their critics and opponents about what was being done. They realized, as some of their critics and opponents did not, that Great Britain, in the abandonment of the Suez Canal

Base, was forfeiting all future possibility of bringing effective British influence to bear either on the foreign or the domestic policies of the Middle East. The Suez adventure was motivated partly by a determination to reverse the decision which had been taken in 1954 and partly by a desire to exercise a power which the British no longer possessed as a result of the decision in 1954.

The illusion of possessing a power which had in fact evaporated was not confined to the British die-hard Tories. Arab nationalist attribution of sundry misfortunes and frustrations to 'imperialist plots' was not entirely a deliberate piece of deception designed to cover up Arab nationalist mistakes and deficiencies; they could not believe that the power which had influenced their lives for so long was no longer able to exercise that influence; they still half-believed the legends about British secret service agents and British espionage rings which they so assiduously propagated, and the corresponding aspirations of the die-hard Tories perpetuated the illusion.

The Baghdad Pact, to which the British Government subscribed some nine months after the Anglo-Egyptian Agreement of 1954, was founded on the assumption, and only made sense on the assumption, that Great Britain wielded the same potential for effective intervention and the same power to protect friends and to punish enemies which she had possessed when the Suez Base was in being, and not in process of being dismantled, as it was at the time of the signature of the Baghdad Pact. The Baghdad Pact represented a British decision to 'take sides' in the internal affairs of the Arab States with the object of restoring that British influence in the Middle East which was falling into abeyance as a result of the abandonment of the Suez Canal Base. But, since there was no intention and no possibility of establishing a powerful military base on the Persian Gulf or on the Tigris to compensate for the loss of the Suez Base, Great Britain was unable to make effective use of the Baghdad Pact for the attainment of that object. From the point of view of the Hashemite regime in Iraq, the Baghdad Pact was a diplomatic liability without having any compensating military advantages. From the point of view of the

British Government, the Baghdad Pact committed Great Britain, in the struggle for power which was going on in the Arab world, to stake her interests on the victory of an ally whose strength she was unable either to augment or to sustain.

The Eisenhower Doctrine, having as its object a shoring-up of the Baghdad Pact after the Suez adventure had exposed its weaknesses, was in its turn, and for the same reason, exposed as an ineffective instrument with which to restore Western influence in the Middle East. The ultimate sanction of usable and overwhelming force was lacking, not because the force was unavailable, but because it was feared that its use might precipitate a world conflict. It was no longer a question of calling out the guard; it was a question of touching off the bomb.

The failure of Abdul Nasr to achieve Egyptian hegemony in the Arab world was in no way due to the existence of 'imperialist plots', although such half-belief as he may have had in the existence of such plots may have dulled his resolution and clouded his judgment at critical moments. His failure to achieve hegemony was due to the same cause as the British failure to retain hegemony—unavailability of physical force to exploit diplomatic successes. For Abdul Nasr, this unavailability of physical force rendered him unable to counteract all the centrifugal forces which were working against his designs. These centrifugal forces owed little to British persuasion, nothing to British compulsion.

The Eisenhower Doctrine policy came to an end with the union of Egypt and Syria into the UAR. The Baghdad Pact policy, which had preceded it, was briefly to survive it; but that too came to an end with the Iraqi revolution in July 1958.[1]

The Iraqi revolution marked the beginning of a new British realism in her relationships with the Arab States. The long period of British hegemony in the Middle East had come to an inconspicuous but not inglorious end with the Anglo-Egyptian Treaty in July 1954. There followed two years of illusion which ended ingloriously and ridiculously with the Suez expedition in October 1956. This was succeeded by some eighteen months of numbed bewilderment during which the British Government could not be said to have had any recognizable policy at all in the Middle East, unless a few half-hearted bets on an outsider, combined with a few ineffective attempts to nobble the favourite, can be accounted a policy.

The disappearance of Nuri as Said left the British Government, as far as the Arab world was concerned, in much the same condition as Mr Pickwick when, after his over-indulgence in cold punch at the shooting picnic, he woke up to find himself sitting in a wheelbarrow in the village pound. 'Where are my friends?' he inquired. 'You ain't got no friends. Hurrah!' was the reply, accompanied with vegetable missiles, from the bystanding village youths.

There are certain advantages, as well as disadvantages, in being friendless. One is under no moral or contractual obligations; one is under no temptation to take sides in circumstances where one is unable to ensure the victory of one's chosen ally. There is no incentive for morality or for prejudice to come creeping in to the consideration of problems which are best dealt with opportunistically and objectively. One can afford that cynical detachment which is the best of all approaches to the problems of foreign policy. In the Middle East particularly, British policy had been bedevilled by conflicting personal preferences and by conflicting senses of moral obligation by those in high office. Now all that was over, or nearly over. On the periphery of Middle Eastern affairs—in the Kingdom of Jordan and in the Sheikhdoms of the Persian Gulf—there remained a residuum of moral obligation towards the Hashemites and contractual obligation towards the Sheikhs in treaty relationship with Great Britain. But as far as the UAR and Iraq—the principal protagonists—and as far as Lebanon and Saudi Arabia—the two neutrals between the principal protagonists—were concerned, the British Government, unencumbered by loyalties which had vanished and unfettered by contracts which had been unilaterally repudiated—either formally or tacitly—were able to appraise the march of events with the same cool objectivity as they were accustomed to display over, for example, Latin America.

It was in this mood that the British Government faced the up-heaval in the Arab world caused by the revolution in Iraq. In the enmity and rivalry which developed between Abdul Nasr and Qasim, between the Nile and the Euphrates, the British Government were tempted neither by the communist threat in Iraq pre-cipitantly to come to terms with Abdul Nasr, nor by the threat of pan-Arabism to lend overmuch support to Qasim. Diplomatic re-lations were maintained with Baghdad, and, with something of the inevitability of gradualness, restored with Cairo. Abuse from both sides, together with a good deal of local 'tail-twisting', was treated as being mainly for domestic edification Although it was possible to regard the shape of things to come in Iraq as being potentially far more menacing than the nationalization of the Suez Canal had been, and although, from the ethical point of view, Qasim was behaving far worse than Abdul Nasr ever did, the fact that no emotional nerve was touched, the fact that no feeling of national pride or imperial proprietorship was con-sciously outraged, assured that this menace was objectively appraised and assisted towards its being effectively contained. By preserving a strict neutrality between the contending parties, the British Government ensured that they had no appreciable stake in the outcome of a struggle over the fortunes of which they no longer had any control.

This sapient policy, pursued by the same Government as had been responsible for, and which had never admitted the error of, the Suez adventure, was both a belated concession to the reality created by the abandonment of the Suez Canal Base and a timely appreciation of two facts which were not immediately and auto-matically apparent—first, that Abdul Nasr's pan-Arab policy had all but exhausted its momentum, and secondly that the com-munist menace in Iraq had been greatly exaggerated by over-excited newspapermen. It was a policy which accepted, and even sought to strngthen, the concept of Arab neutrality as between East and West; it was a policy which accepted the necessity of accommodating oneself to events instead of attempting to shape them, and which concentrated therefore on accurate intelligence

rather than on ineffective intrigue; it was a policy which restricted the definition of vital British interests to the maintenance
of oil supplies and the security of oil investments rather than en-
larging this definition to suit the nostalgia of elderly ex-procon-
suls and the fantasies of peripatetic Middle East experts.

On the fringe of Arabia, along that thin red line stretching
from Aden to Kuwait, remained the only part of the Arab world
where British imperialism could, without abuse of language, still
be said to exist. The Governments of these territories were subjected to, and protected by the British from, three quite separate
threats emanating from various parts of the Arab world. There
was the threat of invasion from, and absorption by, Saudi Arabia
(or, in the case of Aden and the Western Protectorates, Yemen);
there was the threat of pan-Arabism from Cairo; and there was
the threat of communism or near-communism from Baghdad. On
the whole, peoples were in accord with governments in desiring
protection from the first threat, since the standards of freedom
and of justice prevalent in Saudi Arabia and Yemen were even
less attractive than they were in the Sheikhdoms themselves. But
both pan-Arabism and communism, although anathema to the
rulers, had their attractions for many of the subjects of the
Sheikhs whose rule was, in most cases, arbitrary, capricious, inefficient and corrupt. The old story of identification between collaboration and corruption, between imperialism and reaction, was
being repeated. The British Government were once more in danger
of becoming committed to the support, and being identified with
the abuses, of regimes which could not indefinitely be sustained
in the face of increasing popular discontent within and of mounting pressure from without. Two circumstances combined to de-
flect and to delay the convergence of these pressures and to pro-
long the tenuous British hold on these territories. First, the
rivalry between pan-Arabism and communism, usually seen as
dissension between Nasserites and Qasimites, which divided 'progressive' elements in the Sheikhdoms into two bitterly disputing
factions. Secondly, the reactionary nature of the regimes in Saudi
Arabia and Yemen, which made it difficult for 'progressive' ele-

ments to look towards these regimes as potential liberators from the British and from their own domestic tyrants. Thus it could be said that the British position in the Persian Gulf—the last ditch of British imperialism in the Middle East—rested on the twin pillars of Arab disunity and Saudi-Yemani feudalism. This is an interesting and sobering reflection when one considers that British Middle East policy, in the immediate post-war years, was based on the twin pillars of Arab unity and social reform.

It is a commonplace of imperial history that responsibilities which had originally been acquired reluctantly and, in some cases, almost accidentally, as a necesary means of securing some vital but temporary interest, should continue jealously to be retained long after the original reasons for acquiring them had ceased to exist. New arguments, of varying validity, are brought forward to justify the indefinite retention of these responsibilities. To a large extent, these arguments are a rationalization of an instinctive, and entirely natural, desire, felt by nations as well as by individuals, and particularly by ageing nations as by ageing individuals, not to relinquish what one already holds, irrespective of whether or not one gains any advantage from its possession.

During the nineteenth century British interests in the Middle East had been dictated partly by a desire to preserve the balance of power in Europe, partly by a desire to safeguard communications with India. After the First World War security of communications with the British Empire in the Indian Ocean was the dominant consideration which dictated the attempt to found what was, in effect and in intention, a new British Empire in the Middle East. After the Second World War, the containment of Soviet Russia, the desire to avoid a power vacuum which Soviet Russia might succeed, physically and ideologically, in filling, was the dominant British consideration in their rearguard action against Arab nationalism. When the prospect of nuclear warfare rendered military occupation for the purpose of physical defence against a possible Soviet invasion irrelevant, and when the progress of Arab nationalism made it clear that continued military occupation and the continued exercise of political pressure was an encouragement of rather than a deterrent to the propagation of subversive ideologies, the argument became concentrated on the security of Middle East oil supplies, the maintenance of which had by this time become essential to the British and to the Western European industrial economies. It was this consideration which dictated the violent British reaction to the nationalization of the Suez Canal; it was this consideration which dictated the British policy, in Aden Colony and Protectorates and in the oil-bearing Sheikhdoms of the Persian Gulf, of building up and attempting to sustain autonomous regimes which could stand up against attempts to merge them into a larger Arab unity.

Even after the Suez disaster, British policy continued, seemingly, to be concerned with the maintenance of a 'special' British position in the Middle East on the ground that the security of oil supplies and oil investments necessitated some continued degree of political influence and strategic control. Was this concern based on an objective appraisal of the measures necessary to safeguard vital interests, or was it merely the rationalization of an instinctive urge? On the one hand the concept of political influence and strategic control over the source of an essential raw material cannot be regarded as a tenable reason for political interference with the governments of countries possessing that raw material. On the other hand, the desire for political influence and strategic control was not motivated, as in 'plantation' days, by a desire to get the raw material cheap at the expense of the producing country; it was motivated by the fear lest the possession of the raw material should be used as an occasion for political blackmail. It was not a question of exploiting ignorant natives; it was a question of combating the designs of an extremely astute 'imperialist' dictator. After Suez it could reasonably be argued that British political 'interference' in the Middle East—such as it was—was designed to secure that oil transactions between Western Europe and the Middle East should continue to be regulated on a commercial basis and to prevent such transactions from becoming a political weapon in the hands of Gamal Abdul Nasr.

In other words, British Middle East policy, after Suez, would seem to have reverted from the 'offensive' twentieth century policy of attempting to secure and maintain a British hegemony in the Middle East, to the 'defensive' nineteenth century policy of preventing the attainment of that hegemony by anybody else. Immediately after Suez it appeared that this hegemony was within reach of Gamal Abdul Nasr, and British policy was concentrated on trying to frustrate this. Particularly as a result of the Iraqi revolution, and generally as a result of centrifugal tendencies throughout the Arab world which Abdul Nasr was unable to counteract, the prospect of an Egyptian hegemony receded and finally disappeared. As this happened, British Middle East policy reverted more and more to the nineteenth century one of a 'watching brief', conducted with a competence, objectivity and cynicism which provided (for some observers at all events) a refreshing contrast with the emotional and near-hysterical muddling of the previous ten years.

CHAPTER FIFTEEN

The Future

———◆◆◆◆◆———

At the end of 1959 the rulers of the Arab world could be said to have inherited one tremendous liability which needed to be liquidated and one tremendous asset which needed to be exploited. Up to that time lack of realism had prevented the liquidation of the one and lack of unity had prevented the exploitation of the other. Abdul Nasr's attempt at an Egyptian-dominated Arab unity had failed because he had been unable either to conquer Israel and so liquidate the Palestine liability, or to bring the sources of Middle East oil under his control and so secure a unified policy of exploitation. It remained to be seen whether the liability could be effectively liquidated and the asset fruitfully exploited by other methods.

It was apparent that no one Arab State was in a position to dominate the rest of the Arab world to the extent of being able to impose a unified policy on the Arab world, and to carry that policy into effect, either in respect of Palestine or in respect of oil. The only way to arrive at, and to make effective, such a unified policy was by way of agreement. The appropriate instrument of agreement already existed, in the Arab League. But, in its fifteen years of life, the Arab League had been condemned to sterility, not because of the existence of serious disagreements between the member States, but because of a continual refusal to use the Arab League as a means of attempting to reconcile these disagreements. Instead of building from the foundations upwards, continued attempts were made to lower a roof on to a non-existent house. Time and again the roof came crashing to the ground. These disasters were regularly attributed to imperialist intrigues; nobody dared to point out that there was no house there at all, that the fitting of the roof was the end and not the beginning of the operation, and that the only way to build a house was from the bottom upwards and not from the top downwards.

From the time of the inception of the Arab League, the Arab attitude towards Palestine had been characterized by a refusal either effectively to fight or realistically to negotiate. Palestine was lost to the Arabs because they could not bring themselves to accept the fact that the only alternative to a compromise was a victory which they had neither the will nor the means to achieve. Thereafter, the problem had been bedevilled by the Arab refusal to recognize and to reconcile themselves to the fact of military defeat, and to use the many powerful bargaining counters which they could have devised to mitigate the results of defeat. They still thought in terms of victory, but made no attempt to organize victory. They persisted in regarding the refugee problem as a temporary one, but refused to solve it by either of the only possible alternative methods—by victory over Israel or by negotiation with Israel. They continually and clamorously appealed to a non-existent referee, alleging that Israel had won by a foul and demanding a penalty kick. They demanded that the United Nations should compel Israel to accept the UN Partition Resolution of 1947 (which the Arab League had rejected and which the Jewish Agency had accepted at the time), not as a condition of peace with Israel but as a first instalment in the liquidation of Israel. Simultaneously with announcements of their intention to destroy Israel, and with reminders to the world that they were still at war with Israel, the Arab States protested vigorously about the aggressive intentions of Israel against themselves. In short, they behaved like neurotic children. They had a reasonably good case against Israel, if they had pursued it realistically; instead, they exaggerated it to the point of fantasy, pursued it by means of a series of ludicrous gestures, and so let it go by default.

It is necessary to appreciate the depth of the passions which have been aroused over Palestine. Part of the secret of Abdul Nasr's appeal to the Arab world, and particularly to the educated section of the Arab world, was the belief that the unity preached by Abdul Nasr could result in a solution of the Palestine problem in the only way which was acceptable to the majority of Arabs— by the defeat of Israel. The principal reason for Abdul Nasr's declining popularity in the Arab world has been the slow realization that he was incapable of defeating Israel. Will the Arab peoples continue to dream of a victory which they can never achieve, or will they be prepared to aim at a bargain well within their reach? Will they continue to take refuge in their illusions over Palestine and, so remain politically and emotionally stunted, or will they shed their illusions, and, by acknowledging that the Palestine predicament arises from their own past deficiencies, take the first necessary step towards the removal of these deficiencies?

At the end of 1959 there was very little sign of such realism. The nearest approach to it was Abdul Nasr's offer to open the Suez Canal to Israel in accordance with the Security Council's Resolution provided that Israel obeyed the other two United Nations Resolutions about the boundaries of the State of Israel and the repatriation or compensation of the Arab refugees. This may well have been a tactical move made in the knowledge that there was not the slightest chance that Israel would obey these two Resolutions. But it did, at least, admit the existence of Israel and point to the possibility of an eventual peace with Israel.

An important factor in inducing a more realistic attitude will be the views of the Palestinians themselves, many of the more able of whom are scattered about the Arab world, occupying positions of responsibility and influence. Up to the end of 1959 the Palestinians, so far from having been the victims, had to a large extent been the instigators of the intransigent and futile policy adopted by the Arab States towards the Palestine problem. King Abdullah and Riad Solh, the two Arab statesmen who were suspected of a realistic attitude towards the problem, were both murdered by Palestinians; realism in other Arab statesmen has been inhibited by fear of Palestinian Arab vengeance. But behind the Palestinian Arab attitude was the hope, and even the belief, that Palestine might be reconquered. So long as there appeared to be a reasonable possibility that Abdul Nasr might accomplish this, Palestinian Arabs were among his most enthusiastic supporters. The support which Abdul Nasr enjoyed in Jordan, and in the refugee camps, was almost entirely due to a belief that a federation, or some other form of close alliance, between Egypt, Syria and Jordan would encircle, and might lead to war with and the defeat of, Israel. The slow and bitter realization that this was a pipe-dream, and the futile dispute which broke out between Jordan and Lebanon in the second half of 1959 about the recommendations of the Hammarskjold Report, seemed likely to lead a number of Palestinian Arabs, and particularly those who have managed to get out of the refugee camps into regular and, in some cases, into responsible, employment, to a reassessment of the position. Many of these Palestinians, and particularly those in Libya and Lebanon, are being discriminated against in the Arab countries where they are living and working, and competing in commerce and in the employment market, on the ground that it would be wrong, by offering Palestinians a permanent home, to discourage them and other Arabs from the ultimate objective of a return to Palestine. This movement of discrimination seems likely to spread to the Persian Gulf Sheikhdoms as local nationals begin to covet and begin, however remotely, to become qualified for, the positions now being held there by Palestinians. Palestinian Arabs are thus becoming rudely confronted with the logical consequence of the present Arab attitude towards Palestine. They can no longer have it both ways, having the actuality of being citizens of their adopted countries and the aspiration of becoming once more citizens of Palestine. They can see yawning in front of them the same trap as previously faced Zionism and, like the Zionists, they are faced with the choice either of converting a return to Palestine from a vague aspiration into a practical possibility, or of leading a movement for abandoning the prospect of a return to Palestine as a means of safeguarding their actual positions in the countries where they are living and working.

For this reason it seems possible that there will be a growing movement among the Palestinians themselves to induce the Arab States towards realism. And this realism will necessarily, or almost necessarily, have to take the form of a willingness to negotiate. The process will be a slow one, and will be retarded rather than assisted by good advice from the West, or even by overtures on the part of Israel. There are considerable psychological obstacles to overcome. Much depends on the progress of events in Iraq. A definitive departure of Iraq from the Arab nationalist fold would probably accelerate the process; a return of Iraq into the Arab nationalist fold would probably retard it.

Difficulties in the way of a unified and effective Arab oil policy are less intractable simply because they are more tangible. There are the differences in interest between the 'have' and the 'have not' countries; there are the usual objections to any abdication of national sovereignty; there are differences in emphasis between those who wish to use the oil revenues for purposes of general development and those who wish to use them for acquiring a stake in the international oil industry; there are differences of view between those who wish to maximize immediate oil revenues irrespective of any other consideration and those who wish to adopt a co-ordinated system of conservation and price maintenance; above all there are differences of opinion between those who are quite content to leave the oil industry in the hands of foreign companies provided that they can squeeze more and more money out of them and between those who wish to obtain control of the national oil industry even at the expense of a reduction in oil revenue. But these differences and difficulties, although exacerbated by that feeling of distrust towards and dislike of the West, which induces even intelligent Arabs to regard oil at one and the same time as a stick with which to beat the West and as an instrument of imperialist exploitation by the West, are not bedevilled by those psychological considerations which have so far prevented any realistic approach to the Palestine problem.

These psychological considerations make it unreasonable to regard Palestine as a test case of the ability of the Arab States to adjust themselves to a state of affairs in which their economic progress and even their political independence may no longer be sustained by adventitious aids arising from the continuance of the cold war. But oil can reasonably be regarded as such a test case. The evolution and implementation of a common policy over the exploitation of their oil resources is the obvious first step towards a practical Arab nationalism based on a realistic appraisal and a resolute defence of common Arab interests. It would be an effective foundation for a structure which may eventually be erected into some sort of federation, just as, in Western Europe, the Iron and Steel Community was an effective foundation to a building which is still under construction. The construction of such an effective foundation would provide an indication that the old and futile process of trying to build from the top downwards had been substituted by a more modest but a more rewarding attempt to build from the bottom upwards.

As in the case of Palestine, so in the case of oil, the Arab League is an appropriate and ready-made instrument for the fashioning of an effective common policy. There are already signs of a movement towards such a policy coming, not from rulers or ministers, who are in charge of national policies, but from civil servants and technicians who are concerned with day-to-day administration. A particularly noteworthy development in the Arab world during the last twelve years has been the steady emergence of competent and, in some cases, brilliant administrators in most of the independent Arab States, and a gradual transition from the old tradition of personal and arbitrary autocracy, implemented by a handful of ministers and high officials through the medium of a vast, underpaid, underworked, corrupt, incompetent and entirely subservient band of junior officials, into a newer and Western tradition of impersonal and regulated autocracy, controlled by a new generation of reasonably competent, reasonably honest and ambitious civil servants who regard their ministers with much the same mixture of outward respect and secret contempt as is habitual in the civil services of the West. It is this 'managerial' class in government service, with their counterparts in commerce and industry, who are beginning to make their weight felt both in the administration of their own countries and in the various committees of the Arab League. It may even be said that the Arab world is moving through a phase of military dictatorship into a phase of dictatorial bureaucracy, in which the real masters will not be the 'front men'—the Husains, the Abbouds, the Qasims and the Abdul Nasrs—appearing as father figures or as Big Brothers on the radio, in processions or on balconies, but the 'back-room boys', like Yunis and Tariqi and Salim, who really do know, or who are learning, how to run the complicated apparatus of a modern State. This stage has not yet been reached or nearly reached. Civil servants of this calibre do not make policy, either in appearance or in fact. They merely carry it out, as Mahmud Yunis did in his brilliant improvization of an efficient administration for the Suez Canal at about forty-eight hours' notice. But it seems not unlikely that the next impulse towards Arab unity will come, neither from some ambitious ruler seeking personal glory, nor from some political party or group seeking the fulfilment of a political ideal, but from groups of like-minded civil servants, industrialists and business men pursuing practical advantages and becoming more and more impatient with the sterile attitudinizing of politicians, whose raucously declared ends bear no relation whatever either to the means at their disposal or to the practical needs of the Arab countries in this day and age. It is conceivable that, in the eyes of such an elite, the methods and policies of Gamal Abdul Nasr will seem not less antiquated, and not less impractical, than the methods and policies of the Pashas whom he and his kind have supplanted.

For the time being, the voice of the experts, in oil as in everything else, is a voice crying in the wilderness; the experts are useful only and used only for doing the things which their masters set them to do—to run the suddenly nationalized or confiscated public services, to reduce to some sort of order the chaos created by some arbitrary piece of demagogy, to create for public, and particularly for foreign, consumption a thin façade of competence as a screen behind which to hide a welter of increasing disorder.

One of the few subjects on which the voice of the experts has been heard by the outside world is that of oil. The Middle East oil industry may be said to be in its tertiary stage. The first stage was the honeymoon period of the years immediately following the Second World War, when the access of unexpected and increasing wealth to the oil producing countries opened out hitherto undreamed of prospects of personal extravagance for rulers (in some cases) and of economic and social progress for peoples (in other cases). The secondary stage dates from the nationalization of the Anglo-Iranian Oil Company by Musaddiq during which Abdul Nasr attempted to gain effective control of Middle East oil in order to use that control as a political weapon against the Western Powers. The tertiary stage may be said to date from February 1959, when a sharp reduction in prices paid for Middle East crudes drew the attention of the world in general and of the Middle East oil producing countries in particular to the increasing competitiveness of the crude oil market and to the decreasing dependence of the West on Middle East oil as a result of increasing production elsewhere and particularly in North and West Africa

During the secondary stage the governments of the Arab oil producing countries had concentrated on obtaining the maximum material benefits from the foreign oil companies, in respect both of division of profits and of local expenditure by the concessionary companies; they had not attached particular importance either to increased control of or increased participation in their local oil industries. The governments of the non-producing, transit countries had, understandably, taken a different view, and had concentrated on using their strategic position as a means of exerting political pressure on the one hand on the Arab producing and on the other hand on the Western consuming countries. The declining political influence of the UAR in the Arab world, com-

P

bined with the decreasing dependence of the West on Middle East oil, is compelling a rethinking both of the political sanctions and of the commercial pressures which it is practicable to apply. The problem before the Arab States in what we have termed the tertiary stage is not how they can combine to exploit the political and commercial possibilities of a virtual monopoly in the possession of a vital fuel, but how they can best avoid being exploited, as a result of their lack of combination, in the rough and tumble of what is likely to be an increasingly competitive market. It is a question not of exploiting a temporary and fortuitous advantage but of turning this temporary and fortuitous advantage into a permanent asset. This problem, which involves thinking in terms of investment rather than of blackmail, is typical of many other problems facing the Arab world, and, in dealing with them, the past methods of Abdul Nasr are at least as inappropriate as the past methods of any of his predecessors or contemporaries.

At the first Arab Petroleum Congress held in Cairo in April 1959 it became apparent that a number of Arab experts were thinking along more realistic lines than their sheikhly or dictatorial masters. They had already grasped two essential facts which were hidden from these masters. First, that limited co-operation on specific matters within the existing Arab political framework must precede, and could not be allowed to await the fruition of, large schemes of political unity. Secondly, that the Arab attitude *vis-à-vis* the international oil companies must be one of attempted participation in their international interests and not one of attempted expropriation of their local interests. It was becoming apparent to these experts, as it was not yet apparent to their masters, that under the emerging new conditions—a buyer's market for oil and a gradual thawing of the cold war—denunciations of imperialism on the one hand, and assertions of a non-existent unity on the other, so far from being magic incantations resulting in the miraculous destruction of imperialism and the no less miraculous attainment of unity, were diversions of attention and of energy which both assisted the survival of imperialism and inhibited the attainment of unity.

It may be that these stirrings beneath the surface, these vague discontents with increasingly empty denunciations and assertions, presage the advent of a new movement of Arab nationalism based on a conviction of the practical advantages of certain limited measures of unity which, so far from existing already within the notional framework of a larger, esoteric unity of blood and race and tradition, have to be created from nothing out of a maze of conflicting interests and traditional habits of mind. It may possibly be that Abdul Nasr will be able to use his still considerable prestige, be able to moderate his still considerable ambition, and (most important of all) be able to guide and restrain his still considerable body of supporters sufficiently to enable him to put himself at the head of such a new movement.

With all his habitual violence of speech, and with all his occasional violence in action, Gamal Abdul Nasr is still incomparably the most mature and the most realistic leader in the Arab world today. Even on the most favourable estimate, Qasim would seem to be a bloodthirsty, reactionary and obscurantist tyrant of the type (and possibly also of the survival value) of General Franco. King Husain is a courageous and attractive figure, but the last survivor of a hopelessly lost cause. King Saud is the characterless, feckless and spendthrift son of a great father. The series of military coups in the Sudan have as yet produced no single outstanding figure capable of establishing his authority over his immediate subordinates, let alone over the rest of the Arab world. The rôle of Syria seems to be to produce, not leaders, but ideas.

It may be that the immediate future of the Arab world lies in the slough of political impotence and economic stagnation which seems likely to result from the Tweedledum and Tweedledee struggle between Abdul Nasr and Qasim—a struggle in which the Fertile Crescent plays the classic rôle of the rattle. Qasim has already given notice that he is ready and anxious to continue the traditional struggle between the Euphrates and the Nile for the control of the Fertile Crescent. Abdul Nasr has responded suitably to the challenge and it seems possible that a kind of stability —the stability of an eternal tug-of-war in which two evenly

P*

matched teams devote their entire energies to maintaining the same relative position *vis-à-vis* the other will descend on the Arab world. But the more that Abdul Nasr and Qasim revert to the Tweedledum and Tweedledee attitudes of their predecessors, the more they will provoke the resentment of the forces which brought them into power. And the whole dreary cycle of discontent, repression, revolution, reform, reaction and discontent will start all over again. By all the omens this seems the most probable immediate destiny for the Arab world. But there are signs of a possible alternative. The policies adopted by the Arab States within the next few years towards Palestine and towards oil will be decisive.

The all-important question is not 'Who will be the rulers of the Arab world in the immediate future?' but 'Who will rule the rulers of the Arab world in the immediate future?' For, in the last analysis, dictators are the creatures of those upon whom they rely for keeping them in power. The essential strength of Abdul Nasr as a possible future influence in the Arab world lies in the fact that his position in his own country—unlike that of Qasim—is sufficiently secure to enable him to choose his friends. For this reason, and in spite of the political and diplomatic failures experienced in pursuit of his pan-Arab ambitions, he still has enormous potentialities for influence in the Arab world, provided that he adapts his ends to the means at his disposal. In trying to emulate Saladin he has merely succeeded in looking like Tweedledum. A more modest ambition might be to emulate one of his predecessors who, after his pan-Arab ambitions had been frustrated, and his armies forced to evacuate the Fertile Crescent, applied himself successfully to the task of developing Egypt as a modern State.

Notes

———◆●◆———

CHAPTER ONE

Page 11 [1] The Capitulations originated in a series of Treaties made between various European Powers and the Ottoman Empire from the sixteenth century onwards, by which European communities living in the Ottoman Empire were granted certain extra-territorial privileges, based on the Turkish 'milli' system applied to Christian minorities, by which these European nationals had the right to have disputes between themselves settled by their own consuls, and by which consuls had the right to be present at any proceedings taken against their nationals by the Ottoman authorities. In nineteenth-century Egypt a steady and stealthy enlargement of these privileges gradually placed members of most European communities outside the Egyptian law in respect of such matters as taxation, which could not be imposed on European foreigners without the consent of their governments, and crime, for which European foreigners could not be tried except before their own consular courts. These privileges were often grossly abused.

Page 11 [2] The 'Mixed Courts', which were a branch of the National Courts of Egypt, although presided over mostly by foreign judges nominated by the Capitulatory Powers, were set up by Nubar Pasha in 1875 for the purpose of trying civil suits between Egyptians and foreigners and between foreigners of different nationalities. The Mixed Courts, together with the Capitulations, were abolished at the Montreux Conference in 1937.

CHAPTER TWO

Page 20 [1] A holy war which had been proclaimed by the Sultan in his capacity as Khalif-al-Islam. According to Islamic tradition, such a summons by the Khalif was binding on all Moslems. In fact, very little notice was taken of it.

Page 20   ² Known as the 'McMahon correspondence'. It culminated in what became known as the 'MacMahon pledge', after Sir Henry McMahon, the British High Commissioner in Cairo at the time.

Page 22   ³ The descendants of Husain, the Sherif of Mecca, are usually known as the Hashemites and will be referred to as such in this book.

Page 25   ⁴ Almost continuous. The Saudi province of al-Hasa lies between the Sheikhdoms of Qatar and Kuwait.

CHAPTER THREE

Page 33   ¹ The religious law of Islam which is still, in Saudi Arabia and Yeman, and in some of the Persian Gulf Sheikhdoms, the basis of both the civil and criminal codes.

Page 49   ² The Husainis were one of the three leading Arab families of Jerusalem (the other two being the Khalidis and the Nashashibis). Haj Amin was the leading member of the family, and his chief lieutenant was his cousin, Jamal Husaini.

CHAPTER FOUR

Page 52   ¹ A small Saudi contingent was attached to the Egyptian army.

Page 53   ² Prayer, almsgiving, fasting, the pilgrimage to Mecca, and the declaration of faith, 'There is no god but God and Mohammed—the Prophet of God.'

Page 54   ³ It was generally believed that he was murdered by the secret police on the orders of the Government.

Page 56   ⁴ An important factor in Arab politics was that, in the pre-revolutionary era, the military profession in most Arab countries carried with it no exalted social status and did not normally attract young men of the ruling families.

Page 57   ⁵ In his book *The Philosophy of the Revolution.*

CHAPTER FIVE

Page 59   ¹ On the ground that it constituted a danger to peace.
Page 65   ² It had been occupied by Mohamed Ali and his successors during the course of the nineteenth century.

Page 65 ³ Under the 1899 Sudan Agreement between Great Britain and Egypt, the Anglo-Egyptian Sudan, as it was termed, had been declared a Condominium, in theory jointly ruled by Great Britain and Egypt, in practice administered almost exclusively by Great Britain.

Page 65 ⁴ As a result of the 1937 Montreux Conference at which the Capitulatory Powers, as a result of the 1936 Anglo-Egyptian Treaty, and at the instigation of HMG, agreed to the abolition of the Capitulations and Mixed Courts.

CHAPTER SIX

Page 80 ¹ The Revolutionary Command Council, the executive body of the Free Officers' Movement which had engineered the military coup in July 1952 and which, for the first two years of the Revolution was, in practice, the executive government of Egypt. In the early days of the Revolution, it was popularly referred to abroad as the Junta.

Page 88 ² Subsequently joined by Iran and Pakistan.

Page 88 ³ The Gaza strip was that small area of Palestine between Gaza and the Egyptian frontier, which was still occupied by Egyptian troops at the time of the Egypt-Israel armistice in 1949, and which has since been under Egyptian military occupation (apart from the short period when it was occupied by Israel in the autumn of 1956).

CHAPTER SEVEN

Page 102 ¹ There are about seven barrels of crude oil to a metric ton.

CHAPTER EIGHT

Page 116 ¹ Plural of 'waqf'. A religious foundation set up for charitable purposes. They were subject to much the same abuses as gifts made to monasteries in pre-Reformation England.

CHAPTER NINE

Page 126 ¹ The Algerian government-in-exile had been established in Cairo.

Page 131 ² An international Convention providing for freedom of passage through the Suez Canal.

Page 131 ³ Which was due to run until 1968. The Canal was then to revert to Egypt, with the Egyptian Government paying the Canal Company for the book value of the physical assets at the date of the termination of the Concession. The compensation eventually agreed on was based on the current book value of the physical assets, without any allowance for loss of prospective profit as a result of the period of the Concession having been cut short by thirteen years.

Page 131 ⁴ British Prime Minister at the time.

Page 137 ⁵ Conveyed as a joint Anglo-French ultimatum addressed to both sides calling on them each to withdraw their forces to a distance of ten kilometres from the Canal. The Israelis, who were not in fact within ten kilometres of the Canal, signified their compliance, the Egyptians rejected the ultimatum, which called upon the Egyptians militarily to evacuate part of their own territory.

CHAPTER TEN

Page 149 ¹ According to Lebanese custom the President is always a Maronite Christian, and the Prime Minister a Sunni Moslem.

CHAPTER TWELVE

Page 184 ¹ Brigadier Abdi.

Page 184 ² This disagreement did not prevent the subsequent negotiation of a Russian loan to Egypt of 35 million sterling equivalent for starting the construction of the High Dam.

CHAPTER THIRTEEN

Page 189 ¹ Located in Cairo under the protection of Abdul Nasr.

Page 189 ² In January 1959.

Page 193 ³ In July 1959.

Page 193 ⁴ Early in 1960 it was announced that Russia had agreed to finance the whole of the foreign currency required for the completion of the High Dam. Previously Russia had only agreed to finance the first stage.

Page 194 ⁵ At the end of December 1959 the Baathist members of the UAR Government, led by Arram Hourani, the Vice-President, resigned, and their resignations were accepted.

Page 194 [6] Towards the end of 1959 this proposal was, without acknowledgment, vigorously adopted by Abdul Karim Qasim.

Page 196 [7] Two of Abdul Hakim Amer's first actions were (i) to appease Syrian landowners by modifying the land reform regulations which, modelled on Egypt, had been imposed on Syria, and (ii) to appease Syrian industrialists by some liberalization of Syria's trade which had been adversely affected by the 'dirigiste' Egyptian system which had been applied to it. These measures of economic appeasement were accompanied by much tighter political control.

Page 197 [8] A loan for this purpose was obtained from the World Bank in December 1959.

Page 197 [9] Qasim subsequently accused UAR of appeasement towards Israel and claimed himself to be the foremost champion of Arab rights in Palestine.

Page 198 [10] Under the 1929 Agreement Egypt had the right to 44,000 million cubic metres and Sudan to 4,000 million cubic metres out of estimated total available water amounting to 48,000 million cubic metres per annum. Under the 1959 Agreement Egypt has the right to 55,500 million cubic metres and Sudan to 18,500 million cubic metres out of an estimated total supply of 74,000 million cubic metres per annum.

CHAPTER FOURTEEN

Page 203 [1] It was not formally denounced by Iraq until 1959. It was then renamed CENTO.

Bibliography

Abbas, Mekki. *The Sudan Question. The Dispute Over the Anglo-Egyptian Condominium 1884-1951*. Faber, 1952.

Adams, C. C. *Islam and Modernism in Egypt*. Oxford Univ. Press, 1933.

Antonius, George. *The Arab Awakening*. Hamish Hamilton, 1938.

Barawi, Rashid al. *The Military Coup in Egypt*. Renaissance Bookshop, Cairo, 1952.

Barbour, Nevill (ed.). *A Survey of North-West Africa*. Oxford Univ. for RIIA, 1959.

Bromberger, M. and S. (tr.). *Secrets of Suez*. Pan Books, 1957.

Bullard, Sir Reader. *Britain and the Middle East*. Hutchinson, 1952.

Bustani, Emile. *Doubts and Dynamite*. Allan Wingate, 1958.

'Caracatcus' (pseud.). *Revolution in Iraq*. Gollancz, 1959.

Connell, John. *The Most Important Country*. Cassell, 1959.

Cromer, Lord. *Modern Egypt* (2 vols.). Macmillan, 1908.

Dodwell, H. H. *The Founder of Modern Egypt*. Cambridge Univ., 1931.

Faris, N. A. *The Arab Heritage*. Princeton, 1944.

Faris, N. A. and Husain, M. T. *The Crescent in Crisis*. Kansas Univ., 1955.

Gibb, H. A. R. *Modern Trends in Islam*. Chicago Univ., 1947.

Gibb, H. A. R. and Bowen, H. *Islamic Society and the West*. Oxford Univ., 1950.

Glubb, Sir J. B. *Britain and the Arabs*. Hodder & Stoughton, 1959.

Hitti, Philip. *A History of the Arabs*. Macmillan, 1938.

—— *A History of Syria Including Lebanon and Palestine*. Macmillan, 1951.

Hourani, A. H. *Syria and Lebanon*. Oxford Univ. for RIIA, 1946.

—— *Minorities in the Arab World*. Oxford Univ. for RIIA, 1947.

Issawi, Charles. *Egypt at Mid-Century*. Oxford Univ. for RIIA, 1954.

Kaddourie, E. *England and the Middle East: The Destruction of the Ottoman Empire*. Bowes, 1956.

Kimche, Jon. *Seven Fallen Pillars*. Secker & Warburg, 1953.

Kirk, G. E. A *Short History of the Middle East* (3rd ed.). Methuen, 1955.

Lacouture, Jean and Simon. *L'Egypte en Mouvement*. Ed. du Seuil Paris, 1956.

Laoust, Henri (tr.). *La Caliphate dans la Doctrine de Rashid Rida*. Beirut, 1938.

Laqueur, W. Z. *Communism and Nationalism in the Middle East*. Praeger (New York), 1956.

Lenczowski, G. *The Middle East in World Affairs*. Cornell (USA), 1956.

Lewis, Bernard. *The Arabs in History*. Hutchinson, 1950.

Little, T. R. *Egypt*. Benn, 1958.

Lloyd, Lord. *Egypt Since Cromer* (2 vols.). Macmillan, 1934.

Longrigg, S. H. *Four Centuries of Modern Iraq*. Clarendon Press, 1925.

—— *Iraq 1900 to 1950*. Oxford Univ. for RIIA, 1953.

—— *Oil in the Middle East*. Oxford Univ. for RIIA, 1954.

—— *Syria and Lebanon Under French Mandate*. Oxford Univ. for RIIA, 1958.

Longrigg, S. H. and Stoakes, F. *Iraq*. Benn, 1958.

Marlowe, John. *Anglo-Egyptian Relations 1800-1953*. Cresset, 1954.

—— *The Seat of Pilate*. Cresset, 1959.

Nasr, Gamal Abdul. *Egypt's Liberation: The Philosophy of the Revolution*. Public Affairs Press (USA), 1955.

Nuseibeh, Hazem. *The Ideas of Arab Nationalism*. Cornell (USA), 1956.

Philby, H. St. J. *Saudi Arabia*. Benn, 1955.

Royal Institute of International Affairs. *Great Britain and Palestine 1915-45*. 1946.

—— *The Middle East in the War Years*. 1948.

—— *The Middle East 1945-1950*. 1952.

—— *The Middle East — A Political and Economic Survey* (ed. Sir Reader Bullard). 1958.

—— *British Interests in the Mediterranean and Middle East*. Oxford Univ., 1958.

Sadat, Anwar. *Revolt on the Nile*. Wingate, 1957.

Salter, Lord. *The Development of Iraq*. Caxton Press, 1955.

Shwadran, B. *Middle East Oil and the Great Powers*. Praeger (New York), 1955.

Stewart, Desmond. *Young Egypt*. Wingate, 1958.

Twitchell, K. S. *Saudi Arabia*. Princeton (USA), 1953 (2nd ed.).

Utley, T. E. *Not Guilty*. MacGibbon & Kee, 1957.

US Dept. of State. *The Suez Canal Problem, July 26—Sept. 22, 1956*. 1956.

Warriner, Doreen. *Land Reform and Development in the Middle East.* Oxford Univ. for RIIA, 1957.

Watt, D. C. *Britain and the Suez Canal.* RIIA, 1956.

—— *Documents on the Suez Crisis, 26 July to 6 November, 1956.* RIIA, 1957.

Williams, K. *Ibn Saud.* Cape, 1953.

Wilson, Sir Arnold. *The Suez Canal.* Oxford Univ., 1933.

—— *The Persian Gulf.* Allen & Unwin, 1937.

Wint, G. and Calvocoressi, P. *Middle East Crisis.* Penguin Books, 1957.

Ziadeh, N. A. *Syria and Lebanon.* Benn, 1956.

Index

Abadan, oil refinery, 63, 201
Abboud, General Ibrahim, President of the Sudan, 188, 216
Abdi, Brigadier, Military Governor of Baghdad, 184
Abdu, Mohamed, 13
Abdul Hadi, Ibrahim, Prime Minister of Egypt, 54
Abdul Nasr, see Nasr
Abdul Rahman Kawakebi, 14
Abdulillah, Amir, Crown Prince of Iraq, 172, 177
Abdullah, Amir of Transjordan, King (1946), 19-20, 22-3, 34, 36-8, 40, 42, 48-50, 52, 92, 94, 212
Abu Nawar, Lieutenant Colonel Ali, 150
Adana, 21
Aden Colony, 99, 208
Aflak, Michel, 95, 157
Africa, 190
al Ahd, 19
al-Azhar, University of, 14
al Fatat, 19
Alamein, Battle of, 41-2
Alawites, 9, 152
Albanians, 10
Aleppo, 15
Alexandretta, Sanjak of, 152-3
Alexandria Protocol, 1944, 47
Algeria, 106-8, 199
Algerian Government-in-exile, 189-90, 199
Algerian rebels, 125-6
Ali ibn Husain, Amir of Medina, 29
Amer, General Abdul Hakim, 136, 196
Amman, 151
Aneizeh tribe, 153
Anglo-Egyptian Agreement, 1954, 67, 75, 78, 85, 88, 132, 201
Anglo-Egyptian Sudan see Sudan
Anglo-Egyptian Treaty, 1936, 26, 32, 37, 59, 65, 67, 70

Anglo-French ultimatum, 137-8, 141
Anglo-Iranian Oil Company, 63, 103, 122
Anglo-Iraqi Treaty, 1930, 26, 32
Anglo-Jordanian Treaty, 125, 144, 150
Anglo-Persian Oil Company, 101-2
Anglo-Transjordan Treaty see Anglo-Jordanian Treaty
Aqaba, 29, 147
Aqaba, Gulf of, 135, 143, 147-8
Arab Collective Security Pact, 88, 179-80
Arab Congress, 1913, 16, 110
Arab League, federal aims of, 24; formation, 42; Pact of, 1945, 45, 47; and Syrian and Lebanese independence, 46; relations with Britain, 47, 59; Egyptian policy towards, 69, 78, 119; Libya, Morocco and Tunisia join, 107; Lebanese policy to, 168; Iraq and, 178-9; Tunisia boycotts, 189; Egyptian domination of, 190; Political Committee meeting, Beirut, 191; Political Committee meeting, Casablanca, 194; lack of policy, 199; future role of, 210-1, 215
Arab League Boycott Committee, 197
Arab Legion, 51
Arab nationalism, origins, 1, 4, 6-16; since 1942, 41; and Egyptian military regime, 78; in Syria, 95; and independence of Maghrib States, 108; in 1950, 110; defined by Abdul Nasr, 111-2; after Egyptian revolution, 120; and Syrian post war policy, 154; Baath and, 157, 164; and federal union between Egypt and Syria, 163; new movement in, 219
Arab Petroleum Congress, 1959, 218
Arabian Peninsula, 27, 29, 87
Arabic language, 2-4, 6, 8-9
Aramco, 104

Aref, Colonel Abdul Salem, 181-2, 184
Arisi, Abdul Ghani al-, 16
Ashigga, 73, 80
Asir, 23
Aswan High Dam, and Nile Waters
    Agreement, 1929, 80; and Egyptian
    press, 87; financial assistance for,
    123, 127-9; financed from Suez Canal
    revenues, 130, 134; Russian loan,
    193, 198; and conclusion of Nile
    Waters Agreement, 1959, 198
Awqaf, 116
Azm, Khaled al, 96, 158-9, 162
Azzam, Abdul Rahman, 190

Baath Party, 95, 157
Baath Socialist Party, 95, 155-9, 162-4,
    188, 193, 200
Baghdad, 15, 21-2, 24
Baghdad Pact, 88, 90, 114, 122, 124-5,
    146, 151, 180, 182, 186, 202-3
Bahrain, 100, 125
Bahrain Petroleum Company, 102
Balfour Declaration, 23
Bandoeng Conference, 1955, 90
Banias, oil terminal, 103
Banna, Hasan al, 53-4
Barzani, Mullah, 182
Basra, 15, 21-2, 24
Beduin, 15, 153
Beirut, 151, 153; meeting of Political
    Committee of Arab League, 1959,
    191
Bikdash, Khaled, 55, 95, 161
Bludan, pan-Arab Conference, 1937,
    36
Boghdadi, Wing Commander Abdul
    Latif, 74
Bonaparte, Napoleon, landing in
    Egypt, 1798, 7
Bourguiba, Habib, President of
    Tunisia, 107, 111, 126, 175, 193
Bq'a, 168
Brioni, 129
British Petroleum, 104
Buraimi dispute, 98-9
Butler, R. A., 142

Cairo, Government Press, 8; centre of
    British zone of influence, 17;
    Colonial Office Conference, 1921,
    31; pan-Arab Conference, 1938, 36;
    Pact of the Arab League, 1945, 45;
    riots, 1952, 70; meeting of Arab Col-
    lective Security Pact, 1955, 88; im-
    portance in Arab world, 112; Arab

Petroleum Congress, 1959, 218
Canal Users Conference, London,
    1956, 133-4
Capitulory privileges, 11, 65
Casablanca, meeting of Political Com-
    mittee of Arab League, 194-6
Catholic missions, in Syria, 8
CENTO (Central Treaty Organization),
    182
Chamoun, Camille, President of
    Lebanon, 97, 111, 148-9, 169, 171-4
Christian missionaries, in Syria, 8
Christians, in Lebanon, 9, 149, 167-9
Circassians, 2, 10
Colonial Office Conference, 1921, 31
Communism, Eisenhower Doctrine
    and, 146, 159; penetration in Syria,
    161, 166; in Iraq, 180, 184
Communist Party, in Middle East, 55;
    in Syria, 96, 161; in Iraq, 111, 182-3;
    in Egypt, 117
Compagnie Française des Petroles,
    101, 104
Congress of Vienna, 8
Conservative Party, attitude to Suez
    Canal, 74-5, 130, 201
Constantinople, transfer of Caliphate
    from, 17
Cyprus, troops sent to, 131, broad-
    casting station, 138
Cyrenaica, 107
Czechoslovakia, arms deal with Egypt,
    87, 89, 123, 126-7, 129; contract for
    oil refinery, 157

Damascus, 15, 21
'Damascus Protocol', 21
de Gaulle, General Charles, President
    of France, 199
Dhahran, US air base at, 148
Druzes, 9, 152, 167-8
Dulles, John Foster, Secretary of State
    of US, 133-5, 137, 161

Eden, Anthony, Prime Minister, 131,
    133, 137, 142
Egypt, population of, 2; Bonaparte
    lands in, 7; nationalism in, 10;
    foreign influences in, 11; occupa-
    tion by Britain, 11-2, 17; advent of
    Dual Control, 12; riots, 31; British
    connections, 32; and Palestine
    White Paper, 35; and Greater Syria,
    38; resentment towards occupiers
    and rulers, 39; hegemony in Arab
    world, 43, 119, 172; and Arab unity,

44, 47; and Arab League, 45, 48; political parties in, 53-5; Army coup, 57, 68, 71; appeals to UN against 1936 Treaty, 59; attitude to Suez Canal Zone bases, 63-5; and the Sudan, 65-7, 79; declared independent, 1922, 67; war with Palestine, 69; relations with Britain in 1952, 72; as a Third Force, 85; attitude to Israel, 113-14; Joint Military Command with Syria and Jordan, 125, 136; loan for High Dam agreed, 128; Israel invades, 135; diplomatic relations broken with Great Britain and France, 140; seizes British and French property, 144; sends troops to aid Syria, 160; union with Syria, 165; Iraqi rivalry with, 178; Iraqi breach with, 179; competes with Iraq for control of Fertile Crescent, 184; concentration on domestic affairs, 193; and division of Nile waters, 198

Egyptian Army, 11-2, 70, 89
Egyptian Socialist and Democratic Party, 54
Eisenhower, Dwight D., President of the US, 146, 151, 159, 161-2
Eisenhower Doctrine, intentions of, 146-7; importance to Lebanon, 149; effect of, in Jordan, 150-1; effect of, in Iraq, 151; denounced by Syria, 157; as plot against Arab independence, 160; Nasr counter attacks with UAR, 165-6; Lebanese reaction to, 170; Lebanon renounces, 175; and Baghdad Pact, 203
Elath, 135, 147
Euphrates, 43, 83, 87, 124, 185, 219

Faruk II, King of Egypt, 47, 69, 70-2, 92
Feisal I, King of Iraq, 19, 21-3
Feisal II, King of Iraq, 172, 177, 186
Feisal ibn Abdul Aziz, Amir, Crown Prince of Saudi Arabia, 188
Fertile Crescent, 7, 15, 23, 26, 43, 82, 87, 94-5, 98, 124, 158, 164-5, 179, 184-5, 191, 219
Fezzan, 107
France, encourages Mohamed Ali, 8; claims Syria and Palestine, 18; expels Feisal, 22; French Mandate in Syria, 25; treaties with Syria and Lebanon, 26; evacuates Syria and Lebanon, 45; demands treaties with Syria and Lebanon, 46; and Israeli-Arab conflict, 89; Algerian problem, 106-7, 109, 126, 190, 199; and Suez Canal nationalization, 130; Suez Canal Zone occupied, 136-8; Egypt, Syria, Saudi Arabia, Iraq, Sudan and Jordan break off diplomatic relations with, 140; evacuates Egypt, 141, 143-4
Free Officers' Movement, 71, 73

Gaza Strip, 88-9, 127, 143-4
Gemeyel, Pierre, 171
Glubb, General John, 125, 150
Great Britain, intervenes against Mohamed Ali, 8; occupation of Egypt, 11-2, 17; war with Turkey, 17; negotiations with Sherif of Mecca, 18, 20; and Hejaz revolt, 21; position after 1914-18 War, 24; strategic interests of, in 1936, 31; Middle East policy in 1936, 34; and future of Palestine, 35, 39, 42; Arab collaboration with, 44; Zionist pressure on, 45, 50; secures evacuation of France from Syria and Lebanon, 46; and Middle East power vacuum, 61-2; garrisons in Middle East, 62; and Egyptian independence, 67; Nasr's policy of conciliation, 87; and Israeli-Arab conflict, 89; importance of Middle East oil, 103, 108-9; anti-colonial attitude of US to, 121-3; and loan for High Dam, 128-9; reaction to Suez Canal nationalization, 130-1; reoccupies Suez Canal Zone, 136-8; Egypt, Syria and Saudi Arabia break diplomatic relations with, 140; evacuates Egypt, 141, 143-4; reactions to Iraqi coup, 173, 185-7; attitude to Nasr's change of policy, 189-90; relations with UAR resumed, 198; decay of power, 201-9
Greater Syria, 37-8, 42-4, 49, 52, 153
Greenshirts *see* Misr al Fatat
Gulbenkian, Calouste, 101
Gulf Oil Company, 102

Hadhramut, 99
Haifa, importance to Britain, 18; oil terminal, 102-3
Haj Amin al Husaini, Mufti of Jerusalem, 38, 49, 92, 94, 110, 192
Hama, 15
Hamidian despots, 10, 19

Hammarskjold, Dag, Secretary General of UN, 194, 197
Hashemites, 21-2, 25, 29, 32, 37-8, 42-3, 48-9, 93, 179
Hassuna, Abdul Khaliq, 190
Hejaz, Mohamed Ali master of, 7; revolt in, 20-1; annexed by ibn Saud, 22, 28
Henderson, Loy, 159
High Dam, *see* Aswan High Dam
Hinnawi, Sami, 57, 94
Hodeibi, Hasan al, 54
Homs, 15, 157
Hourani, Akram, 95, 157, 193
Husain, King of Jordan, succeeds to the throne, 94; and nationalist propaganda, 111; dismisses General Glubb, 125; coup, 148; dismisses Nabulsi, 150; forms new government, 151; requests military assistance from Britain, 173; evacuation planned, 174-5; as leader of Arab nationalism, 176, 194; considers 'rescuing' Iraq, 185; changing status of, 216; as survivor of a lost cause, 219
Husain, Sherif of Mecca, King of the Hejaz, 18-20, 22, 25, 28-9
Husain, Ahmed, 54
Husaini family, 43
Husaini Party, 49, 93

ibn Rashid, Amir of Shammar, 28
ibn Saud, Abdul Aziz, King of the Hejaz and of Nejd, annexes the Hejaz, 22, 28-9; as powerful factor in the Arabian Peninsula, 27; and the Palestine Arab problem, 34; opposition to Greater Syria, 37, 42; attitude to occupying powers, 40; and Egyptian leadership of Arab League, 48; develops oil resources, 52; death, 92, 98, 123
Ibrahim Pasha, Governor of Syria, and Arab nationalism, 7; encourages missions, 8; invades Asia Minor, 8
Ibrahim, Wing Commander Hassan, 74
Idris al Senussi, King of Libya, 107
Indo-Egyptian Treaty of Friendship, 90
Inge Toft, 197
Iran, Russian pressure on, 60; oilfields, 61, 63; expropriates Anglo-Iranian Oil Company, 103-4; US alliance

with, 122; Iraq quarrels with, 184
Iraq, population of, 2; British Mandate, 23-4; sovereign state, 26; insurrection, 31; British connections, 32; and Palestine White Paper, 35; and idea of Greater Syria, 37; resentment against occupiers and rulers, 39; Egyptian pressure, 44; signs Pact of the Arab League, 45; Egyptian and Syrian hostility, 48; political parties in, 55; Army coup, 57, 68, 118; anti-British demonstrations, 59; defence pact with Turkey, 84, 88; Nasr's policy of conciliation, 87; dependence on Britain, 93; oilfields, 101; oil pipe lines, 103, 124; and Nasr's expansionist policies, 109; Baghdad Pact and, 114; and Arab nationalism, 125; isolationism of, 126, 146, 179; breaks diplomatic relations with France, 140; troops in Jordan, 150; and Eisenhower Doctrine, 151; plot against Syria, 156; support for Baath in, 164; union with Jordan, 165, 173; army and the revolution, 170, 172; revolution in, 177-87; relations with UAR, 189; defies Nasr, 191; after Casablanca Conference, 196; effect of revolution on British policy, 203
Iraq Petroleum Company, 101-2, 126, 140, 151, 156, 158, 183, 186
Islamic modernism, 13, 32-3
Islamic Socialist Front, 55
Ismailia, 130
Israel (events prior to 1948 *see* Palestine), war with Arab States, 49, 52, 154; war with Egypt, 69; Arab attitude to, in 1954, 83-4; mounting Arab hostility, 87; raid on Gaza Strip, 88, 127; in 1955, 97-8, 109; Egyptian attitude to, 113-4; ships denied use of Suez Canal, 133, 147, 197; invades Egypt, 135-6; evacuates Egypt, 143-4; army and Lebanese revolution, 174; Iraqi attitude to, 178; refugee problem, 194; UAR attitude to, in 1959, 197; Suez Canal opened to ships of, 212
Istiqlal Party, in Iraq, 55; in Morocco, 107

Jaffa, 153
Jamal ad-Din Afghani, 13

Jewish Agency, 197, 211
Jewish National Home *see* National
  Home in Palestine
Jezireh, 152
Jidda, Treaty of, 1927, 29
Jihad, 20
Jordan (events before 1949 *see* Transjordan); in 1955, 93-4; dependence
  on Britain, 124; sucked into
  Egyptian orbit, 125; Joint Military
  Command with Egypt and Syria,
  125, 136, 150; breaks diplomatic
  relations with France, 140; receives
  aid from Egypt, Syria and Saudi
  Arabia, 144; and Eisenhower Doctrine, 150-1; and Syria, 159; support
  for Baath in, 164; union with Iraq,
  165, 173; diplomatic relations with
  UAR broken off, 170; army and the
  revolution, 170; British troops
  flown to, 173, 175; British troops
  leave, 176; Iraqi relations with, 178;
  effect of Iraqi revolution on, 185;
  defies Nasr, 191; diplomatic relations with UAR resumed, 192; and
  refugee problem, 194

Karami, Rashid, Prime Minister of
  Lebanon, 174
Kawakebi, Abdul Rahman, 14
Khalif-al-Islam, 6, 28
Khalil, Abdullah, Prime Minister of
  Sudan, 188
Khedive Ismail, 12
Khoury, Bishara, P r e s i d e n t of
  Lebanon, 96-7, 149, 169
Kirkuk, 101, 183
Krushchev, Nikita S., 195
Kurds, 2, 178, 180
Kuwait, 100, 102, 104, 125
Kuwait Oil Company, 102
Kuwatli, Shukry, President of Syria,
  42, 96, 156

Labour Opposition, condemns Suez
  operation, 141
Lebanon, population of, 2, 9, 14, 48;
  French Mandate, 23; treaty with
  France, 26; resentment against
  occupiers and rulers, 39-40; independence, 42, 45-6, 52; Customs
  Union with Syria dissolved, 94; in
  1955, 96-7; and Egyptian influence,
  148-9; territorial extent of, 153;
  support for Baath in, 164; civil war

in, 167-76; effect of Iraqi revolu-
  tion on, 185; refugee problem, 194
Liberalism, 12-4, 33
Libya, 107
London, Canal Users' Conference,
  1956, 133-4

Maan, 29
Macmillan, Harold, Prime Minister,
  142
Maghrib, States of the, 107-8, 125
Mahdist revolt, 1882, 65
Majali, Haza, Prime Minister of
  Jordan, 194
Malik, Charles, Foreign Minister of
  Lebanon, 149, 169
Mecca, 7
Mecca, Sherif of *see* Husain
Medina, 7
Menzies, Robert, Prime Minister of
  Australia, 133
Mersine, 21
Mesjid-as-Suleiman, 101
Metawalis, 9
Misr al Fatat, 54
Mixed Courts, in Egypt, 11
Mohammed V, King of Morocco,
  106-7
Mohamed Ali, ruler of Egypt, 7, 66;
  encouraged by France, 8; and
  Egyptian Army, 11-2
Mohieddin, Zakaria, 74
Morocco, 106, 189, 199
Moslem Brotherhood, 53-5, 70, 76, 111
Moslem religion, 3, 6, 16, 116
Moslems, and British Empire, 17, 20;
  in Lebanon, 149, 168-9
Mosul, 22, 24, 101, 183, 196
Mount Lebanon, Sanjak of, 153, 167
Murphy, Robert, 174
Mussadiq, Mohamed, Prime Minister
  of Iran, 104, 122, 201
Muskat and Oman, 100, 102

Nabulsi, Suleiman, Prime Minister of
  Jordan, 125, 150, 151
Nahas Pasha, Mustafa, Prime Minister
  of Egypt, 42, 45, 47, 53, 92
Napoleon *see* Bonaparte, Napoleon
Nasr, Colonel Gamal Abdul, President
  of Egypt, and Arab nationalism, 5,
  57, 78, 90-1, 111-2; becomes Prime
  Minister of Egypt, 73; becomes
  President, 74; Tory distrust of, 75;
  purge of Moslem Brotherhood, 76;

pan-Arab ambitions of, 77, 82-7, 188, 199, 210; attitude to Sudan, 81; Czech arms deal, 87, 89-90, 123; invited to join Baghdad Pact, 88; and Israeli raids, 89; designs on Jordan, 94; struggle for power in Middle East, 109; impact on Arab world, 115-7; nationalist propaganda, 117-8; ambitions for Egyptian hegemony, 119, 172, 203; elected President of Egypt, 126; as world figure, 127; nationalizes the Suez Canal, 129-32; rejects international control of Suez Canal, 134-5; British and French distrust of, 137; attitude of US to, 142; challenged by Iraq and Saudi Arabia, 152; attitude to federal union with Syria, 163; regains initiative in Fertile Crescent, 165; effect of pan-Arabist policy on Iraq, 179; attitude towards Iraqi revolution, 184; Qasim as rival to, 186, 205; changes policies, 189-90, 192-3; loses influence in Arab world, 191, 212; and division of the Nile waters, 198; changing status of, 216; as realistic leader, 219; potential for future influence, 220
National Bloc, Syria, 37, 94, 155-6
National Home in Palestine: Jewish National Home, sponsored by Britain, 18, 22, 25; British policy towards, 23
Neguib, General Mohamed, President of Egypt, 73-4, 80
Nehru, Shri Jawaharlal, Prime Minister of India, 129
Nejd, 28
Neo-Dustour, 107, 111
Nile Valley, 10, 43, 83, 87, 124, 185, 219
Nile Waters Agreement, 1929, 80, 198; 1959, 193, 198
Noqrashy Pasha, Prime Minister of Egypt, 54
Nuri as Said, Prime Minister of Iraq, 42, 44-5, 57, 84, 92-3, 111, 172, 177, 186
Nuseibeh, Hazem, The Ideas of Arab Nationalism, 16

Oil, importance to Western Europe, 1, 41; Iraqi, 44, 48, 101, 178; Persian Gulf, 58-9, 100-2, 104; Saudi Arabian, 61, 102, 104; Iranian, 61,

63, 104-5; Middle East production, 102; and nationalization of Suez Canal, 131; buyers' market for, 199; British interest in, 206, 208; as foundation for Arab federation, 215; declining importance of, to West, 217
Orabi rebellion, 9, 12
Ottoman Empire, territorial integrity, 1, 6; influences from Western Europe, 7; threatened by Mohamed Ali, 8, 66; in 1914, 17

Pakistan, 151
Palestine, Mohamed Ali master of, 7; claimed by France, 18; British mandate, 23, 26, 33; Arab rebellion, 34, 39; Jewish immigrants, 35; as part of Greater Syria, 37; Zionism and Arabs, 40; Arab attitude to, 43, 211; and Palestine White Paper, 49; British withdrawal, 122 (events after 1948 see Israel)
Palestine Arab Higher Committee, 34
Palestine Rebellion, 1936, 33-4, 36, 38-9
Palestine White Paper, 1939, 35, 39, 42, 44-5
pan-Arab Conference, 1937, 36; 1938, 36
pan-Islam, 110, 116
pan-Turania, 10
Paris, Arab Congress, 1913, 16, 110
Partie Populaire Syrien see Syrian Popular Party
Peel Commission, 35
Persia see Iran
Persian Gulf States, 25, 40, 99-100, 126, 164, 186, 190, 199, 206, 208, 213
Phalange, Christian Youth Movement in Lebanon, 171
Port Said, 141, 197
Protestant missions, 8

Qailani, Rashid Ali al see Rashid Ali al Qailani
Qasim, General Abdul Karim, Prime Minister of Iraq, and Cairo propaganda, 111; leads Iraqi coup, 172; develops own policy, 181-3; assassination attempt, 184-5, 196; as rival to Nasr, 186, 205; changing status of, 216, a tyrant, 219
Qatar, 100, 102
Quran, 3

racial consciousness, 14-5
Rashid Ali al Qailani, coup 1941, 39,

49, 55, 177; leads pan-Arab plot in Iraq, 182
refugees, 93, 97, 124, 165, 194, 197, 199, 211-2
Rifai, Samir, Prime Minister of Jordan, 151, 194
Royal-Dutch Shell Group, 101, 104
Russia, proximity to Middle East oil, 1, 41; and Constantinople, 8; pressure on Turkey and Iran, 60, 84; propaganda and subversion, 86; arms shipments to Egypt, 126, 129; finance for High Dam, 128; and Suez crisis, 141-2, 145; influence in Syria, 146, 158-9; diplomatic relations with Jordan, 150-1; commerce with Syria, 157; champion of Arab independence, 160-1; technicians and arms in Iraq, 182; Iraqi disagreement with, 184; loan for High Dam, 193

Saade, Anton, 38, 96
Saida, 153
Salem, Gamal, 74
Salem, Sa'eb, 171
Salem, Major Salah, 74, 80, 84
Salim, Mohammed, 216
San Remo Conference, 1920, 21
Sarraj, Colonel Abdul Hamid, 95, 162-3, 174
Saud, King of Saudi Arabia, 76, 98, 125, 148, 151, 174, 193, 219
Saudi Arabia, foundation, 23; and Palestine White Paper, 35; attitude to Greater Syria, 38; and Arab unity, 44; signs Pact of the Arab League, 45; oilfields, 61, 102; deplores purge of Moslem Brotherhood by Egypt, 76; end of influence in Arab world, 98; and US policy, 123; breaks off diplomatic relations with Britain and France, 140; troops in Jordan, 150; Iraqi relations with, 178; effect of Iraqi revolution on, 185; neutral policy of, 188
Saudites, 22, 38
Shammar, 23, 28
Sharia Law, 33, 53, 116
Sharm as Sheikh, 147
Sharq al Adna broadcasting station, 138
Shatt-el-Arab, 184
Sherifian family see Hashemites
Shia, 180

Shihab, General Fouad, President of Lebanon, 171, 174
Shishakli, Colonel Adib, 57, 94-6, 155, 157
Sidqi, General Bekr, 177
Silo, Colonel Fawzi, 155
Sinai Peninsula, 135-6, 140, 143-4
Solh, Riad, Prime Minister of Lebanon, 92, 96, 149, 169, 212
Solh, Sami, Prime Minister of Lebanon, 169, 171
Stalingrad, Battle of, 41
Standard Oil Company of California, 102
Sudan, 7, 24, 69, 72-3, 79, 81, 140, 188, 191, 198
Sudan Agreement, 1953, 67, 73, 80
Suez Canal, British bridgehead on, 18, 24; nationalization of, 129-32; Israeli ships denied use of, 133, 147, 197; blocking of, 140; repair, 144; opened to Israeli ships, 212
Suez Canal Board, 133
Suez Canal Company, 130-1, 134
Suez Canal Convention, 1888, 131-2
Suez Canal Users' Association, 134-5
Suez Canal Zone, British bases in, 61, 63-5, 69; evacuation of bases in, 67, 88, 90, 122; sabotage in, 70; Egyptian negotiations over, 73-4; and the 'imperialist' plot, 114; Conservative Party and, 130, 201-2; reoccupation of, 136-8; Nasr seizes British bases, 144
Sultan, 6, 20
Sunni Moslems, 9-10, 32, 180
Syria, Arab blood in, 2; Mohamed Ali master of, 7; missions in, 8; Arabic language in, 9; boundaries of, 9, 152; racial consciousness of, 15; claimed by France, 18; French mandate, 23, 25; treaty with France, 26; and Palestine rebellion, 34; and Greater Syria, 37; resentment against occupiers and rulers, 39; independence, 42, 45-6; and Arab League, 45; interest of Transjordan in, 48; political parties in, 55; Army coup, 57, 68; asylum given to Moslem Brotherhood, 76; in 1955, 94-6; pro-Egyptian alignment of, 124-6; Joint Military Command with Egypt and Jordan, 125, 136, 150; breaks diplomatic relations with Britain and France, 140; blows up

IPC pumping station, 140, 151, 156, 158; Russian influence in, 146; troops in Jordan, 150; post war policies of, and the Syrian crisis, 154-66; union with Egypt, 165; smuggles arms to Lebanon, 171; Iraqi relations with, 178; effect of Iraqi revolution on, 185; relations with Egypt, 188; Egyptian influence in elections, 193; after Casablanca Conference, 196; as originator of ideas, 219

Syria, Greater see Greater Syria

Syrian Popular Party, 38, 96, 155-7, 162

Syrian Socialist Party, 95, 157

Tallal, King of Jordan, 94

Tariqi, Abdullah al, 216

Taufiq, Abu Huda, Prime Minister of Jordan, 124

Taufiq as Suwaidi, 34

Templer, General Gerald, 125

Texas Oil Company, 102

Tito, Marshal, President of Yugoslavia, 129

Transjordan, population of, 2; British Mandate, 23; and Palestine White Paper, 35; and idea of a Greater Syria, 37, 49; resentment towards ocupiers and rulers, 39-40; Pact of the Arab League, 45; Palestine war and, 50; regarded as under British influence, 59 (events after 1949 see Jordan)

Tripartite Agreement, 1950, 89

Tripoli (Lebanon) oil terminal, 102-3

Tripolitania, 107

Trucial States, 100, 102

Tunisia, 106-7, 189, 191, 199

Turkey, war with Britain, 17; Russian pressure on, 60; defence pact with Iraq, 84, 88; US alliance with, 122; adheres to Eisenhower Doctrine, 151; threatens to invade Syria, 158, 160

Turkish Petroleum Company, 101

Turko-Iraq Agreement, 1955 see Baghdad Pact

Turks, 2, 10

Umma, 73, 81

United Arab Republic, formation, 165; diplomatic relations broken off with Lebanon and Jordan, 170; fo-

ments Lebanese rebellion, 171; Iraq and, 182, 184-5; disagreement with Russia, 184; and Iraqi imperialism, 185; diplomatic relations re-established with Iraq, 186; loan for Suez Canal improvements, 187; diplomatic defeat at Arab League meeting, 191; resumes diplomatic relations with Jordan, 192; after Casablanca Conference, 196; declining influence of, 217

United Nations, Egyptian appeal against 1936 Treaty, 59; Security Council discusses Suez Canal nationalization, 135; calls for cease fire in Egypt, 141; compels Great Britain, France and Israel to withdraw from Egypt, 143; observation team in Lebanon, 171; Partition Resolution for Israel, 1947, 197, 211

United States of America, and Zionist pressure, 45; interests in Arab world, 61-2; and Israeli-Arab conflict, 89; presses Britain to leave Canal Zone, 90; interest in Middle East oil, 103; supports Middle East nationalism, 121-3; alliance with Turkey and Iran, 122; air bases in Libya and Saudi Arabia, 122; and loan for High Dam, 128-9; condemns Anglo-French intervention in Egypt, 141-2; policy in Middle East, 146; Sixth Fleet sent to Beirut, 151; alarm at Syrian interest in Russia, 158; reaction to Iraqi coup, 173, 186-7; policy towards Nasr, 190; visit of Krushchev to, 195

United Nations Emergency Force, 143-4

USSR see Russia

Wafd, 53, 68-9, 71, 119, 122

Wahhabi sect, 28

World Bank, loan for High Dam, 128; loan for Suez Canal improvements, 134, 187, 197

Yafi, Abdallah, Prime Minister of Lebanon, 169

Yeman, 23, 27, 35, 45, 99, 165

Young Turks, 10, 19-20

Yunis, Mahmud, 216

Zaim, Colonel Husni, 57, 94, 96

Zionists, 18, 25-6, 40, 45, 90, 122, 213

Date Due